Sellotape Legacy

Delhi & the Commonwealth Games

Sellotape Legacy

DELHI & THE COMMONWEALTH GAMES

Boria Majumdar • Nalin Mehta

HarperCollins *Publishers* India
a joint venture with

New Delhi

First published in India in 2010 by
HarperCollins *Publishers* India
a joint venture with
The India Today Group

HarperCollins *Publishers*
A-53, Sector 57, Noida 201301, India
77-85 Fulham Palace Road, London W6 8JB, United Kingdom
Hazelton Lanes, 55 Avenue Road, Suite 2900, Toronto, Ontario M5R 3L2
and 1995 Markham Road, Scarborough, Ontario M1B 5M8, Canada
25 Ryde Road, Pymble, Sydney, NSW 2073, Australia
31 View Road, Glenfield, Auckland 10, New Zealand
10 East 53rd Street, New York NY 10022, USA

Typeset in 11/14 Bembo Std
Vision One Knowledge Resources Pvt. Ltd.

Printed and bound at
Thomson Press (India) Ltd.

For the little one who opens his eyes with this book — may he go on to love the city it chronicles

—Nalin Mehta

For Sharmistha and Bnatul — the two controlling influences of my life

—Boria Majumdar

CONTENTS

1 | FEAR AND THE CITY

CHASING THE COMMONWEALTH MIRAGE

It began in an auto-rickshaw. Abhinav Bindra had just ended eighty years of pointless national hand-wringing; Akhil Kumar, he of the magnificent dropping hands, had recently dazzled the country with that special Sehwag-like small-town chutzpah that is defining new India; and Vijender Singh had shown the world that Indian bees carried a sting as well. In the cruel way of Delhi – too self-important and smug in our discussion on sport and the Indian character – we barely noticed the driver as we got into the auto. The two of us had, after all, just released our book, *Olympics: The India Story*. It was our first book together and to us, at least, there was a poetic melody in the unexpected delights of Beijing; and to our lesser selves, perhaps, there was the prospect of greater book sales.

It was oh-so-promising; a glimmer, finally, to light up what had largely been a dismal and soul-crunching story. Suresh Kalmadi had been on stage at the book launch in Delhi and he had used it to paint his own particular version of Indian sport. Now, as the auto slowly crawled under half-complete flyovers and roads dug up ostensibly for the looming Commonwealth Games, something he had said that day kept coming back into the conversation. 'A new dawn', 'Rs 767 crore for training', 'never before in our history', 'we will change everything'. It was the evening of the no-confidence vote on the Indo-US nuclear deal but the Member of Parliament from Pune, taking a break from the Lok Sabha, was at our book launch, facing the cynical arc lights of Delhi's sporting press and preening about a new tomorrow. This was his other self, as the chairman of the Commonwealth Games Organizing Committee. A galaxy of forgotten Olympians badgered him with uncomfortable questions, all of which were diplomatically answered with a smile and a nod by the suave Randhir Singh, the other top honcho of Indian sport.

We had been fairly content then, happy with our little launch. It fit the corporate definition of what constitutes such an event in Delhi – just enough names to gather journalists, just enough discussion and back-slapping before the drinks begin, just enough to make small news items that everyone but the authors forgets. Everybody goes home happy. Now we were dissecting the speech again, talking of lonely athletes and powerful babus, the Games and Delhi, sports and nationalism.

It was then that he burst in, '*Sab bakwaas hai*' [This is all nonsense]. The auto-driver had been listening. '*Barah din ke liye hazaron perh kaat diye inhone. Barah din ke liye, saab*' [They have cut thousands of trees for twelve days].[1] We were crossing Siri Fort and his arm swung in a disgusted arc as the words came out in staccato. He was angry, he wanted to have his say and he knew his stuff in the way that only those who are truly affected know. The statistics rolled off his tongue, mixed with incantations to *maa-behen* in glorious Benarasi Hindi. What he was saying was not new; it had been culled from a public sphere created by a vibrant media that has hungrily analysed most aspects of the Games. It was his passion that bowled us over. He had hit upon a cardinal truth about sporting events: they are rarely about sport in itself. They are about cities and nations and their place in the world. Sport is about athletic achievement but, at its heart, it is also about what it means and does to people, to societies. That is why we love it, or hate it so – but can never ignore it. The auto-driver was showing us a street-side view of the Games in a manner that textbooks rarely capture. It underscored to us why a detailed story of the Delhi Games must be written.

The Cambridge historian Christopher Bailey, writing in the 1980s, described similar epiphanies on Indian streets:

> In this poor society, some forms of political and social knowledge were remarkably diffused: apparently uneducated people would come up to one in the bazaar to discourse on the demerits of Baroness Thatcher or Mr Gorbachev, while educated people in east and south-east Asia, let alone Britain, seemed to struggle to understand anything of the external world.[2]

It is precisely this tendency that Amartya Sen noticed and developed into his 'argumentative Indian' thesis. The auto-driver was now giving us our Christopher Bailey moment and it was this moment – for twelve days, he had said – that crystallized the path that has led to this book.

The newspapers had long since been moaning about the delays in setting up the Commonwealth Games infrastructure – daily after national daily had published special reports on its alleged mismanagement and the increasingly difficult race the organizers were running with deadlines. A week or so after our exchange with the auto-driver, the *Hindustan Times*, for instance, flatly declared: 'What is actually needed for it [CWG 2010] to materialize without our embarrassing ourselves is a miracle.'[3] The reporters' verdict was based on an extensive survey of the construction sites. But the success or failure of an endeavour is one thing. We wanted to go into the heart of the matter. We wanted to ask the big questions that journalists – prisoners of the exigencies of their medium – sometimes don't have the luxury of asking. Why are we hosting the Games? Who benefits from it? Who pays? Who gains? Who loses? Where does Delhi 2010 stand in the larger history of sport? And, yes, whose city is this after all? These are the questions that this book answers.

The story of the Commonwealth Games holds up a mirror in which we see a reflection of contemporary India. There is a telling story that exemplifies much of this. In the early summer of 2009, as India's political parties jostled with each other in a bruising battle for the throne in Delhi, the capital's newspapers were suddenly flooded with a curious slew of full-page advertisements extolling the Congress for its developmental work for the Commonwealth Games. The advertisements were put out at a time when the idea of Dr Manmohan Singh storming back to power with such a decisive mandate was still a daring dream, even for the staunchest of Congress supporters. At such a time, the crores being spent on Games-related infrastructure in Delhi clearly had its political uses. The advertisements did not specify the issuing authority, but unashamedly used the peg of the Games to praise Dr Manmohan Singh and Sheila Dikshit, chief minister of Delhi, 'regarding the [related] development works carried out in the capital, like, twenty-four flyovers, seventy-five aerobridges airport, 1285 km of better roads, 5,000 low floor buses, etc (sic).'[4] An angry Election Commission issued strictures for violation of the poll code – even going so far as to threaten officials who had cleared it to pay from their own pockets. The Delhi government denied any hand in the affair. The matter eventually blew away, a forgotten sidelight from a historic election that will be remembered for much else.[5] As it turned out, the organizing committee of the Commonwealth Games had issued the politically loaded advertisements on its own accord. Its office bearers 'profusely apologized'[6] to the EC but not before the Commission summoned the Union sports secretary to 'define the linkage between the ministry and the Commonwealth Games organizing committee'.[7] The case of the Commonwealth advertisements in the middle of the 2009 general election campaign was instructive because it offered a window into what the Games are really all about – politics, plain and simple.

The Commonwealth Games have been dismissed by many as a posthumous celebration of a long-forgotten Empire. Others have mistakenly played up their potential to revive Indian sport, offering rosy visions of an assembly line of Indian sportsmen and women turning us, overnight, into the next China. This is all just window dressing. At their heart, the Commonwealth Games are about the politics of development and the raging ambitions of a rising India that so animate the middle classes and many decision makers in this country. Fuelled by the unrelenting fear of global ridicule that so drives our weak egos – and by the colour of money – politicians, bureaucrats and India's sports czars have taken the citizens of Delhi on a ride that will change their city forever. Notions of a fragile national pride are inherent in this debate. India must show its best face, we are told. Delhi has been dug up, bamboos have been brought in from the North East to hide its poor, and the organizers have had a free run on many things.

This book is the story of the politics of these Games. It is the story of the money that has been spent on it and how it has been spent. Delhi is changing and this is a book about the city, about the idea of First World development and the work around the Commonwealth Games that has been such an important subtext in Sheila Dikshit stomping back as chief minister for a historic third consecutive term. We want to state our position clearly: the reshaping of Delhi is surely welcome and the Games have provided the trigger that was needed. We have few sympathies with some of the *jhola-walas* who see eternal bliss in notions of struggle and poverty. Our concern is with the manner in which much of this work has been driven, the priorities which have shaped it – and they have not always been driven by only altruistic desires – the people who have shaped it and the direction in which the Games are taking Delhi and India.

Over the past few years of non-stop construction, virtually each one of Delhi's fourteen million denizens has been touched by the Games in one way or the other, but never before has the entire saga of the Games been revealed in its entirety.

GLOBAL CITY, GLOBAL ASPIRATIONS

Throughout history, rulers have sought to build their cities in their own image. If Lutyens's New Delhi was a metaphor for the might of the British Empire, Nehru held up Le Corbusier's spanking new city of Chandigarh to reflect the new rationality and the planning ethos of the Nehruvian state.[8] In the same vein, many of Delhi's current ruling elites see the Commonwealth Games as an opportunity to refashion Delhi into what they call a 'global city', one that will adequately reflect India's ever-increasing power and prestige in the world order. The notion of projecting the capital city as a shining beacon of India's global power play has always been at the heart of Delhi's bid for the Commonwealth Games. It explains why the rest of the political class, and not just the sporting netas, bought in to the idea of the Games. National pride is on a premium in post-liberalization India, more so in India's capital. Internal documents of the organizing committee made available to us are unambiguous on the 'bidding rationale' of Delhi 2010:

> *These Games will showcase New Delhi, the capital of India, to the world and promote it as a global city of an emerging economic power.* These Games will act as a medium for the development of the country. New sports venues will be built, existing venues will be modernized and a range of

infrastructure projects such as a comprehensive roads programme and a new metro system will be initiated. The 2010 Games in Delhi will provide a unique sponsorship opportunity for the Commonwealth Games movement within Asia, particularly South Asia, which is fast becoming a focus region for investments.[9]

Delhi wants to do a Beijing, albeit on a smaller scale. One of the key missions of the organizing committee is to project India as 'an economic superpower'[10] and in late 2006, its officials made a presentation to Prime Minister Manmohan Singh. Describing this presentation, the organizing committee's official newsletter listed six points in a slide entitled 'Impact of hosting the Games'. Only one made a cursory reference to sport. The rest of the listed aims, laid down in those pre-global recession days, are self-explanatory: 'enhance the image and stature of India', 'project Delhi as a global destination', 'act as a catalyst for sustained development of infrastructure', 'add to the prevailing upbeat mood in the Indian economy' and 'create opportunities for trade, business and investment for Delhi and India'.[11] It could have been written by the Ministry of Tourism or Commerce. The writer noted, almost as an afterthought, that the prime minister also wanted India to win more medals than ever. Sure, but those would only be the icing on the cake.

The tale of Delhi's ambition comes through in virtually every Games document one touches. The original Delhi bid, submitted to the Commonwealth secretariat, was designed virtually like a tourism brochure, with pious statements of commitment sitting easily with the language of hyperbole:

> One of the world's oldest living cities ... conquerors have fallen in love with it, marauders have plundered it and kings and princes have pampered it. A city that has held its own – in the past and even today in the 21st century. Where age-old monuments rub shoulders with modern chrome-and-glass skyscrapers. Where mouse-clicks enticingly co-exist with horse-cart clips ... Delhi today leads the country's progress, charting out new vistas in globalisation and economic growth for this mammoth country of over one billion ... Where huge, landscaped gardens created by emperors of yore suddenly give way to air-conditioned, glitzy shopping malls.[12]

It is this new India of shopping malls and flyovers that the organizers want to propagate. Even the Games logo is a case in point. Inspired by the Gandhian charka, its official explanation goes: 'spiralling upwards, it depicts the growth of India into a proud, vibrant nation, her billion people coming together to fulfil their true destinies. India's journey from tradition to modernity, her economic transformation into a superpower ... reaching out to the world and leading the way ...'[13]

The Games are about Brand India. As Suresh Kalmadi, the chairman of the organizing committee puts it, 'We are now living in a world that is increasingly global. We are always wired and connected to the rest of the world. Our comparisons are no longer with the past or with just our neighbours, but with the best in the world.'[14] Nothing symbolizes India's deepest-felt desires and pretensions better than this.

'MANY THINGS WERE NOT FACTORED IN BEFORE': COUNT THE MONEY, BE AFRAID

So, how much will the Commonwealth Games cost us? That is the first big question that this book grapples with. It is not an easy question to answer because the work is spread across diverse sectors and the money is being spent by a bewildering morass of multiple agencies. To enter the story of the Commonwealth Games is to enter into a labyrinth of overlapping controls – Ministry of Sports, Ministry of Home Affairs, Ministry of Urban Development, Ministry of Tourism, Government of Delhi, Planning Commission, New Delhi Municipal Corporation (NDMC), Municipal Corporation of Delhi (MCD), Sports Authority of India (SAI), Delhi Development Authority (DDA), and so on. There are several high-level committees to coordinate their work,[15] but like it often happens in government, many things remain unclear to the very end.[16] The result is that even many among those involved in organizing the Games do not have the full financial picture in front of them, with each government agency pursuing its own targets.

When we first started looking for the Games' bill, we thought Olympic Bhawan would have all the answers. The brand-new headquarters of the Indian Olympic Association and the original home of the Games' organizing committee – before it shifted to its even swankier new office opposite Jantar Mantar – is a recent addition to Delhi's Qutub Enclave. Nestled amid private hospitals and corporate offices, the skyscraper looks like a metaphor for the self-image of the Delhi Games – modern, efficient, organized. Standing outside its gates, a visitor would not blink if told that this white building, with its Manhattan air, was the home of an IBM or a Microsoft. Once inside, however, Olympic Bhawan has the smell of Gurgaon, the new hick town which has one eye trained on New York but is implanted surgically in the confusing reality of Delhi. In Olympic Bhawan you have the interiors of a fast-moving corporate office – orange walls, slick colour-coordinated decorations – juxtaposed with a staff that often moves to the rhythms of a moribund government office.

When we first walked into its precincts in mid-2008, the entry was from the basement. It was one of the few parts of the building that was really ready. As we lounged around, talking to our contacts, someone pointed to the high-profile foreign consultant, sitting with his laptop on a makeshift table in the corner. He didn't notice us, totally absorbed in his computer in a very harried sort of way, but he seemed horribly out of place. Around us, the room was full of the revered names of Indian sportsdom, their corners littered with favour-seekers – out-of-luck former athletes, wannabe managers, contractors – in the time-honoured manner of Indian sport. Someone brought in cups of tea, and sounds of construction hammered in from every pore of the building as labourers raced against time to complete their work. It seemed like an apt picture of the external reality of the Games: a whole lot of gloss, a great deal of confusion, and some *Casablanca*-style figures working like mad to make it work.

That was then. The next time we went in, the basement was no longer the entry, and many of the floors were functional. A kindly official had promised us the financial documents. We strolled through the corridors, walking past nameplates of ex-generals, high-profile bureaucrats and sporting politicians. There is nothing secret about these documents, but it was something of a minor triumph to get our hands on them. Access to information in Olympic Bhawan – as indeed in NDCC Tower – is often a function of access to power. Compounding the apparent veil of opaqueness is the fact that the organizing committee has in the past refused to impart information under the Right to Information Act, arguing in the Delhi High Court that the RTI does not apply to it. This is especially jarring when parliamentary records on the Commonwealth Games are available at the click of a mouse button, a legacy of the delightful digitization of those records that was started by the late Bharatiya Janata Party (BJP) leader, Pramod Mahajan.

The financing of the Commonwealth Games has been the subject of parliamentary questioning since 2004 and it took us just twenty minutes to download the entire details from the parliamentary website after a month of running around in circles to find the organizing committee's records. Juxtapose these two realities together and a curious dichotomy emerges. The organizing committee's slickly prepared plan, its annual reports and its budgets are prepared using best-practice templates taken from consultants who have worked on similar events the world over. If you had only these documents – with their nice diagrams, futuristic timelines and jazzy graphs – to rely on, you would think that the Commonwealth Games are the most well-organized event ever. Compare these with actual performance data submitted by various ministries and you enter the reality of India, with too many overlapping ministries, huge cost overruns and estimations going crazily haywire. The organizing committee is a clearing house, but, on its own, it is only responsible for the twelve days of the event itself. It does not control the rest – the flyovers, the airport, the roads, the stadiums – and with so many stakeholders, counting the money is a tricky terrain.

Parliamentary records show that at the time of government approval for the Games, the Games budget estimate had been only Rs 617.5 crore.[17] This was a very preliminary original estimate and the Vajpayee government agreed to fund any future shortfalls between revenue and expenditure.[18] It was a virtual blank cheque. By March 2003, when Delhi submitted its official bid, the cost estimates had tripled to Rs 1895.3 crore.[19] As Sunil Dutt, the sports minister at the time, told the Lok Sabha in 2004, everybody knew that these were only early projections that could only go up later.[20] What is shocking is just how much they went up. Table 1.1 charts how the budgets have kept rising, sector by sector, ever since.

Table 1.1: Commonwealth Games Estimated Costs (2003–09) (Figures in INR Crore)[21]

Year	Operating Expense (OC)	Infrastructure	Publicity in Melbourne (Bollywood show)	Security/ Services	Pune Cth. Youth Games	Athletes	Others/ Overlays	Broadcasting	TOTAL
Dec. 2002	399.05	218.5							617.55
Mar. 2003	655.5	1085		154.8					1895.3
Dec. 2005	896.04	3376.4							4272.44
Nov. 2006	767	2669	29	264	110	300			4139
Aug. 2007	767	2707	29	264	110	661			4538
Dec. 2008	1628	4109.77	29	277	351.48†	678	400	463	7936.2
July 2009	1628	9764	29	277	351.48	678**	405*	463	13595.48
Final 2009 -incl. Delhi Govt. infrastructure cost estimate	1628	67181.55	29	277	351.48	678		463	70608

For *, **, † see footnote 21.

Note: 2006 figures were estimated by GoI with a variation of 10–25 per cent under various heads.[22]

In last row, column on infrastructure, we have added estimated official cost of Games Village (Rs 631.55 crore) to Delhi government infrastructure cost estimate of Rs 66,550 crore.

By 2005, the estimated costs had shot up by more than six times from the original figure. By 2008, the minister of sports was estimating a figure of over Rs 7,000 crore and in 2009, the comptroller and auditor general provided a calculation of about Rs 13,000 crore. This was more than twenty times the original cost estimate and even this figure did not include spending by many agencies (See Table 1.1).[23] If you were running a company, such sharp cost overruns would, in most cases, be seen as management failure. But this is only half the story.

In early 2009, we were discussing these rocketing estimates with a senior Delhi government official when he dropped a bombshell. We had met about something else over lunch on a lazy Sunday afternoon. The Games came up in passing and he listened to our calculations before calmly pointing out: 'The total Games spending on city infrastructure is Rs 65,550 crore.' It didn't square at all with any of the other financial data. But he was way up in Delhi's power circle and clearly knew what he was talking about. So we asked him for a detailed breakdown and there it was in fine print: Rs 65,550 crore clearly marked in an internal Delhi government note on what it calls 'Commonwealth Games–related work'. The state government subsequently published these figures officially[24] and when clubbed together with other costs, they pushed the total amount to more than Rs 70,000 crore.

Our problem was that between 2003 and 2009, this estimate on infrastructure spending calculated by Sheila Dikshit's government did not figure in any of the data submitted by successive sports ministers in Parliament or in the internal records of the organizing committee that were made available to us. This new information, passed on by the office of Delhi's chief secretary, had us completely flummoxed. Why was it invisible?

A close analysis of the financial data reveals that the Games infrastructure budgets submitted in Parliament between 2003 and 2008 had only listed a little over Rs 1,300 crore (for building civic infrastructure) against the Delhi government's name. This was the amount that the Delhi government said it needed extra funding for, asking the Planning Commission[25] for a grant. This was the amount

Figure 1.1: CWG 2010: Escalation in Cost Estimates (2003–09), Figs. in Rs Crore[26]

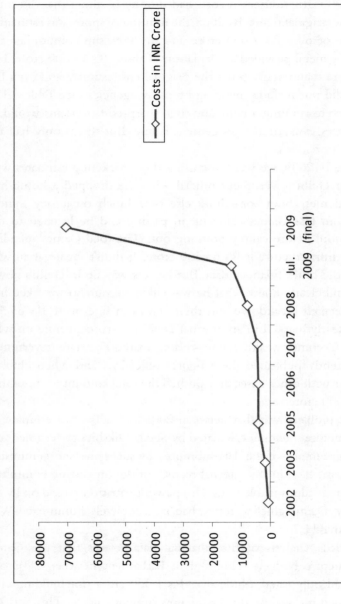

(The massive escalation in 2009 is due to the addition of consolidated figures from the Delhi government on infrastructure spending that were hitherto absent from other records.)

that got reflected in budget estimates by sports ministers in Parliament, instead of the state government's total Games-related estimate. The Delhi government and other agencies were spending far more from their own coffers – the CAG also pointed this out – but this spending escaped all other reporting. The organizing committee and Central government budget records, therefore, never reflected the rest of the Rs 65,550 crore that was being spent on the Games. If you include this amount, overall Games expenditure estimates shoot up to a whopping Rs 70,608 crore (Table 1.1 and Figure 1.1). This is more than 114 times the original calculation made in 2002!

In a sense, Table 1.1 and Figure 1.1 also illustrate the problems in any budget tabulation of this massive endeavour. It really depends on how you calculate these things. And, remember, the Delhi government is just one of many stakeholders in this whole business.

Table 1.2 further breaks up the Rs 65,550 crore that the Government of Delhi says is being spent on Commonwealth Games-related work.

Some might say that much of the money listed in Table 1.2 would have been spent anyway. Projects like new power stations account for nearly half of this budget and is it misleading to account for these in a CWG estimate? No, it is not. There is good reason why the office of Delhi's chief secretary chose to put all these costs under the heading 'Projects Related to CWG 2010'. This is their language, not ours. The fact is that most of this infrastructure construction is being put on the fast-track only because of the Games and the kind of money that is being spent on Delhi's infrastructure would not have been possible in ordinary times. Power, for instance, is being fast-tracked due to the lofty promise of showcasing a capital city with twenty-four-hour power during the Games. Delhi is to be India's marquee. As V.K. Verma, director general of the organizing committee puts it:

> For all the huge infrastructure projects which either would have been really slowed down or there would have been a huge time overrun on those projects, we now know that there is a timeline to it. This is a huge legacy advantage for Delhi. Now, whether it is creation of world-class venues or it is the widening of roads and new flyovers or

metros or general sprucing up of the city or cityscaping, in every facet –
building of new hotels, hospitals, everything is like as if a city is being
rebuilt. So that is the big legacy advantage of the Commonwealth
Games.[27]

Table 1.2: Approximate Cost of Projects Related to CWG 2010
(Govt. of Delhi data)[28]

S. No.	Name of the Project	Cost (in Rs Crore)
1.	Flyovers and Bridges	5,700.00
2.	Road Overbridges/Road Underbridges	520.00
3.	Stadia	650.00
4.	HCBS	1,518.00
5.	Augmentation of DTC Fleet	1,800.00
6.	Construction of Bus Depots	900.00
7.	Widening of Roads, Strengthening and Resurfacing	700.00
8.	Street Lighting	650.00
9.	Street Scaping	525.00
10.	Improved Road Signage	100.00
11.	Metro Connectivity	16,887.00
12.	New Power Generation Plants (instrument from NTPC, DVC, THDC, PPCL, Aravali Power Corporation)	35,000.00
13.	Water Supply (STP, WTP, Munak Canal, etc.)	950.00
14.	Health	50.00
15.	Parking Facility by Covering *Nallahs*	400.00
16.	Communication and IT	200.00
	Total	66,550.00

Why does all this matter? Well, for one thing, most of this money is the
taxpayers'. The Vajpayee government had guaranteed the Commonwealth Federation that it would pay for any shortfall between revenues
and expenditure of the organizing committee.[29] We have already seen the
huge cost overruns outlined. Remember that even these escalated costs
do not cover the entire expenditure. For instance, the crores being spent
on building new hotels, on the Games Village by Emaar and elsewhere
by the private sector on its own or in public – private partnerships are
not part of the budgets reproduced here.[30] Remember also that the
Central government has given funds to the organizing committee as an
unsecured loan to be repaid only after revenues start coming in. Under

the terms of the Games contract, the schedule and other details of this governmental loan *'will be worked out later'*.[31] The organizing committee, a private non-profit body, has got a virtual blank cheque in perpetuity. Suresh Kalmadi defends himself, saying:

> We will return every penny we've received from the government by collecting money ... We will only return the amount given to the organizing committee. Why should you count the expenses incurred on infrastructure, airport, flyovers, metro, Games Village, malls, etc.? This will be a legacy from the Games. All these developments move the city five to ten years forward.[32]

Sure, but is anyone willing to bet on when the money will make its way back to the government's treasury?

There are some who say that cost overruns always happen in big sporting events like this one. The Beijing Olympics were a good example of this and London, which is preparing for the 2012 Olympic Games, is another. However, if these cities got their fiscal management so wrong, why is it necessary that we should do so as well? A pertinent example here is Melbourne which hosted the 2006 Commonwealth Games. Unlike Delhi, Melbourne's total spending of $2,913,157,000 was just 0.6 per cent above its estimate.[33]

The big question is, why were the cost estimates so far off the mark? Was it because of mismanagement or because of unavoidable circumstances? Sheila Dikshit has a plausible point when she argues that the global downturn is partly responsible. 'There are many stakeholders. The estimates given were approximations but, because of the current economic situation, things have changed. Both cement and steel are costlier,' the chief minister argues.[34]

But wait till you hear what the director general of the organizing committee has to say in his defence. Speaking to us in January 2009, he admitted that the costs have escalated so sharply because the original estimates were based on total ignorance. It was such a chilling admission that it deserves to be reproduced in full:

> All of us made a budget. We, [the] organizing committee, made a budget. The Delhi government made a budget, we all made a budget. The first budget was made two years back [i.e., four years after the bid

was submitted]. At that time the OC was a fledgling organization. It was finding its feet. Nobody had past Games' experience. Watching Games, seeing Games is one thing but nobody was inside it. The budget was made on very basic things. So if you want to present a very basic Games, the budget was made like that [sic]. Similarly the other arms, Delhi government, all the budgets were very rudimentary budgets. As you really take the plunge, as you get more and more into it, you begin to look at the other websites, you begin to get more documents as to what was done. Then your estimations also keep going up, so now a more detailed exercise has been done.

We are in the process of revaluating our budgets and of course input costs have gone high ... steel has become more expensive, cement is a problem. These are normal escalations which happen. But many things were not factored in. Now one has become wiser because everybody is into the Games more, everybody has read more about the Games. Everybody has got more data and information about the previous Games. So now we are benchmarking with respect to that. [sic]³⁵

Frankly, then, the organizing committee never had an idea what it was doing. Delhi hosted the Asian Games in 1982 but there was no institutional memory of it, or if there was, it wasn't tapped into. The Government of India signed a blank cheque based on shoddy budget estimations made by amateurs who didn't seem to know what they were doing. And are we supposed to be happy that now, six years later, the organizing committee is claiming to get its act together? Shouldn't all of this have been done earlier? And who will be held accountable?

The problem is that we can't get out of it now. 'What will the world think', they all say, and so the money keeps flowing. Let it be clear that this is not a party-specific attitude. It is no accident that the idea of the Games has always enjoyed political support, cutting across the party divide. The 2003 bid was guaranteed by the then BJP-led National Democratic Alliance government but the Congress party, then in Opposition,³⁶ backed it fully. So did the lieutenant governor of Delhi,³⁷ the Congress-led state government of Delhi,³⁸ and the MCD, also controlled at the time by the Congress.³⁹

The last time so much money was floating around in Delhi was during the Asian Games in 1982, when Indira Gandhi, staging a comeback from the opprobrium of the Emergency, pulled out all stops to refashion her and the capital's image in front of the world.[40] The Delhi of 2010 is a very different place from the Delhi of 1982 but one thing has not changed: money is aplenty and everybody wants to be in on the party.

REMEMBER MONTREAL: DID WE REALLY NEED THESE GAMES?

With costs rising the way they are, Delhi's masters would do well to remember what happened to Montreal. The 1976 Montreal Olympics was sold to its citizens as an event that would rejuvenate the city, with all kinds of administrators hard-selling its long-term benefits. When people started doubting the tall promises that were being made and the heavy cost overruns, Mayor Jean Drapeau dismissed them, haughtily declaring, 'The Montreal Olympics can no more have a deficit, than a man can have a baby.'[41] Well, the Canadians were paying off the debt from those Games until November 2006. Delhi should take heed.

The question is: can India or Delhi really afford this huge cost? In 2009, the Delhi government was hit by such a cash crunch that it sent an SOS to the Centre, demanding a share of the profits earned by the DDA through sale of land in the capital region. Squeezed in by the economic downturn and by the rising costs of the Games, the state government announced that its stamp duty collections had dipped by Rs 750 crore and VAT collections by Rs 500 crore.[42] Overall revenue collections had dipped by 12 per cent,[43] which meant that the government was facing a financial shortfall of approximately Rs 1,500 crore in early 2009. The cash crunch was expected to lead into the 2010–11 financial year. Appealing to the Centre for help, the Delhi government demanded a fee from the DDA for developing infrastructure in the city. With the Games looming ahead, Delhi Finance Minister A.K. Walia's worries were adding up. As he put it:

> We have the Games coming up which is a prestigious event for the country, and our revenue collection has hit a slump because of the economic slowdown ... Our funds are depleting and we may not have

enough for the next financial year, in the thick of the Commonwealth
Games. How are we going to carry out transport, education and even
social welfare projects next year?[44]

This was a state government on its knees despite the fact that it had
received a lavish budgetary grant (Rs 2,360 crore) from the Centre
in the Interim Union Budget of 2009–10. This was a full Rs 1,600
crore more than the previous year and much of this money was for
Games infrastructure.[45] Delhi also got a massive Rs 1,000 crore fuel
injection under the Jawaharlal Nehru National Urban Renewal
Mission (JNNURM). Again, this was Rs 600 crore more than what
it had received in 2008 for low-cost housing and for redeveloping
the arterial Connaught Place.[46] Yet, it was not enough and the city's
finances were in trouble.

'SAME AS PUTTING A MAN ON THE MOON': THE DELHI VS. INDIA DEBATE

This brings us to the second big question we are asking in this book: did
Delhi really need the Games at all? If the Delhi government's figures
are correct, the amount being spent on Commonwealth Games-
related development projects in Delhi is four times the amount being
spent annually on the entire National Rural Health Mission.[47] This is a
sobering thought and one that should make all right-thinking Indians
sit up and take notice. Wouldn't we have been better off putting these
vast resources where they were really needed?

For all our great power pretensions, can a country where 28.3
percent of the people still live below the poverty line[48] really
afford this kind of expenditure on a sporting event of this kind?
These are important questions, especially for a government that
came back to power on the vote of the *aam aadmi*. The coffers of
the Government of India are not bottomless. The heavy spending
on Delhi comes at a time when the Dr Manmohan Singh-led
government was dealing with a fiscal deficit of 6.8 per cent of
GDP in 2009 – that is what it was spending over and above its
revenues. Between 2007 and 2009, it was estimated by at least one
eminent economist that total government spending was as much
as nine times its income.[49] At such a time – and for a government

whose first priorities are to sustain India's high growth trajectory; to focus on social development programmes like the National Rural Employment Guarantee Scheme (NREGS), NRHM, the National Rural Livelihood Mission, the new National Food Security Act, and so on – does the heavy spending on Commonwealth Games not appear like too expensive a diversion?

Develop Delhi by all means but remember also that India's capital city is already one of the most developed regions in the country. Within the city, its citizens often complain about the divide between them and the pampered denizens of Lutyens's Delhi, where the power elite reside and where electricity and water run twenty-four hours a day. Outside the city, many would be justified in thinking that it has always been a favoured place. For instance, the capital already had 1,749 km of road length per 100 sq. km area in 1996–97, compared to the national average of 73 km per 100 sq. km area (1995-96).[50] Writing in 2000, the social anthropologist Anita Soni pointed out: 'As the supreme centre of political power, Delhi has assured itself of preferential treatment in the allocation of national resources. The Central Plan Outlay for Delhi is more than for the entire state of Assam, for instance.'[51] The capital was already one of the most well-funded and most developed places in India. Now, it is even more so.

But the Games are more than just a simple arithmetic calculation about resource allocation. They are more about a rising India and its global power projection. When Pranab Mukherjee rose to present the Union Budget for 2009–10 he was clear on this: 'The Commonwealth Games present the country with an opportunity to showcase our potential as an emerging Asian power.' So the finance minister pumped in another Rs 1,360 crore into the Games budget.[52] International power projection doesn't happen for free.

In a sense, the Government of India has no choice now. The die has long been cast. The overwhelming impression one gets while sifting through the Games records is of power elites who bought into the idea of the Games without really thinking through its implications and detailed costs. They successfully sold the notion of development through the Games and we have been presented with a fait accompli. The 'Games train' has left the station.

Studying similar sporting events in the past, sport historian David Black has shown that once such events are set in motion, the costs of failure 'become too ghastly to contemplate'. They have a dynamic of their own, weighing particularly heavily on emerging and/or smaller centres – often hosting second-order events – who do not have an established reputation for successful event management and who may be subject to more or less prejudicial doubts about their ability to do so, particularly in post-colonial contexts.[53]

Delhi is certainly not a small centre but the argument holds true. We are terrified of failing before the glare of the world's cameras and in that sense, India is falling prey to the same self-destructive sentiment that Havana had given in to during the Latin American Games in 1991, Kuala Lumpur during the 1998 Commonwealth Games and Athens during the 2004 Olympics.

Social historians of sport have a word for what Delhi is going through: the 'winner's curse'.[54] Every city that wins an event like the Commonwealth Games talks up its benefits, while talking down the downside. This becomes part of a narrative that is progressively enriched, without critical examination. It does benefit a few, but does that really translate into the greater good?[55]

Responding to this criticism, the organizing committee's director general has an interesting response, drawing an analogy with India's moon mission:

See, it is like saying that whatever money we are spending on putting a man on the moon, from that standard that should not be done. Because what relevance is there for putting a man on the moon when there is poverty? One-third of the country is quite poor. These are extreme notions. The country has to move forward on all facets. And I think we have already been behind in sports. Sports has become a brand now. Sports prowess is a reflection of the general health, general well-being of the advancement your country is making. So far we have scored a blank. At least, with the Beijing Olympic Games we made a beginning. Commonwealth Games is the opportunity to take that, to build on that to take it to the next, higher level. Surely India should be looking in the next twenty years to be at least in the top ten or top twenty of the Olympic table ... Everything has to move together.[56]

The mission to the moon is part of a larger scientific thrust with deep-seated strategic and defence implications.[57] But there is a wider claim being made here about the potential of the Commonwealth Games to turn India into an Olympics predator. This is a claim that merits detailed examination.

DREAMING OF OLYMPIA: SPORT AND THE NATION

In 2007, when Delhi was making a bid for another big-ticket event, the 2014 Asian Games, the then sports minister, Mani Shankar Aiyar, was categorical in his opposition to hosting another event which would do nothing for Indian sport. He went public with his objections, arguing instead for investing money in rural sports. Aiyar was right and as sports minister, he must also have been privy to the inside story and the escalating costs of the CWG projects. He vehemently argued for a comprehensive national sports policy, one focussed on rural development, instead of such events.[58] His objections were brushed aside by the Union Cabinet and Delhi made its Asiad bid, one that it eventually lost to Incheon, partly as a fallout of Aiyar's public opposition. Aiyar may have lost the battle in the Cabinet but at least he had the last laugh: Delhi was not to play host to another mega event.

The argument for hosting the Asian Games followed a similar trajectory as that given for the Commonwealth Games. The organizing committee argued that hosting the Commonwealth Games 2010 in Delhi will result 'in the process of developing sports infrastructure which will make India one of the powerhouses in the world's sporting arena'.[59] This was a sentiment also echoed by the BJP's Vikram Verma, who signed off on Delhi's original bid as Union sports minister.[60] Justifying their intentions, the organizers, therefore, told the Commonwealth Games Federation (CGF) that 'sports and games propagated at the highest levels have a miraculous capacity to percolate even to the grassroots and also achieve the widest coverage'.[61]

Unfortunately, we were told similar things before the Asian Games of 1982 and India still remains a poor performer in international sport. The event that the Games' organizers called the 'Super Asiad'[62] fundamentally changed the infrastructure of Delhi. The most obvious manifestation of 1982 was in the new stadiums – five constructed in two years – which were referred to by their creators as the 'temples of Indian sport':[63] the Jawaharlal Nehru Stadium, with a seating capacity of 75,000; the Indraprastha Indoor Stadium with a seating capacity of 25,000; the Velodrome; the Talkatora Swimming Stadium and the Tughlakabad Shooting Range.[64] The Games came and went, Delhi became the best endowed of Indian cities in terms of sporting infrastructure and its entire skyline changed as a result, but India remained a laggard in international sport.

Everyone in India knows this and even the sports ministry seemed to recognize the obvious in 2008, when an internal report pointed out: 'The achievement in this sector has not been significant largely on account of policy lacunae and inadequate budgetary support.'[65] When the Games' organizers wrote their vision statement in 2007, its first line noted that their aim was 'to boost sports culture as a part of daily life of every Indian, particularly the youth'.[66] Let us examine the evidence of this on the ground.

In 2008, the sports ministry came out with a draft Comprehensive National Sports Policy which sought to 'broad base' sports with the slogan 'Sports for all'.[67] At the heart of the new blueprint was a grand vision to encourage rural sports through the flagship Panchayat Yuva Krida aur Khel Abhiyan (PYKKA) programme.[68] This made sense: less than 5 per cent of the Indian population has access to sporting facilities and organized sports. The answer to India's sporting woes lies in its rural areas and the idea of developing rural sports has been raised in the Parliamentary Standing Committee as well as the Eleventh Plan Document.[69] The sports ministry, quite sensibly, therefore, decided to provide substantial financial assistance to rural youth and sports clubs.[70]

So far so good. The problem now is that the Commonwealth Games seem to have deflected attention from all these big plans. The ministry's budgetary figures tell a sad story. A performance review of the sports ministry in 2006–07 showed that Rs 4.4 crore was to be spent on the PYKKA and the rural sports programme and this was indeed done. In 2007–08, however, the ministry allocated nearly double the amount (Rs 7.9 crore) but none of this money was actually spent. In contrast, the ministry's spending target for the CWG in that year was Rs 150 crore, and it managed to spend 96 per cent of this money.[71]

It got worse in 2008–09. Of the ministry's total budget estimates of Rs 1082.14 crore, Rs 356 crore was allotted to the Commonwealth Games alone and nothing at all to the rural sports programme or to rural sports clubs.[72] A detailed look at the Outcome Budget for 2008–09 tells us the real picture. In the ministry's work plan, every activity has a column next to it, specifying the quantifiable deliverables/physical outputs for the money spent. But in the line for CWG 2010, this column has a telling legend: 'Since the items of work for the CWG 2010 are not quantifiable, no physical targets were fixed as such.'[73] This is the crux. Anything goes for the CWG. Rural sports and everything else will have to live on crumbs.

WHY NOT HYDERABAD? WHY NO NATIONAL GAMES?

Sporting successes can only be built on sustained investments towards creating a sporting culture, and not by one-off events. Take the example of Hyderabad, which hosted the Afro-Asian Games in 2003. The organizing committee's internal documents are replete with copious references to the success of these Games and they are repeatedly held up as proof that India can deliver on such high-level sporting events. Former Chief Minister Chandrababu Naidu created a brand-new sports complex on the outskirts of the city specifically for these Games. Built on the outskirts of the city of Hyderabad, the Gowchi Bowli Sports Complex is a world-class complex and crores were spent on creating it. In May 2009, when we went to visit it, we only found bored maintenance workers who told us that the still sparkling complex was used only by the children of local government officials.

The complex has no doubt been used since 2002 for holding a few events – like the World Military Games or the Indo–Dutch hockey series and, more recently, the world badminton championships – but as a real and regular sporting centre for the general public, it has largely been a closed shop.[74] To see its brand-new badminton and boxing stadium lying unused and largely inaccessible was to see the tragedy of Indian sport. If a sports event could really change our destiny, why not hold it here in Hyderabad, where the facilities had just been built! Surely, that would have saved a great deal of money and still given us a great

Games. Instead, we chose to refurbish the facilities in a city whose sports infrastructure was already more massive than any other in India.

Some of the arguments that the organizers give are rather disingenuous. The bid document, for instance, extols the value of the National Games, drawing a direct link with the Commonwealth Games: 'If National-level games can have such a profound impact, the Commonwealth games would definitely transform the sports scenario not only in India, but, in fact, in the entire region.'[75] Well, if anyone had bothered to consult the sportsmen and women of the country, they would have told our sports mandarins that only two National Games have been held in the last seven years. Andhra Pradesh hosted the 32nd National Games in 2002 and the country had to wait till 2007 for the 33rd Games in 2007. The National Games have not been held since. What talent hunting are we really talking about? And what sports culture?

It is pertinent to mention here that we did hold a National School Games in 2008. Delhi was the proud host. With less than two years to go for the Commonwealth Games, the National School Games should have been a dress rehearsal. Instead, an investigative report in a city tabloid pointed out the grim reality of the city: 600 school-going athletes were housed in the Sarvodya Co-Educational School in Civil Lines. The band of 600 budding sportspersons had only five toilets between them and thirty-six players each were crammed in one classroom. Any of them wanting to have a warm bath in Delhi's cold winter mornings had to shell out Rs 5 from his own pocket for a bucket of warm water.[76] As a letter writer to a newspaper put it:

> Is this the kind of facilities we are providing to our young athletes? Is this the way to promote young talents? After such horrific experience, who will really come forward for sports? And then we blame our country of a billion people for not getting us gold medals in the Olympics. It's really a matter of shame for the government that is preparing so rigorously for the Commonwealth Games, but has few facilities to extend towards National School Games.[77]

That is the real sporting tragedy of our times and the Commonwealth Games is not the solution. Yet, its organizers are looking ahead confidently at a potential Olympic bid. As one top official told us:

> If the Commonwealth Games are delivered well I think India will enhance its take for getting the Olympics Games. Now we can't really hazard a guess as to whether it is happening in 2020 or 2024 but it will be in close proximity. Today India is nowhere in reckoning because we haven't had a delivery, a showcase and now that will happen.[78]

BUREAUCRATS, SPORTSMEN AND THE REALITY

As the city is dug up and its sports administrators dream of Olympia, let us do another reality check on our sports scenario. In February 2008, the government announced that it was spending Rs 802 crore on elite sportsmen for improving their performance at the Commonwealth Games.[79] This was later revised to a spending of Rs 678 crore[80] and with the Games in sight, the sports ministry created a separate International Sports Division headed by a joint secretary and with a twelve-member staff.[81] Ministry mandarins have made much of its Long Term Development Plan (LTDP) to train athletes for big events. This includes the provision of foreign coaches, equipment provision, need-based and performance-based funding.[82] Table 1.3 lists the number of sportspersons being trained specifically for the Games.

A total of 1,280 athletes were trained with the CWG money by 2009.[83] At the same time, the number of trainees in Centres of Excellence has gone up from 10,000 at the beginning of the Tenth Plan to 18,000 at the end of 2008.[84] The figures look good until you begin to probe a little more. Champions take years to be made and much of this money is a little too late in the day, at least for 2010. The real problem, though, is deeper.

Government figures show that it gives virtually peanuts at the district level to schools – Rs 75,000 per district and Rs 3 lakhs per state to hold inter-school competitions.[85] Without a real school-level nursery, where will we find our future champions?

After much hue and cry, at least there is now a reward system in place for international medal winners – ranging from Rs 30 lakhs for an Olympic gold to Rs 3 lakhs for a Commonwealth gold – but the real story is in the pension plan for these champions: Rs 1500 – 5000

Table 1.3: Number of Sportspersons to be Trained in Each Discipline of Commonwealth Games, 2010 (as in March 2008)[86]

S. No.	Discipline	No. of sportspersons to be selected for training	
		Men	Women
1.	Archery	32	32
2.	Athletics	100	100
3.	Aquatics	60	45
4.	Badminton	20	20
5.	Boxing	44	0
6.	Cycling	75	42
7.	Gymnastics	24	36
8.	Hockey	48	48
9.	Lawn Bowls	15	15
10.	Net Ball	0	36
11.	Rugby 7s	36	0
12.	Shooting	100	50
13.	Squash	15	15
14.	Table Tennis	20	20
15.	Tennis	20	20
16.	Weightlifting	32	28
17.	Wrestling	56	28
18.	EAD★	36	18
	Total	**733**	**553**

*EAD: Elite Athletes with Disability

for gold /silver / bronze in Olympics/ World Cup / Asiad / Commonwealth Games / Para-Olympic Games.[87] Clearly, we are yet to treat our non-cricket sporting champions with the respect they deserve.

Look more closely at government figures and you realize that the malaise runs deep. Take the sports scholarship scheme which aims to assist sportspersons with '[a] nutritious diet, sports equipment support'. All it offers budding sportspersons is Rs 700 per month for a national-level scholarship and Rs 850 per month for college- and university-level scholarship.[88]

Even in the elite programme, a look at the salaries for foreign coaches shows that the highest salary paid till 2008 was for rifle shooting — $4500 per month. In most cases, the salaries of our much-touted foreign coaches were less than $3000 per month. For instance, two judo coaches were paid a princely sum of $950 per month (2006–07) and an athletics recovery expert was paid $1500 per month (2007–08).[89] You will only get poor-quality foreign coaches for this kind of money. They may make up the numbers in official reports but nothing will change on the ground with these kinds of investments.

SLUMS 'WE DON'T WANT TO SEE': THE GAMES AND DELHI'S BAMBOO MODERNITY

While supporting the city's bid for the Games, the then lieutenant governor of Delhi was ebullient in his choice of words. Harking back to the city's ancient heritage, he elegantly summed up: 'Delhi is a unique city, built with the stones of myth and tradition and the mortar of modernity … It is a city inspired by its heritage, while remaining open to innovation and modernity.'[90] There is that word again: modernity. The question is, whose idea of modernity are we getting through these Games and who will drive it?

In mid-2009, the newspapers reported that the Delhi government was so ashamed of the poverty on its streets that it was importing bamboo poles from the jungles of Mizoram and Assam to hide the poor from foreign visitors during the Games.[91] The plan was confirmed by the state's chief secretary to a British journalist. This is juvenile, short-sighted nationalism. Potemkin villages could do well in the nineteenth century but not in the age of the television camera and YouTube.

But the bamboo-curtain view of Delhi is shared by many of the movers and shakers of the Games. In early 2009, we visited Olympic Bhawan again to meet the director general of the Commonwealth Games. V.K. Verma is a sports administrator in the typical Indian mould; a director in the combined Air India and Indian Airlines conglomerate, he has also headed the Badminton Federation of India for years and been executive director of the Sports Authority of India.[92] If anyone knows the ins and outs of the logic of Indian sport, it is him. Receiving us in his office, the director general was charming and hospitable, but unapologetic when questioned about the massive displacements among the city's underclass because of the Games:

> We know that when a plane lands in Mumbai, the view of the slums sometimes create the first wrong impression about India … If I see from the viewpoint of a global traveller or somebody who is looking at India as a tourist destination, the slums must move out … Because we have to look at Delhi as the capital of India. We cannot present to the world a capital of the second-biggest global economy dotted with slums, and dotted with pockets that we don't want to see.[93]

His message is loud and clear: Delhi's guardians don't want the slums.

This is India and this is not the first time Delhi has been subjected to the draconian tendencies of some of its minority elites. This is a new modernity that has no space for the downtrodden. The city's silent majority is suddenly an eyesore. Tourism brochures are suddenly more important than the reality of the city.

But let us be fair to Verma. He did emphasize that those being moved out to show the world a better city were indeed being compensated to allow them a 'better start in life', but when we asked him about the compensation package, his answer was revealing: 'We are not into that. Organizing committee is not responsible. That is the Delhi government. I am sure Delhi government, more than anybody else, than any government, would look at how those people would respond and that is their direct responsibility.'[94]

It occurred to us that this wasn't just something that Verma was saying. He genuinely believed in his vision for Delhi. The fact is that it did not even occur to him that such statements could be seen as insensitive and elitist; that was the real punch in the guts.

The director general's aspirations for Delhi are not surprising. As a perceptive account of the city argues, Delhi's history shows that 'there is only a fine line to be drawn between the desire to create a totalizing image of the city and the confusion of that image with reality – hence the various attempts made by those in power to make the capital correspond to their desired image, and to suppress those aspects which do not conform'.[95]

The Commonwealth Games are merely another in a long line of such events that seek to change this ancient city completely.

'WHAT IMAGE WILL THE CAPITAL PRESENT?': THE FEAR OF SMALLNESS

India is not the first, nor will it be the last country, to use sports to project its power. Dubai's ruler Sheikh Mohammad bin Rashid al-Makhtoum has long used sport as part of a multi-billion-dollar charm offensive. The Gulf states have amassed a number of sporting events for precisely this reason: golf (four events), tennis (Qatar and the Dubai Open), the WTA Championship 2008 – 10, horse racing (the Dubai World Cup), motor sport (Bahrain GP, Qatar Moto GP, Abu Dhabi GP) and soccer (2011 AFC Asian Cup in Qatar).[96] All kinds of governments, representing every type of political ideology, have endorsed international sporting competition as a testing ground for the nation or for a political system – German Nazis, Italian fascists, Soviet and Cuban communists, Chinese Maoists, Western capitalist democrats, Latin American juntas – all have played the game and believed in it.[97]

Sporting events are so important for national pride that when Paris lost the bid to host the 2012 Olympics, *Le Monde* predicted that 'the current malaise in France is likely to get worse'.[98] We do not doubt that big sporting events have an appeal for cities and nations – that is why they are so popular. There are indeed benefits, but as one study of big games warns:

> Their benefits continue to be chronically oversold and their opportunity costs minimized and overlooked. Their continued – indeed growing – popularity therefore presents a puzzle that can at least partly be accounted for by the particular appeal and usefulness of such events as a strategic response to the conditions of globalization ...
>
> ... there are predictable patterns of hyperbolic promotion, collective gullibility and underappreciated opportunity costs and distributional impacts that deserve much closer attention from responsible policy-makers than they typically receive.[99]

These words ring true for Delhi. India's capital is looking to graduate from 'developing country' status with these Games and the organizers are simultaneously promoting an internal appeal to patriotism.[100]

The fear of failure pervades the city. It occurs in unlikely places. In December 2008, ruling on a case dealing with a contractor's poor quality work, Justice Kailash Gambhir of the Delhi High Court exemplified it well:'The MCD and other agencies taking care of roads in Delhi should now be on tenterhooks because Delhi is hosting the Commonwealth Games. What image will the capital of the country project if the roads are not of international standards and remain in such poor conditions?'[101] This is the gnawing ache that is changing a city and changing it irrevocably. But how? It is to this story that we now turn.

2 | DELHI'S SELLOTAPE LEGACY

FOR A MONSOON WEDDING

The Bird's Nest burst into a breathtaking kaleidoscope of colours and as the triumphal swansong of Beijing concluded on the television screen, the news anchors turned and asked if Delhi would do an encore. We were in different television studios, discussing the successes of Beijing as the closing ceremony of the Olympics faded out. Both of us got the same question. It was an obvious comparison to make, but even more pertinent because China, at some level, has come to symbolize some of India's deepest insecurities and fears. In a different context, Shekhar Gupta, editor-in-chief of the *Indian Express*, has noted that in our discourse on China it is as if we psychologically 'continue to fight the 1962 war' in one form or another; somehow 'the scar refuses to fade away'.[1] To fail is one thing, but to fail where the Chinese have succeeded is quite another. The Commonwealth Games, of course, hardly compare with the scale of an Olympics. But this is precisely why the heady success of Beijing seemed to have added an even greater stench of failure to our Games effort.

With the exception of Suresh Kalmadi, everyone who has had anything to do with the Games – the Commonwealth Games Federation, the comptroller and auditor general,[2] a parliamentary panel on tourism and culture,[3] the Delhi High Court and the Delhi Urban Arts Commission – has at some point or the other waved a red flag and invoked the spectre of impending disaster. Now, Delhi is not Beijing and India is not China – socially, culturally and politically – so at one level, the comparison only serves puerile nationalist notions. Yet, it is a useful barometer and we cannot ignore our own oversights and failures. More is at stake here than the fate of a sporting event, and the world has watched a country that sees itself as an emerging great power tying itself up in knots over things that should have been simple. In mid-2009, the prime minister was forced to step in and ask his sports minister to take on a bigger role, providing additional 'assistance' to the organizing committee.[4] The question is, how did we get here? Why does the Commonwealth Games Federation demand prime ministerial intervention and why do Indian sport officials call it an 'imperial federation' for its insistence on retaining a foreign CEO in Delhi?[5]

The television programme on Beijing ignited something in the veteran sports presenter Charu Sharma. He had been on the discussion panel, and walking out of the studio, began reminiscing about the things he had seen in twenty years as a sports presenter in India:

> We don't have a culture for institutions. It happens again and again. No one bothers about processes, policies, about getting it right, in the right way, as you would expect in something as big as this. Then, suddenly, everyone wakes up and panics because there is this huge event looming in front. You can't fix the fundamental things any more so what do you do – you put sellotape over the cracks and somehow manage to pull it off. And then we go and do it all over again, again and again. We don't learn anything. *What we have is a sellotape culture* and people say, '*chalta hai*'.[6]

Talk of the Games crops up in unlikely places. More often than not, it leaves a horrible sinking feeling – a bit like watching a car crash in slow motion and hoping like hell that somehow, something will save it. A week after that television show, we found ourselves in the Army headquarters on personal business. The spit and polish of the Army's corner in South Block was a far cry from the maddening confusions of the Games. Officers in shining medals walked around smartly. There was an air of order in the musty colonial corridors and brass flower-pots sparkled as only army brass pots can.

Waiting to see a general in his anteroom, we struck up a conversation with one of his senior staff officers. The Games came up, and the moment he heard about this book, he shook his head in exasperation. 'You know, we already have our contingency plans ready,' he said. 'We know they may well ask us to sort the mess out in the end. They always do.' He saw our puzzled looks – the Army doesn't figure in any of the official Games plans – so he added with a smile, 'Oh, we just haven't told them yet. Because then they will ask us to get involved immediately.' This conversation took place some time in August 2008 but before we could quiz him further, we were ushered in for the appointment with his boss, who refused to comment. What happens when all else fails? Can the Army be the last resort, if it comes to that? The Army, of course, played a big part in the logistics of the 1982 Asiad and whether our officer in South Block was right or not about its 2010 contingency plans, he was pointing to a much deeper problem.

Sports Minister M.S. Gill, who has been trying to solve a problem that he didn't create, acknowledged this in early 2009 when he compared the Games to the madness and the spectacle of the great Indian wedding. 'Never mind the delays,' he promised. 'Like a seemingly disorganized arrangement in an Indian marriage – just like in the movie *Monsoon Wedding* – we will have a grand Games.'[7]

Gill has been acting as a virtual troubleshooter since October 2009, when a worried prime minister asked him to sort things out. The question is, why did the minister's 'monsoon wedding' reach such a pass? What did Delhi promise in the euphoria of the Games bid and what has been the reality on the ground? When did things start going wrong and why? Who will pay the price? Can it finally be salvaged as the government puts its collective might behind the Games effort in its final lap? These are the questions that this chapter explores.

OF THE PEOPLE, BY THE PEOPLE BUT NOT RESPONSIBLE TO THE PEOPLE

In December 2008, a lawyer representing the Commonwealth Games organizing committee made an astounding statement before a Delhi court. Refusing to provide information under the Right to Information Act, Advocate B.P. Singh, appearing for the committee, argued, '*We are not responsible to people*. We get loans from the governments so we are responsible only to them and the government [is in turn] responsible to the public.'[8] The organizing committee was refusing to reveal information about its affairs even though it is funded almost entirely by the government and *despite* strictures from the sports ministry.[9]

It was an extraordinary argument to make, and quite telling about the proprietary mindset of those who were running the show at the organizing committee. The Games are ostensibly about bettering Delhi but here were its organizers arguing that they didn't think they were responsible to the city's people. As their lawyers argued in the Delhi High Court:

> The committee does not fulfil the criteria of being declared a State under Article 12 of the Constitution and hence it cannot be declared a public authority. The committee has not been established or constituted as an institution of self-government or under the Constitution. It has not been created under the law made either by Parliament or state legislature.[10]

The organizing committee had no qualms about taking thousands of crores of public money but refused to be bound by the rules that govern public institutions. The Central Information Commission's definition of public authorities subject to the RTI Act clearly includes organizations substantially financed by the Central government or state governments. Its manual states clearly that the 'financing of the body or the NGO by the government may be direct or indirect'.[11] The organizing committee claimed exemption because its funding is in the nature of government loans but why this extreme reticence for any transparency with the public? Whose interest does it serve? Technicalities apart, if the organizing committee had been performing well, would it have opposed the RTI requests so vehemently? There was, perhaps, too much to be embarrassed about. In January 2010, the Delhi High Court dismissed the organizing committee's arguments and forced it to disclose information.

The discord between the Ministry of Sport and the organizing committee over the disclosure of information also reveals a great deal about the complex management structure put in place for the Games. Even though the Games have always enjoyed the support of Delhi's ruling governments – at the Centre and at the state – there is a clear distinction between the government per se and the organizing committee. With Kalmadi at its head, the organizing committee was created in February 2005 as a registered society vested with the responsibility of delivering the Games. Its executive board is a fifteen-member body which includes the chairman and vice chairman, two nominees each of the Central and state governments and the IOA, four nominees from national sports federations and three nominees of the CGF.[12]

Despite the presence of dozens of other governmental committees to oversee the Games effort, in practice, the organizing committee's secretariat virtually drove its own furrow until the prime minister's office decided to act in October 2009 and got the sports ministry to take greater control. We will examine this complex administrative structure in detail later in this chapter but, for now, this distinction between the sports ministry, the Delhi government and the organizing committee is an important one to keep in mind.

THE HOSTEL THAT WASN'T

Delhi may still have its miracle, but there were structural reasons for the quagmire it found itself in, just a year before the Games. The story of the Games Village characterizes all that went wrong and deserves a close look. In 2003, Delhi was in serious danger of losing its Games bid to Hamilton, the Canadian city that hosted the first version of the Commonwealth Games in 1930 (it was called the British Empire Games then). In a two-horse race, both cities submitted detailed plans to the CGF in May 2003. When they were opened, Delhi found itself on the back foot on one of the most important questions that determine sporting mega-events: legacies and long-term impact on the city. Hamilton had put the local McMaster University at the centre of its Games concept. It put academic partnerships as the second-most important objective of the Games and the university was slated to benefit from the entire new infrastructure that was to be built.[13] The Games Village and three of the other five new sporting venues that Hamilton proposed were to be built on the 300-acre campus of McMaster University.[14] The idea was to create a permanent legacy of world-class and accessible sporting infrastructure for students in this small city of 500,000.[15]

In contrast, Delhi's original bid proposed to build a Games Village and to sell it as luxury apartments after the Games concluded. Compared to Hamilton's focus on its university, Delhi seemed on shaky ground. Even more seriously, India's sporting czars said that they would finance almost 40 per cent of the then–estimated cost of the Games from the sale of these flats.[16] This looked decidedly risky. The flats could only be sold after the Games. If they were also supposed to pay for the Games, how would the Games be held in the first place? And what if the flats failed to yield the expected revenue? The CGF's technical experts rightly saw this as a major financial risk for Delhi.

Delhi needed to win the bid. So, when the CGF's experts raised these questions, Delhi's organizers agreed to a major change. The plan to sell the flats to finance part of the Games was 'subsequently amended' to ensure that the budget would not be reliant on the sale of the accommodation.[17] By October 2003, Delhi submitted a revised budget wherein the Delhi Development Authority (DDA) took over the risk and responsibility of the Village and the CGF Evaluation Commission reported that the 'sale of residential apartments is not [any more] a risk to the Games budget'.[18] Basically, government agencies agreed to pay for the money that the flats' sale would have provided.

One of the most disturbing but little-known stories of these Games is that at the same time, Delhi's organizers also promised that its Games Village would be turned into hostel accommodation for Delhi University after the Games. CGF documents are unambiguous on this count. Leading up to the crucial vote of Commonwealth countries in November 2003, when Delhi finally won the Games, it gave an undertaking that 'post-Games, the Village will provide hostel facility for the Delhi University'.[19] This was done, it seems, to make Delhi look as committed to education as Hamilton did with McMaster University. India's sports managers championed this idea and the notion of the Village as a university hostel was prominently displayed in Delhi's revised bid documents. As the CGF noted, 'The Games Village will provide an excellent hostel facility for the Delhi University and will remain available for residential use during hosting of future international events.'[20]

This plan was published in cold print but was never heard of once Delhi won the bid. Delhi's Games masters had always intended on selling the real estate and the much-needed DU hostel plan was given a quiet burial. Few people knew of the commitment to the Delhi University and there was virtually no public protest when it was cancelled. Instead of creating a student hostel for the overcrowded university, the organizers now focussed again on getting in a private builder to create ridiculously high-priced apartments that would be sold to rich Indians after the Games. As the organizing committee's director general told us proudly: 'It is not what the 1982 Asian Games Village was. It is not being constructed by a government agency with a government vision. It is totally private luxury apartments [complex] that is coming up in March 2010 [sic].'[21] Marketing posters for the Village apartments are even more indicative. Enticing Delhites to buy the flats, the posters proclaim the Village as 'the finest address in Delhi', one of the 'finest concepts in luxury living' and one that will 'set new standard in fine living'.[22]

It is pertinent to ask what would have benefited the city more: a student hostel or yet another gated enclave for the rich? The answer is obvious but when we asked the organizing committee's director general about why the student hostel commitment was dropped, he seemed to dismiss the question: 'No. That must have been superseded because now the Games Village will be auctioned to private bidders; a major part of the Games Village is private accommodation which will be sold by the builders, by the developers, to the public.'[23]

THE GREAT VILLAGE MUDDLE

The U-turn on the Games Village is at the heart of a central question on who these Games are intended to benefit: the city as a whole or a tiny, elite minority? Linked to this is the heated debate over the location of the Village. Rising on the east bank of the Yamuna, the sixty-hectare Village site[24] has been pilloried by activists on environmental grounds. Eventually cleared by the Supreme Court after a tortuous legal battle, its story is reflective of the shadows that have characterized the Games effort since its early stages.

As early as 2003, the lieutenant governor of Delhi announced that the government had set aside land for the Village.[25] The 2003 bid document did not name the site but helpfully explained that it would be 'just twenty-five minutes from the airport, thirty minutes from the central business district and twenty minutes from all major venues'.[26] Subsequent events were to show, however, that the location was chosen prior to conducting detailed impact studies. The permissions were to come later. At the height of the environmental row that was later to engulf the Village, the minister of urban development told the Parliament that even though an expert appraisal committee of the Ministry of Environment and Forests had, in October 2006, mentioned the Safdarjung Airport as a possible alternative Games Village site, the authorities had gone ahead with the Yamuna riverbank site because the Commonwealth Games Federation had already approved it in November 2003.[27] From the beginning, then, the Yamuna site seems to have been a fait accompli. This is a crucial point, when set against the backdrop of the high decibel environmental debate around the Village and the legal twists and turns that followed.

To simplify a complex argument, environmental activists claim two things. First, the flood plain of the Yamuna is crucial for Delhi's ecological security and should be left free from construction. It is a safety valve that protects the city – especially the east Delhi region – preventing water from flooding outside the river bed into populated areas. Any permanent structure over it will seriously damage the region's ecology and have catastrophic consequences in the future.[28] The claim is that the Village is precisely such a structure. Secondly, the site is a water recharge zone and permanent construction on it could damage levels of ground water, which Delhi depends on.[29]

How valid are these arguments and how were requisite clearances given to DDA for the Village? Let us examine the sequence of events. There are three key milestones that have defined the debate.

First: in 2005, the National Environmental Engineering Research Institute (NEERI) submitted a general report to the DDA on the rejuvenation of the Yamuna. It argued that no permanent structures should be built on the riverbed or in its immediate vicinity. This was based on an earlier study of the area carried out in 1999.[30] In 2008, the NEERI revised its opinion, arguing that the Village was not a threat to the environment because a bund built in the year 2000 to prevent floodwaters from reaching the Akshardham temple had altered the river's flood plain and the Village site no longer lay within the threatened zone.[31]

Second: an expert committee of the Ministry of Environment and Forests had at first expressed reservations and suggested an alternative Games Village site.[32] Later, on 14 December 2006, the ministry did give construction clearance, but subject to certain conditions. Initially, the ministry only gave the DDA clearance to construct temporary structures ruling that 'actual work on permanent structures shall not start till mitigation/abatement measures against upstream flooding are identified through studies'.[33] Subsequently, though, through a series of letters culminating on 23 April 2007,[34] the ministry altered the nature of its permission, allowing permanent constructions, and, hence, the Village to go ahead.[35]

Third: as *India Today* reported, the DDA made a key change in land use for the site in its 2021 Master Plan, 'changing the description of the proposed site for the Village from "agriculture and water body" to land for "residential" and "commercial" use'.[36] Steps for changing the land use had been initiated as early as 1999.[37] Table 2.1 details the changes of stand affected by the major agencies concerned.

The Delhi High Court was outraged by the volte-face of the agencies concerned. Ruling on a Public Interest Litigation, on 3 November 2008, it raised serious questions over the Village by ordering the formation of a four-member committee, headed by Nobel laureate R.K. Pachauri, to gauge its environmental impact. The court ruled that the agencies pursuing the construction were doing so 'at their own peril' and that the future of the site would be subject to the findings of the report. The divisional bench consisting of Justice A.K. Sikri and Justice R.K. Sharma was particularly angry at the NEERI,[38] which, according to the court, went against its own stand to say that the bund created for the Akshardham temple was sufficient to prevent flooding of the area.[39] As Justice Sikri opined, 'It was not expected from an institution of this repute that a report of this kind would be submitted.' Justice Sharma was even more acerbic: 'Reports of NEERI show how it has changed colours…' She also criticized the Union Ministry of Environment and Forests for changing its position, arguing, 'It is a sad story of men in haste fiddling with major issues

Table 2.1: The Village and the Environmental Permissions: Timeline[40]

Institution	Initial Stand	Revised Stand
Ministry of Environment and Forests	• Expert committee in 2006 suggested alternative venue. • In December 2006 gave permission for temporary structures only. Asked for studies against upstream flooding before any work on permanent structures could begin.	In April 2007, amended order to allow construction of permanent structures.
NEERI	In 2005, argued against any permanent structures on river bed. Based on 1999 study.	Revised opinion in 2008, arguing that a bund built in 2000 had redefined the Yamuna's flood plain.
DDA	Proposed land use for the Village site was for 'agriculture and water body'.	2021 Master Plan changed the proposed land-use description for the Village site to 'residential' and 'commercial projects'.

and resultantly playing havoc … neither NEERI nor the ministry nor the DDA can be said to have acted fairly and objectively. Their hands appear to be tainted.'[41]

The Delhi government, of course, claimed that all due clearances were taken[42] but the question was about the manner in which this was done. As the convenor of the Yamuna Jiye Abhiyan [Yamuna Lives Campaign], Manoj Mishra said: 'This whole case is regarding River Yamuna and its security … A nine-day event is important or security of Yamuna flood plains?'[43] Environmentalists pointed to the Central Ground Water Authority and the Yamuna Standing Committee, for instance, which, in response to an RTI application in 2007, said that it had never given any permission for any bore wells or tube wells for the Village.[44]

As the environmental debate was raging, a new factor entered the mix: a private developer and a first-of-its-kind public–private partnership. The DDA followed up the Ministry of Environment's clearance by awarding the contract for building the accommodation in the Village to Emaar-MGF in June 2007. Under this agreement, Emaar-MGF could sell 768 of the 1,168 premier flats being built on the site for profit, while the rest would be held by the DDA after the Games. Bookings for these luxury flats opened in 2008 but Emaar-MGF soon ran into serious financial trouble.[45] Pointing to major cost overruns and the economic slowdown, it put up its hands in December 2008, asking for a huge loan.[46] With the clock ticking and the deadline drawing closer, the DDA agreed. In the first such bailout plan for a private developer in the city,[47] in May 2009, the DDA announced a bailout package of Rs 766 crore, under which it agreed to buy an additional 333 flats from Emaar-MGF, apart from its existing share of one-third of the total apartments.[48]

Though the argument was ultimately lost, one of the lawyers for the environmental groups went so far as to say in the Supreme Court that 'a real estate activity is going on there under the garb of the Games'.[49] This is the fear that has animated environmentalists and activists in the city ever since the Games plans were unveiled. Sociologist Amita Baviskar summed up these general apprehensions in 2007:

For Delhi's ecological security, it is of paramount importance that the flood plain be left untouched. It should be a no-go zone for construction. But the Dikshit government is committed to channelizing the river and turning the river bed into real estate. Think of the Thames Embankment, it says, what a glittering jewel in London's crown. But the Yamuna is not the Thames; its rhythm is harmonized to the distinctive tempo of the Indian subcontinent's seasons. With the bulk of its flow concentrated in the monsoons, the Yamuna is liable to breach its embankments if denied its present expanse … As the [Yamuna Jiye] Abhiyan points out, we already have too many buildings on the riverfront that shouldn't be there: three power plants, the Delhi Secretariat and the Akshardham temple. We don't need more, and certainly not a sprawling 150-acre strip of Games Village houses, hotels and malls …

First they take a stupid decision like locating the Games Village on the eastern flood plain of the Yamuna. Then they make it worse by piling up other foolish schemes on top of it …'[50]

The Supreme Court, though, found such apprehensions about the Village untenable. At about the same time as when Emaar was asking the DDA for a bailout – December 2008 – the apex court stepped in and stayed the Delhi court's orders stalling construction work in the Commonwealth Games village.

The Supreme Court's ruling came after the DDA forcefully argued that scientific evidence was on its side. The sports ministry, the Delhi government, the DDA and the builders, all agreed that any delays in constructing the Village would seriously jeopardize the holding of the Games, which had already sucked in thousands of crores of rupees.[51] Implicit in the government's plea was a real fear of failure and the impending deadline. This was also about the time that the CGF issued the first of its public criticisms of the Games arrangements. Its chairman, Austin Sealy, said in November 2008 that he was concerned about the state of preparation and the dispute over the Games Village, so much so that India could lose the Games. He said, 'Any change at this late stage to the Games Village arrangements would seriously jeopardize India's hosting of the Games.'[52] The stakes were just too high.

Cancelling the Games would not only cause serious embarrassment but also make the government liable to pay crores in damages to Commonwealth countries and private stakeholders.[53] By now, the financial implications had also become a huge factor, including those for private builders. The DDA pointed this out, saying that if construction did not resume, 'people would be reluctant to come forward to purchase the flats and therefore fund generation in these troubled economic times would be a serious problem'.[54]

The legal battle was ultimately resolved only in July 2009, when the Supreme Court gave a definitive green light to the Village. It said in no uncertain terms that the High Court had 'disregarded and ignored material scientific literature and the opinion of experts and scientific bodies which have categorically held that the Commonwealth Games Village (CGV) site is neither located on a "river bed" nor on the "flood plain"'. It gave a clean chit to the project, saying that 'at every stage, the ecological integrity of the river, the concepts of "river bed", "flood plain" and "river zone" were duly considered' and faulted the High Court for even entertaining the PIL because it was filed after a long delay.[55]

The legal battle exposed all the fault lines in the Games effort: the absence of a single window for clearances and the resultant maze of complex red tape and the lack of transparency, which led to a distrust of the organizers and, ultimately, caused significant delays in construction (Table 2.2). Sample this: the Village was to have been ready by December 2009. Even the process of finalizing the construction companies for some of the venues and the Village was not completed till mid-2007.[56] This meant that construction did not begin till October 2007.[57] Valuable lead time went by, there were several bureaucratic delays and virtually every step of the way was littered with complex legal callisthenics.

THE BID AND THE REALITY

It is no secret that the organizing committee has always been woefully behind most of Delhi's own targets. Delhi's glossy 2003 bid document had promised that 'all major Games facilities either exist or would be created by 2007, except for the Games Village'.[58] This included a grand commitment by the Central and state governments to 'complete' new venues (one outdoor and two indoor stadiums) by 2007.[59] The evaluation committee of the Commonwealth Games Federation did push the original timelines a little forward. Even according to this, however, most venues were to be delivered by 2008, some even by 2005.[60]

The reality on the ground has been very different. Conscious of the delays, the government shifted the goalposts in 2007, when the urban development minister presented a revised deadline schedule before the Parliament (See Table 2.3).[61]

Anyone who has been to any of these sites, of course, knows that, in practice, many of these deadlines meant little. In a suo motu audit published in July 2009, the comptroller and auditor general of India reported a dismal rate of progress. Its auditors characterized thirteen

Table 2.2: Main Delays/Problems in Games Village Project[62]

Agency/Issue	Problem	Status/Response
Litigation on environmental issues	PIL filed in October 2007 in Delhi High Court. Court ordered committee on environmental impact in November 2008.	Supreme Court stayed order and judgment of Delhi High Court in December 2008. Gave clearance in July 2009.
DDA and private partner for construction of residential accommodation (1186 flats)	• DDA took 10 months to select the private partner due to a delay in finalizing the list of bidders and preparing the RFP. • DDA entered into PPP with Emaar-MGF in September 2007. • Targets not achieved even after shifting and revision of deadlines. • Private builder slowed construction in December 2008 citing fund problems and global slowdown.	• DDA: Many procedures new to it in public–private partnership. • DDA: Milestones had to be revised due to objections from NGOs, Akshardham temple, litigation, configuration of rooms/flats. • DDA announced bailout package of Rs 766 crore in May 2009 for additional share of 333 flats from project developer's share of apartments, in addition to DDA's existing share of one-third apartments.
DDA	DDA engaged a third party for quality assurance only in May 2008, by which time 25 per cent of the period of execution was already over.	• DDA: No substantial delays and all facilities will be handed over to OC by stipulated timeline of June 2010.
DDA	Venue briefs were received in December 2006, but DDA appointed technical consultants for the project only in February 2007.	• Many procedures new to DDA in public–private partnership.
Construction work for the swimming pool, training hall, fitness centre, athletic track and internal development (roads and subways)	Was awarded only in April 2008, after a year's delay.	
Proposed Entry Roads	Two separate entry roads from NOIDA link road were planned but these roads pass through 15-metre strip of land owned by the Uttar Pradesh government, which had not given permission till July 2009.	DDA: Proposal for land acquisition was sent in July 2009 to Land Acquisition Collector.

Table 2.3: Targets and Progress of Competition Venues of Commonwealth Games 2010[63]

Project	Target dates of completion (Set in 2007)	Revised Deadline	Progress in July 2009 (As reported by CAG)
A. DDA			
1. Games Village			
a) Residential	1.3.2010		
b) Practice Venue	1.5.2010		30 – 55%
c) Temporary Overlay	1.5.2010		
2. Siri Fort Sports Complex (Badminton and Squash)	31.12.2009		46%
3. Yamuna Sports Complex			
a) Table Tennis	31.12.2009		46%
b) Archery	15.12.2009		7%
B. SAI/CPWD			
1. Jawaharlal Nehru Stadium			
a) Main Stadium (athletics)	15.11.2009		54%
b) Wada Admn. Block	21.9.2008		
c) Hostels	31.8.2009		
d) Weight Lifting Hall	15.11.2009	Dec. 2009	43%
2. Major Dhyan Chand National Stadium	30.9.2009		75%
3. IG Stadium			
a) Wrestling Hall	31.10.2009	Dec. 2009	43%
b) Gymnastics Hall	31.10.2009		56%
c) Cycling Velodrome	30.10.2009	Feb./March 2010	35%

Contd.

Project	Target dates of completion (Set in 2007)	Revised Deadline	Progress in July 2009 (As reported by CAG)
4. Dr Karni Singh Shooting Range	31.3.2009	Dec. 2009	42%
5. SPM Swimming Pool Complex	31.10.2009	March 2010	42%
C. Government of NCT of Delhi			
1. Thyagaraj Sports Complex	19.9.2008		69%
D. New Delhi Municipal Council			
1. Talkatora Indoor Stadium	30.11.2009		73%
E. Delhi University			
1. Main Ground Rugby 7s	15.11.2009	Jan. 2010	34%
F. All India Tennis Association			
1. R.K. Khanna Tennis Complex	31.12.2009		45%

of the nineteen competition and training venues as medium-risk – with a shortfall of 25 to 50 per cent with targets – and expressed serious concern about the Shyama Prasad Mukherjee Aquatic Complex in particular. This was termed especially high-risk – with a shortfall of over 50 per cent – and the auditors ruled that even the revised deadline of February or March 2010 'would be challenging'. In addition, of the thirty-five flyovers and bridges directly related to the Games, the CAG reported that as many as twenty-three were running behind schedule. Twenty of these projects were critical due to slow progress, with nine at high and two at medium risk.[64] Table 2.3 details the original deadlines vis-à-vis the July 2009 progress rates of construction. Months before the CAG's damning verdict virtually forced the prime minister's intervention, the *Hindustan Times* summed up the collective fear that seemed to be building up:

> What is actually needed for it [the Games] to materialize without our embarrassing ourselves, is a miracle. And even more money ... What we face is a race against time. The ambitious airport project is facing a cash crunch. Roads and flyovers to be completed by 2008 have hit a dead-end. The DDA is yet to find a contractor for the Games Village flyover. The elevated corridor connecting the Games Village to the Nehru Stadium has barely begun. The venues are officially 40 per cent complete, but walk by them and all you can see is a mess.[65]

THE PROBLEM

In *The Great Indian Novel*, Shashi Tharoor famously observed that India is not 'an underdeveloped country' but 'a highly developed one in an advanced state of decay'. It was a phrase that captured the overwhelming despair and shabbiness that had come to characterize the worst excesses of the licence–permit raj. The rise of the Azim Premjis and Narayan Murthys in the 1990s shattered that grand narrative of fallen greatness, ushering in a new era of self-belief. This is an India that is fast emerging as one of the new pillars of the world economy; an India that gives billions of dollars to the International Monetary Foundation (IMF) in return for a greater say at the global high table;[66] an India that has the chutzpah to create a cocky global brand like the Indian Premier League (IPL) from scratch. Delhi certainly has the talents and the abilities, yet it made a mess of the Commonwealth Games. As always, in India, opposites coexist. Just as the Naxals and their voiceless, excluded multitudes continually remind us of our dark underbelly, threatening to engulf the shining lights of Manmohan Singh's brave new India, so do shibboleths from the past coexist with the promise of a brighter tomorrow. The story of the Commonwealth Games in its first few years is a case in point.

We watched incredulously in Melbourne when the organizing committee flew in Aishwarya Rai, Saif Ali Khan and Rani Mukherjee to dance to the drumbeats at the closing ceremony of the 2006 Commonwealth Games. The stars were meant to showcase Delhi, to somehow put it on the map. No one quite understood why, but the ten-minute Bollywood trailer cost the Delhi government a whopping Rs 29 crore. In contrast, the entire Indian sports contingent at the Melbourne Games cost the government less than Rs 3 crore.[67] In a sense, though, this lopsided spending was rather symbolic of the Games effort. When they should have been focussing on the script, the organizers have often seemed to focus on the item number. What should have been *Sholay* has been looking horribly like Ram Gopal Varma's high-octane but shoddy replica.

To begin with, Delhi got off the starting block rather late. Beijing 2008 and London 2012, for instance, followed a seven-year time cycle: two years for planning and approvals, four years for construction and development and the last year for test events and trial runs.[68] In the case of Delhi, though, the first few years were utterly wasted. As per the contract with the CGF, Delhi's OC was to be in place by May 2004, but it was not formed until as late as February 2005. In contrast, the OC for the 2014 Commonwealth Games in Glasgow was formed even before the award of the Games.[69]

This rendered most of the original timelines redundant. The bid document had four phases: 2004–06 for planning, 2006–08 for creating, 2008–10 for delivering and 2010–11 for concluding. The CAG's auditors found 'no evidence of the four-phase approach being translated into action during the first phase years of 2004 to 2006'. Planning commenced only from late 2006.[70] Part of the problem was the serious lack of expertise within the OC for organizing an event of this magnitude. It had set itself the target for recruiting key functional heads by April 2007.[71] Yet, several posts at this level were only being advertised for and filled up by the end of 2008. An important unit like communications did not get an ADG until mid-2009. The first steps to fill the gaps were only taken with the appointment of technical consultants in 2007.[72] The organizing committee's director general was quite candid about the learning curve his organization had been on:

> Most of us have been to several Olympic Games, several Asian Games. When you go to these Games, you are not really becoming a part of their workforce. You are not becoming an insider. What you are experiencing is much more than a spectator but you are still a guest. So you are seeing the brighter side, the happier side of the Games. The toil, the sweat that is inside, you have not been a part of …
>
> We also have consultants … but again consultants can only take you that far … then you have to run.[73]

But the Games effort didn't run. It crawled. There was a serious problem of coordination between a virtual jungle of government agencies. The organizing committee's own SWOT analysis in 2007 had highlighted a 'general apprehension' about the problem of 'inadequate formal or established protocols' to coordinate between multiple stakeholders and government agencies.[74] This is exactly what went wrong. Twenty-one major organizations and agencies were involved, each with different roles, budgets and reporting lines. According to the CAG, 'Many agencies were either unaware of their role or refuted the role expected of them.' Many even had different timelines for the same project.[75] Even though the government set up a core group of ministers to coordinate the work, pulling together so many moving parts proved to be a bureaucratic quagmire with as many as twenty-two sub-committees.[76] The PMO was involved at sporadic intervals, taking status updates in 2006 and 2008,[77] but one gets the overwhelming impression that the entire impetus lacked a strong centre of the kind that Rajiv Gandhi gave to the 1982 Games.

In 1982, the prime minister's young son, cutting his political teeth, had spearheaded the effort, giving the Buta Singh-led organizing committee a focussed coherence from the highest level. In contrast,

2010 seemed to lack such a concentrated direction, leaving everything to the Kalmadi cohorts until the sports ministry began taking charge in 2009.

Cumulatively, this caused serious problems. For instance, the organizing committee submitted its budget to the government in November 2006, but it received approval only in April 2007.[78] Similarly, basic planning documents were way behind schedule. The Games Organization Plan and Games Master Schedule were to have been ready by May 2004. These were only finalized for the CGF's approval in August 2007 and May 2008.[79] The test event strategy was to be ready by October 2008 but it wasn't – even by mid-2009. Out of thirty-four functional areas in the General Organization Plan, draft operational plans had been prepared for only sixteen by March 2009.[80]

One has to ask: just what was happening? The managerial limbo translated into chaos at the venues. Until February 2009, construction had not begun on lawn balls and archery sites. Construction work for the velodrome only began in January 2009.[81] As the CAG pointed out, on the ground, this laxity meant that '[the] organization committee had given only conditional approval to the final designs for most venues'. Shockingly, in thirteen cases, at eleven venues, agencies began construction even before conditional approval of the final designs by the organizing committee.[82] With the government failing to evolve a single-window clearance system, a great deal of construction activity got stuck in a sticky bureaucratic swamp. In five major venues – Jawaharlal Nehru Stadium, the National Stadium, IG Stadium, SPM Aquatic Complex and Karni Singh Shooting Range – applications for twenty-four NOCs were submitted up to eleven months after the stipulated date of completion of the related consultancy work of which they were supposed to be part. Jamia Millia Islamia had still not applied for clearances for rugby 7s and TT training venues in March 2009.[83]

Not surprisingly, the old chestnut of national pride became the last defence for infrastructural delays. Time and time again, when the administrators have been accused of not following the rules, they have responded with the same basic argument – forget the rules now, the nation's pride is at stake. As a Delhi Urban Arts Commission (DUAC)

Table 2.4: CAG Findings on Finalization of Basic Planning Documents (up to May 2009)[84]

S. No.	Milestone Originally Specified	Original Deadline	Approval by CGF	Delay in months
1.	Formation of OC	May 2004	February 2005	9
2.	General Organization Plan, OC	May 2004	August 2007	39
3.	Master Plan of OC and the Games	May 2004	Nov. 2008	54
4.	Written approval of joint marketing agreement	December 2005	Pending	41
5.	Approval for sports programme	October 2007	Nov. 2007	1
6.	Approval of cultural programme	October 2007	Pending	19
7.	Approval of international and national business programme	October 2007	Pending	19
8.	Branding strategy encompassing the designs and usage of Games emblem and other Games symbols	October 2007	Pending	19
9.	Implementation plans for technology and IS with statement of requirements	October 2007	Pending	20
10.	Test event strategy and plan for organizing the test events	October 2008	Pending	8
11.	System of distribution of admission tickets	October 2008	Pending	8
12.	Plans for Games corporate hospitality programme	October 2008	Pending	8
13.	System for accreditation for written consent of CGF	October 2008	Pending	8
14.	Outlines of official reports	October 2008	Pending	8
15.	Corporate hospitality plan	October 2008	Pending	8
16.	System of distribution of admission plan	October 2008	Pending	8

member told the *Times of India*: 'There is no overall planning and they want us to clear projects in a hurry before the Games and compromise the city ultimately.' The DUAC had been at loggerheads over projects like the Barapullah Nallah, East–West Corridor, Salimgarh Bypass Road and the Airport Express Line. A Commission panel was accused of blocking Commonwealth projects. As DUAC Chairman K.T. Ravindran said:

> Suddenly the government bodies like Public Works Department seem to have woken up to a Commonwealth Games deadline and there is time pressure. So, they want DUAC clearance at the earliest. These projects should have been planned years in advance. There is simply no planning strategy ... In any foreign country, projects are completed much before the deadline and trials are also run on them.[85]

Delhi's PWD Minister Raj Kumar Chauhan had a different spin on it: 'No one will blame the DUAC if the government fails to complete the project by Commonwealth Games; it will all come down on us and the country. India will get a bad name for poor preparedness.'[86] Chief Minister Sheila Dikshit had a similar take after the DUAC held up clearances for the Ring Road bypass and the East – West corridor. 'I am worried,' she said in early 2009. 'It is not as if aesthetics don't matter but there are ugly structures in Delhi despite the DUAC. We are also concerned about the green cover, but as a government we need to move on.'[87] The pressure was beginning to show.

A classic example is the bitter dispute over the construction of the basketball and squash complex at Siri Fort. It led to large-scale felling of trees in the Siri Fort 'green area', strong protests by resident welfare societies and a court case. The Supreme Court, on 27 April 2009, finally cleared the project arguing that too much time had been lost and the damage to the environment could not now be undone. The decision came after two stinging reports. First, a central empowered committee appointed by the Supreme Court found 'serious pitfalls' in the project. It noted that 'at the outset, it should have never been taken up at the present location as it involved felling of a huge number of trees with all its inevitable serious adverse environmental impact, including destruction of the massive green areas'. Accusing the DDA of 'mindless planning', the committee also found the controversial underground parking plot on the site to be 'wasteful expenditure'.[88] The police had raised security questions over it and there were also fears that it would lead to traffic congestion. 'It would put the final seal of destruction on the greenery forever,' said the experts and recommended a fine of Rs 5 crore on the DDA if the site couldn't be relocated.[89]

Following this, the Supreme Court bench appointed architect and town planner Charles Correa to review the project in its totality. He too criticized the DDA for flouting norms. His report found that ten hectares of forest land had been encroached upon and there had been indiscriminate uprooting of trees. As he put it, 'The site selection was not proper and the design far from satisfactory.'[90] Correa wanted the project to be relocated and the forest area restored.[91]

The DDA, of course, maintained that no rules were broken and that 8,000 trees had been planted in lieu of the 700 that were cut down. Additional Solicitor-General Amarendra Saran emphasized the impending deadlines, pointing out in court that 'we cannot stop the Games. We are building an international-standard sports stadium in that area. Several alternative suggestions were considered and only thereafter this area was selected'.[92] The latter argument did not find many takers among the experts but in the end the deadlines seemed to leave little room for manoeuvre.[93]

There seems little popular enthusiasm in the city for an event of this magnitude. Ironically, it was a police officer who summed up the city's indifference at a public function to mobilize support in March 2009. Speaking at the event, Kulvinder Singh, DCP, Gurgaon, was quoted as saying, 'There is no excitement in Delhites about the 2010 Games. It is almost like it is being imposed on them.'[94] His words seemed to ring true. By the end of 2009, then, Delhi's great white hope lay in what north Indians call *jugaad*, that wonderful yet utterly untranslatable word that roughly means a propensity to improvise; in short, in a 'sellotape legacy' that may well deliver the Games without inherently solving the great divides that have underpinned this effort since the beginning.

WILL SHERA FLY?

Long before he became a politician, Suresh Kalmadi was an Air Force pilot. Among his favourite memories, he says, was landing planes in Leh when there were no proper runways. Given this, the pertinent question is: can he deliver the Games with poorly finished stadiums? Responding to such queries in public, Kalmadi has always been gung-ho, insisting that 'we will be fully prepared'.[95] Sheila Dikshit has generally been more upfront about the challenges – even admitting her nervousness at times but she has usually backed up these assertions.[96] When television news channel NDTV questioned her about the stinging critique by the CAG report, for instance, she brushed it aside as an old report that wasn't up-to-date.[97] The big question is: will Shera fly? Will it be remembered fondly like Appu – the tubby elephant mascot of the 1982 Asian Games – or will it be flung into the dustbin of India's collective consciousness?

Interviewing Kalmadi in October 2009, Shekhar Gupta bluntly described him as 'somebody who will decide whether' by 2010 'we are a very proud country or a very embarrassed country'.[98] Brand Kalmadi, as Gupta implied, has come to symbolize the Games effort and his fortunes are indelibly linked with the Games. In the end though, if Delhi fails, it would be seen globally as India's failure, and not just the organizing committee's. The world doesn't remember the Chinese manager who delivered the headiness of Beijing. Or, for that matter, the Greek officials who fixed up Athens at the last minute. What remains is the memory of the city itself. Ever since the huge public row between the CGF and the organizing committee in October 2009 – Kalmadi even accused the chief executive of the CGF, Mike Hooper, of 'throwing keys at our staff' – this realization has hit home. As the sport historian Brian Stoddart puts it: 'This underlines dramatically the impasse that sees the rest of the world, the Commonwealth included, in awe of India's economic might but convinced of her inability to overcome bureaucratic delay, local intrigue and a combative approach.'[99]

It is this continuing tension and the need to prove India's credentials that led to V.K. Malhotra's over-the-top outburst against the CGF:

'These are the Commonwealth Games, not the Imperial Games.'[100] Edward Said might have seen it as a classic Orientalist expression. As Stoddart argues, though, 'it certainly seems now that India's need for the Games to be a success has gone up several notches.'[101]

This is why M.S. Gill, with a direct mandate from the prime minister, has been virtually working in crisis management mode ever since the Manmohan Singh government woke up to the urgency of the problem in October 2009.[102] The government's tightening of control has been self-evident. The appointment of former bureaucrat Jarnail Singh as CEO[103] and the move to bring in more IAS officers at senior levels was the first step. The group of ministers, which used to meet once a month, has now begun to meet more often. As one senior organizing committee official told us, 'It is quite clear, the sports ministry is tightening its control.'[104] A case in point is the Cabinet decision to set up a three-member sub-committee to take charge of Games finances. Consisting of the urban development secretary, the sports secretary and additional secretary from the expenditure department, this committee was approved to create 'a guarantee mechanism' in the organizing committee and to ensure spending 'according to the guidelines laid down'.[105]

A lot of things remain unresolved at the time of the writing of this book but by November 2009, there were some signs of catching up. Kalmadi claimed that from being behind in twenty out of thirty-five functional areas in early 2009, they were now behind in only five.[106] As a senior official told us:

> This is India and the *sarkaar* is a big thing in this country. By hook or by crook, they will manage somehow by the end. The two real issues are venues and security. They should have the venues under control by mid-2010. You can never predict security but usually security agencies do their jobs well at such events, though they may not be good at communicating it.[107]

Serious questions remain. In the bid document, for instance, the Delhi government committed to an exclusive lane for Games vehicles on all major roads.[108] No one quite knows how that will be possible in a city bursting at its seams, one where even the Bus Rapid Transit System

(BRTS) has been a disaster. As political scientist Robin Jeffrey says, 'They may just shut down the city, if that is what it takes.'

Delhi will have its Games. The real question is: will it really be world-class? Linked to this, of course, is the question of who defines what is world-class. At the Commonwealth Games General Assembly in Delhi, Kalmadi overwhelmingly won the support of African delegates who unanimously backed him against what they called 'racist attitudes' within the Commonwealth nations.[109] The Commonwealth Games do not have the kind of global exposure that the Olympics or even the Asian Games enjoy. As one official pointed out to us: 'There are only a handful of rich countries out of the seventy-one in this group who will keep complaining. The rest may well be quite happy with our five-star treatment and if things are more or less passable.' Try as we might, Charu's observation about a 'sellotape legacy' keeps coming back to mind.

In 1982, the Indira Gandhi-led government was so serious about feeding its guests in the Indian spirit of hospitality, it decided to impose 'controls' on the export of bread from Delhi to other areas, to ensure that there were no shortages during the Games.[110] The rest of India could eat rotis; the foreign athletes had to get their bread. The India of 2010 is very different from the India of 1982. It's a safe assumption that there won't be any bread controls this time round, but Delhi certainly needs an all-out collective effort of the kind that it saw in 1982.

3 | THE NINTH DELHI

THE POLITICS OF CONSTRUCTING A 'GLOBAL CITY'

There is something visceral about great cities, something that intoxicates rulers, compels them to leave their own mark. Delhi, in this sense, has been special. The pulsating heart of Hindustan for a thousand years, it has been a particularly fertile playground for ambitious kings with an eye on immortality. The magnificent ruins of their fantasies – the remains of at least eight different cities – are now a part of the lived existence of the present-day Dilli–wala, and they pop up delightfully at roundabouts, behind parking lots and inside illegal residential colonies. These ruins stand testimony to the proclivity of ruler after ruler of this timeless city to fashion it in his or her own image. Just think of the British creation of New Delhi. Lutyens and Baker may have got the slope of the Rashtrapati Bhavan wrong – it was meant to be visible for miles around and not just from its base, but the Viceregal Palace, as it was then known, and the flanking Secretariat buildings, were designed as giant phallic symbols of power. They were to be awe-inspiring testaments, in red Bharatpur stone, to the might of the British Empire. Independent India quickly replaced the statue of King George V on the India Gate lawns with one of Mahatma Gandhi, but never quite had the time or the money to significantly rebuild the city in its own manner. It was the Partition refugees who took over Delhi and fashioned it into the monster city that it is today. The city has been a Punjabi one for decades, and now, increasingly, it is acquiring the flavour of Bihar and Uttar Pradesh.

Through all this, administrative power played a powerful role in Delhi's urbanism in a way that is distinct from any other Indian metropolis.[1] The city's post-independence rulers – of all political hues – have always dreamt of building a 'ninth Delhi'[2] or of 'reconstructing Shahjahanabad'.[3] Political power is intrinsic to the way Delhi is run.

Indira Gandhi vastly reshaped the city for the 1982 Asian Games in order to showcase her vision of modernity to the world. Twenty-eight years later, Sheila Dikshit, and all kinds of sports officials and administrators, are using the 2010 Games to sell the idea of what they call a 'global city'.

'LIKE A CITY BEING REBUILT': CHASING A CHIMERA

In 2007, the CWG 2010 organizing committee made a SWOT analysis of the Games as part of its planning exercise. Listed prominently in the opportunities section was a clear statement of belief that the Games would 'present the image of India as an emerging economic power and Delhi as a global business hub city'.[4] Drawing a clear link with India's vocal ambitions of becoming a major global power, the planners also highlighted the connections between the city's sporting history and its recent evolution. The sales pitch for Delhi's bid took care to present the city's post-1947 history as one that had chugged along on the engines of the two Asian Games it had hosted. According to this view, the 1951 Delhi Asiad – the first ever – was central to the original nationalist project.[5] It led to the creation of new sporting infrastructure as well as a 'future plan to guide the country, on the drawing board'.[6] This was the strand that linked it directly to 1982. As the bid document boasted, the 1982 Asiad turned Delhi into a 'changed and modern city' with 'one of the swankiest stadia in the world'.[7] The motif of modernity was present in all talk of Delhi's sporting venue history, just as it is now.

Both of us have hazy childhood memories of Asiad '82. We remember the cheerful dancing image of Appu and the brilliant rubber-like gymnasts on television. In our minds, the Asiad has always been special, for it gave us our first memories of organized sport. The politics of it came later. It was only as we grew into adulthood that we realized how fundamentally it had changed Delhi and its skyline: ten stadiums, thirteen new sporting venues, numerous flyovers – necessary and unnecessary – new and upgraded hotels.[8] As the 2010 bid document put it, somewhat too poetically: 'Along with the spires and heritage buildings piercing the skyline, rose gargantuan structures, the modern arenas of fierce yet friendly sporting contests.'[9] But 1982 was more than just about the city; it also transformed the rest of India by ushering in the foundations of the first real nationwide television service. It seems unimaginable in today's India, swamped as it is by satellite television and the never-ending chatter of news channels, but until 1982, only the four metros, and Amritsar and Srinagar, had localized television centres. There was no 'national' television service as we know it. The fear of foreign ridicule and the quest to showcase a new India at the Asiad changed all that. Delhi had to broadcast the Games to the rest of Asia, and Vasant Sathe, the then information and broadcasting minister, realized that even Sri Lanka had a colour television service. So we had to have one too.[10] A nationwide service in colour might have happened eventually anyway, but it was the pressure of the Games that cast the die.

Ashok Kumar's monologues in *Hum Log*, Arun Govil's beatific smile in *Ramayana*, the spectacle of *Mahabharat*, Salma Sultan, Prannoy Roy, satellite television – nothing that followed in the subsequent rise of Indian television would have been possible without the catalytic push of the Asiad. Bollywood composer Anu Malik was trying to be cheesy when he infamously sang '*Doordarshan waah waah!*' in the 1990s' Salman Khan flick *Judwa*, but in a bizarre sort of way he underscored the role Doordarshan has come to play in the popular culture of India. Television turned 1982 into a crucial turning point in India's recent history. CWG 2010 may not yield anything with such far-reaching impact but its planners certainly believe that it will provide a take-off point for catapulting Delhi into the league of the world's best-developed cities.

This idea, of a city with 'world-class amenities', is the blazing flame that has driven the agenda of the Commonwealth Games so far.[11] That term 'world class' always has a special ring in India. Maybe it is the colonial inheritance or an emerging halo of superiority, which comes from decades of inferiority. Being 'like foreign' is one of the best compliments you can receive in India, and Delhi's politicians have a vested interest in painting pictures of a city that would indeed be so. In 2006, Chief Minister Sheila Dikshit told the National Development

Council that she was working towards 'making Delhi a global city'.[12] As she explained:

> Holding of Commonwealth Games 2010 in Delhi is a matter of pride for us … Government of Delhi has already worked out its schedule for timely completion of all identified projects relating to Commonwealth Games 2010 … because of their national importance, we would require the support and involvement of all concerned. We particularly look forward to adequate support from the Union government.[13]

This is the crux of the matter. Not since the 1982 Asian Games have the Central government's coffers opened up for Delhi like they have for this event. The refurbishment of Delhi would have unfolded at its own pace had the Commonwealth Games not come to the city. What they have done is to inject an urgent timeline and the mind-boggling Rs 65,000–crore credit line that government agencies have held out. As one organizing committee official put it, 'Everything is as if a city is being rebuilt.'[14]

This suits the state government and its agenda. A BJP-led government was in power at the Centre when Delhi first bid for the Games, but it is the Congress government of Sheila Dikshit that is reaping the political windfall. Soon after she swept back to power for a record third time in 2008, the chief minister was asked what her priority areas are. 'Commonwealth Games,' she said immediately. 'We lost three months because of the elections and will lose another three because of the Lok Sabha elections [April–May 2009]. Thankfully, we had factored in all these things while planning.'[15] The quality of the planning is debatable but the priorities, at least, give us a window into the dreams of Delhi's current rulers.

'A FACELIFT' FOR DELHI

City of Flyovers

The writer William Dalrymple famously called Delhi the 'city of djinns'. Such metaphysical entities, of course, do not figure in the paper trail of the city's Games effort. Going by the sheer number of construction sites, though, 'city of flyovers' – or more accurately 'city of future flyovers' – might be a more apt description. The biggest chunk of the Delhi government's Rs 65,000-crore cost estimate is being spent on general infrastructure projects: Rs 6,920 crore on flyovers, railway bridges and road widening; Rs 16,887 crore on metro connectivity; and Rs 35,000 crore on new power generation plants.[16] The first two categories are the most visible aspects of the remaking of Delhi as anyone who has driven anywhere in the city in the past five years will testify.

Sheila Dikshit announced big plans in 2006 to build twenty-four new flyovers and to decongest all National Highways entering Delhi ahead of the Games. As she said, 'We will give Delhi a facelift with the commissioning of twenty-four new flyovers, signal-free Ring Road and Outer Ring Road and decongestion of all National Highways at Delhi's entry points from its neighbouring states in the next few years.'[17] The number of flyovers in the 'facelift' has now gone up to twenty-six. The big projects include the link road (tunnel) from the Games Village site to the vicinity of Jawaharlal Nehru Stadium and bypasses at Mahipalpur and Masoodpur to improve airport connectivity.[18]

So, why so many flyovers? Explaining their need, a Delhi government note rightly points out that the number of vehicles plying in the city is now more than those plying on the roads of Kolkata, Mumbai and Chennai taken together. Delhi's traffic problems need big solutions. The flyover spree is also in line with the chief minister's public declaration of making the Ring Road and Outer Ring Road, the two main lifelines of Delhi, signal-free. This is why the government has kept the building of these flyovers on what it calls a 'fast track mechanism'.[19] At the time of writing this book, in early 2009, however, some of these projects were progressing well but construction work in at least six of them had not even started (Table 3.1). The Mahipalpur Bypass was still in the planning stage and the east and west corridors had just been approved by the DUAC in part and had reached the design stage.[20]

In 1982, Delhi got seven new flyovers, some of them unnecessary at the time; widened 290 kilometres of roads; redesigned fifty intersections; developed nineteen areas within the city; and built two new hotels – Kanishka and Ashok Yatri Niwas.[21] However, 1982 was a pittance compared to 2010. Tables 3.1, 3.2 and 3.3 show why.

Table 3.1: Commonwealth Games Related Projects: Flyovers / Bridges [22]

S.No.	Name of the Project	Estimated Cost in Crores (rounded off)	Completion Date	Status as on 01.01.2009
1.	Geeta Colony Bridge	120.00	April 2008	100%
2.	Bridge at Neela Hauz	46.60	March 2010	12%
3.	ITO Chungi	81.80	June 2009	38%
4.	R.R. Kohli Marg	120.90	June 2009	65%
5.	Shastri Nagar Pusta	108.80	June 2009	65%
6.	B.J. Marg/R.T.R. Marg			
7.	Nelson Mandela/Vivekanand Marg	246.50	June 2009	44%
8.	Aruna Asaf Ali/Africa Avenue Marg			
9.	Corridor improvement of Road No.56	123.40	March 2010	Work yet to be awarded
10.	Flyover on NH-24 bypass near Gazipur	246.50	March 2010	11%
11.	Alignment over Barapulla Nallah	498.00	June 2010	5%
12.	Ring Road bypass from Salimgarh Fort to Velodrome Road	653.00	March 2010	Test pile is in progress
13.	Elevated East–west Corridor from East Delhi to Connaught Place area	1680.00	June 2010	–
14.	ROB on Road No. 63	34.15	June 2008	97%
15.	Mukerba Chowk	195.00	November 2008	96%
16.	RUB on Road No. 58-64	37.70	September 2009	13%
17.	Naraina	119.80	November 2009	42%
18.	Mangolpuri	31.00	June 2008	100%
19.	Azadpur	153.60	June 2009	46%

Contd.

S.No.	Name of the Project	Estimated Cost in Crores (rounded off)	Completion Date	Status as on 01.01.2009
20.	Behra Enclave	54.80	March 2009	76%
21.	Nagloi NH-10	78.00	October 2009	61%
22.	Shyam Lal College G.T. Road	93.00	September 2009	21%
23.	Apsara Border	226.40	March 2010	01%
24.	U.P. Link Road	334.00	May 2010	Test pile is in progress
25.	Road No. 68	107.00	April 2010	Tenders called
26.	a) Masoodpur corridor improvement b) Mahipalpur tunnel project	390.00	June 2010	-

The state government's blueprint for creating a global city also includes the construction of eighteen new railway bridges and the widening and beautification of 3,069 km of roads.[23]

The last time Delhi's citizens saw their city being turned into a virtually permanent construction site on anything resembling this scale was in 1982. Describing the state of the city in preparation, the writers of the official report of the Asiad effusively observed:

> For two years preceding the Games, Delhi throbbed with the cacophony of gyrating cement mixers that kept rhythm round the clock with giant pile-drivers and massive earth movers as project engineers, workers, planners and architects went all out to meet the deadline – June 1982! If the pace was frantic, the dedication was total.[24]

They could well have been describing the state of Delhi in the lead-up to 2010. The pace and the dedication, of course, are variable – with many projects horribly behind time.

'Poore Ghar ke Badal Daloonga': Changing the Lights

Like the iconic Laxman-Sylvania advertisement in the early 1980s where the comedian Asrani promised to change every light bulb in his house to one manufactured by the company, Delhi too is going in for a massive overhaul of its lights. 'Poore ghar ke badal daloonga' [I will change everything in the house] was Asrani's punchline. Delhi may not be changing the 'poora ghar' but it is certainly changing a substantial part of it. The numbers churned out by the state government's bureaucrats make for mind-numbing reading. The sheer size of the endeavour, though, is clear. The PWD, NDMC and MCD are planning to change the street lights in 424 lane km, 150 lane km and 960 lane km at the cost of Rs 197 crore, Rs 100 crore and Rs 387 crore, respectively.[25] Similarly, the PWD is undertaking what it calls 'comprehensive streetscaping works' on all the roads around the Games venues. This Rs 400-crore project involves what a note from the chief secretary's office calls 'aesthetic development of the roads and street furnishing with various utilities. It also includes beautification of the area, signage and various items of

Table 3.2: Commonwealth Games Related Projects: Railway Overbridges/ Railway Underbridges[26]

S.No.	Name of the Project	Estimated Cost (in crores)	Completion Date
1.	Level Crossing near Vivek Vihar	40.00	March 2010
2.	Sarai Kale Khan	09.00	March 2010
3.	Samaipur Badli on Auchandi Road	30.00	June 2010
4.	Sultanpuri	64.00	June 2010
5.	Sewa Nagar–Prem Nagar	30.00	March 2010
6.	Najafgarh–Brijwasan Road	58.00	June 2010
7.	Nahari Road Crossing at Narela Lampur Road	15.00	June 2010
8.	Adjacent to Roshnara Garden underbridge Shakti Nagar	40.00	June 2010
9.	G.T. Road Indl. Area approaching towards Sawan Park near overbridge at Ashok Vihar	15.00	June 2010
10.	At back of Sanjay Gandhi Transport Nagar towards Badli Village Level Crossing	10.00	June 2010
11.	Rohatak Road–Rampura	09.00	June 2010
12.	Near Rohatak Road and Zakira (Daya Basti)	40.00	June 2010
13.	Approach from Ring Road upto intersection leading to railway side (Shakur Basti)	08.00	June 2010
14.	Connecting Mangol Puri and Rohatak Road	15.00	June 2010
15.	Kirti Nagar–Prem Nagar	15.00	June 2010
16.	Munkuka Railway Crossing	15.00	June 2010
17.	Kirari Railway Crossing	15.00	-
18.	Rajasthan Udyog Nagar	89.03	September 2010

Table 3.3: Commonwealth Games Related Projects: Widening and Beautification[27]

S. No.	Work	Length	Cost (in Rs Cr)
1.	Strengthening and Resurfacing of Roads by PWD	917 Lane Km	288.60
2.	Improvement of Major Roads by MCD	368 Lane Km	387.00
3.	Street Scaping and Road Improvement Plan by NDMC	100 Lane Km	125.10
4.	Street lighting by PWD	424 Lane Km	197.00
5.	Street lighting by MCD	960 Lane Km	387.00
6.	Street lighting by NDMC	150 Lane Km	100.00
7.	Streetscaping by PWD	150 Lane Km	400.00

street furniture such as information kiosks, public toilets, PCO booths, garbage bins and bus queue shelters.'[28]

This is in addition to the plans for improving road signage on all the major roads in the capital to take them up to what the planners think is the 'international level'. The NDMC is spending Rs 70 crore on this revamp while the PWD also undertook a pilot project worth Rs 2 crore. All the major roads of Delhi will be covered under this scheme.

'Energy-boosting Tonic to a Hyperactive Child': The Tale of the Tourism Tsunami

One of the drivers of the construction bonanza in Delhi is the large number of hotels being built to cater to the tsunami of tourists that the Games will supposedly bring in. Part of a Ministry of Tourism plan for the 'marketing of India as a tourism destination for the upcoming Commonwealth Games',[29] this hotel push is puzzling. Consider this: in the great rush for Games-related construction, the DDA had, by 2007, identified thirty-four sites for hotels that would be built specifically for the event.[30] One would assume that such a massive investment exercise would have been the result of a proper needs assessment. Yet, as late as February 2007, the Ministry of Tourism and Culture admitted in the Parliament that 'no estimate has been made regarding the number of tourists expected to arrive' in Delhi. The minister announced that the only benchmark they were operating with was the approximately 90,000 tourists who, the Indian government estimated, visited Melbourne when that city hosted the Commonwealth Games.

But Delhi is not Melbourne. Where is the guarantee that Delhi will get as many tourists as Melbourne did? It just might, but the fact remains that, without any real study of estimates, the ministry had assessed that the city would need 30,000 hotel rooms and the National Capital Region (NCR) would need 40,000 rooms in order to be prepared for the Games.[31]

A more charitable way of judging the performance of the Ministry of Tourism and the organizing committee is by analysing the arrangements to cater to the tourists expected to be in Delhi for the Games. At the heart of the tourism ministry's Games plan is the push to create more tourist accommodation. In this regard, all hotels being built in Delhi, Faridabad, Gurgaon, Gautam Budh Nagar and Ghaziabad between April 2007 and March 2010 have been given a five-year tax holiday. In addition, the tourism ministry has been pushing various agencies to follow 'investor-friendly land policies and single-window approach' for hotel development in the city.[32] It also floated schemes like the approval of guest houses and Incredible India bed-and-breakfast establishments in order to increase the number of rooms available for rent in the NCR region.[33]

By March 2007, however, the tourism ministry admitted in the Parliament that 'there is a shortage of 30,000 rooms in the city of Delhi and the NCR of Delhi for Commonwealth Games 2010'.[34] The Government of Delhi also admitted in 2009 that 'the present availability of 11,000 rooms in the star-category hotels in the NCR is grossly inadequate and there is a need for an additional 30,000 hotel rooms for the Games'. The only way out of the mess was the bed-and-breakfast scheme but this too looked woefully inadequate. In early 2009, the total establishments registered under this scheme in Delhi totalled 287, with a total room availability of 849.[35] Like much else in India, this is a case of everybody waking up late and then scrambling madly to get to the finish line.

Adding to the problems, the construction industry has been hit particularly hard by the economic recession. At least six hoteliers who

Table 3.4: Total hotel rooms in Delhi in 1–5 star hotels (2003)[36]

Category	No. of hotels	No. of rooms
5 star deluxe	13	4461
5 star	7	1209
4 star	10	959
Heritage	1	20
3 star	10	467
2 star	5	135
1 star	7	676
Total	53	7927

were allotted plots withdrew their proposals by January 2009. The problems in construction were compounded by a general slowdown in the travel industry. Foreign tourist arrivals in India in 2008, for instance, showed a 12.5 per cent negative growth rate.[37] Despite the gung-ho hard sell by the Games organizers, many of the private developers were clearly developing cold feet.

Do we really need this hotel construction drive? Remember that even in Melbourne only 166, 513 visitors came for the Games – exactly 53,927 less than the pre-Games estimate of 220,440.[38] No one would mind additional hotels being built in Delhi if there was a convincing reason for it. But there is a lurking feeling that there isn't one. In a scathing critique of the building blitz, sociologist Amita Baviskar put it best:

> [This] is all very exciting till we recall that Asiad '82 fetched us a grand total of 200 [no, this is not a typo] – two hundred – foreign tourists, according to a National Institute of Urban Affairs study. Why these off-the-wall projections of a tourism tsunami? To create a buzz, because building castles in the air lets the government justify the concrete messes it creates on the ground. No one stops to ask: does Delhi need to grow? Isn't more growth for Delhi like giving a hyperactive child an energy-boosting tonic – a recipe for mayhem? We are already straining at the seams of our infrastructure. Do we need the additional demand of energy-intensive, traffic-congesting, green area-swallowing malls and hotels?[39]

Preserving the Eight Cities

The upside is that as officials work to polish the ninth city of Delhi, the eight Delhis that preceded it are also getting a facelift. Most key heritage monuments of Delhi are being lit up, utilizing energy-efficient technology prior to the Commonwealth Games 2010.[40] This is particularly true of the monuments in the vicinity of sports venues. A total of 250 monuments will be covered under this scheme to showcase the city's rich cultural heritage. The government also plans to hold exhibitions showcasing the lesser-known monuments of Delhi during the Games.[41] A number of agencies have come together for heritage conservation. The Ministry of Tourism, for instance, has put in Rs 23 crore to illuminate thirteen selected monuments such as the Purana Qila, Sher Shah gates, and the Subz Buz.[42] The NDMC is similarly pouring in more than Rs 615 crore as part of its Return to Heritage project, to revamp and redevelop the iconic Connaught Place. This includes the provision of heritage-sensitive signage, sewerage, water supply and sub-stations, development of adequate parking, new-look walkways and more.[43]

In this regard, 2010 is a virtual repeat of 1982, when more than 400,000 trees were planted in the city and all archaeological monuments spruced up.[44] Back then too, special attention was paid to monuments near the stadiums and those near the other venues and the athletes' village. In the athletes' village, the wall of Siri Fort – Allaudin Khilji's thirteenth-century capital – was restored, and monuments like the Tofewala Gombad were renovated and flood-lit. Shahjahan's Red Fort, too, got a lusty scrub.[45] Unauthorized hoardings across the city were removed and new fogging equipment was introduced as an anti-malaria measure.[46] Back then, crazy about putting Delhi's best face forward to international visitors, the organizers had gone to ridiculous lengths. For instance, they wanted to portray a city blooming with flowers. And since November, the month of the Asiad, is generally a poor month for flowers in Delhi, they flew in the requisite flowers from Bangalore. After detailed discussions with horticulturists, Delhi's municipal gardeners were ordered not to water the city's bougainvilleas and to time it in a way that would ensure their flowering in November.[47]

There is no talk of flying in the bougainvilleas from Bangalore this time round – at least none that we know of. The heritage plans accompany what a headline writer at the *Indian Express* chose to call

'Digital Delhi': a state government plan to install information kiosks, wi-fi hotspots and prominent screens at public places.[48] This involves setting up more than 500 kiosks with all necessary information about the city, 24× 7 call centres and Games–related tourist information on touch–screens at the airport, railway stations, bus terminals and major markets.[49]

Delhi on Wheels: Racing for a Transport Upgrade

London is inseparable from the myth of the friendly Bobby. Delhi, likewise, is inseparable from the image of the pot–bellied, rough *thulla*, complete with a Haryanvi intonation. In tune with its slogan 'With You, for You, Always', the Delhi Police has instituted special politeness and courtesy training classes for its personnel with an eye on the Games.[50] We don't know how much this will do to the bearing of the average thulla but there is another Commonwealth project whose results we can be certain of. Transport services are the real gainers. Dilli–walas who have, for years, suffered the dust and grime of the Delhi Transport Corporation buses and killer Blue Lines are seeing the beginning of a new era in public transport. The first phase of the spanking-new Delhi Metro (65 km of route length) has been completed and all Metro lines for Phase II (on six more corridors) were, at the time of writing, on track for completion before the Games.[51] The Metro, of course, began well before the Games were conceived. Its success has been hailed as a shining example of Indian endeavour, but recent accidents have dimmed its halo and put a dark cloud over the rush to complete the projects before the Games.

Delhi's bus services, though, are being revamped specifically for the Games. On 5 October 2006, Sheila Dikshit laid the foundation stone for the high capacity bus system at Ambedkar Nagar. The 14.3-km-long corridor was to run between Ambedkar Nagar and Delhi Gate at a cost of Rs 150.15 crore. As the chief minister said: 'It is a major step towards modernizing the public transport system in the capital before [the] commencement of Commonwealth Games 2010. This would bring improvements in the quality of life, benefiting both residents and tourists.'[52] Similarly, the State Transport Authority procured a fleet of 700 modern, low-floor and disabled-friendly buses ahead of the Games.[53]

The DTC's fleet of buses is also being modernized and nearly doubled. Over 5,000 new state-of-the-art buses are being inducted during 2007-2011. The Corporation procured 650 low-floor buses (including twenty-five with air conditioning) during 2007–08. Further, purchase orders for 2,500 low-floor CNG buses (1,500 non-air-conditioned and 1,000 air-conditioned) have been placed, for delivery during 2009–10.[54] From the end of 2009, the DTC is starting air-conditioned bus services from more than twenty locations to the Delhi International Airport.[55] The plans of the DTC are in tandem with a broader traffic police plan designed by the Delhi police in 2005.[56] Central to it are plans for intelligent traffic signals with sensors that will respond to traffic load.[57] The state government sees these measures as part of a larger public transport policy.[58] How effective these plans will be on the ground, though, is still unclear.

The Great Airport Modernization Project

The Commonwealth Games have also been the trigger for a major reconstruction of the Delhi airport. A brand-new international departure and arrival lounge was built at the Delhi airport in 1982.[59] In 2010, however, the aim is a complete revamp. To handle the expected traffic during the Commonwealth Games, Terminal 3 of the airport will have a new runway of 4.4 km and a new integrated passenger terminal building catering to both domestic and international traffic.[60] According to the minister of civil aviation, the new 4.4-million-sq. ft Terminal 3 will cater to thirty-seven million passengers per annum, increasing Indira Gandhi Airport's total annual capacity to 60 million passengers. With ninety walkalators, forty-seven escalators, seventy lifts, forty-eight immigration counters and fifty emigration counters,[61] this is an airport that will 'become the face of Delhi when the Commonwealth Games are held here in 2010'.[62] Not just Delhi. The Mumbai airport is also being expanded and modernized; it is getting a new domestic terminal and its services are being expanded to cater to 40 million passengers per annum.[63]

While no one in their right minds can oppose the idea of airport modernization, the hurry to beat the Commonwealth Games deadline has also led to serious financial problems. Stuck in a financial lurch, the private developer, Delhi International Airport Pvt Ltd (DIAL), has levied a fee of Rs 1,300 on every international passenger departing from Delhi, and Rs 200 on every domestic passenger. This user development fee is akin to the levy being charged at the new airports at Hyderabad and Bangalore. The civil aviation minister justified the additional tax, arguing that it was necessary to ensure that Phase-1 of the airport modernization is over before the Commonwealth Games:

> The completion of [the] project by March 2010, in time for the Commonwealth Games 2010, was of utmost importance. Keeping in view the position that all other funding options appeared to have been exhausted, there was no option but to levy a pre-funding charge as contemplated so as to ensure timely completion of the project.[64]

The Commonwealth Games have provided the trigger for airport modernization but also some painful and unnecessary financial liabilities.

Switching On: The Promise of Twenty-four-hour Power

In the summer of 2009, the Delhi region witnessed its worst power crisis in years. Many parts of the city suffered from eight to ten hours of power cuts. The last week of June saw power riots in several localities; the Small Industries Association threatened to move units out from Noida to Uttarakhand; and at least one person was killed in the protests that erupted across the city.[65] Straining to control the unprecedented crisis, and with tempers flaring over the severe power outages, Sheila Dikshit was left wringing her hands, issuing ultimatums to private suppliers and blaming 'the course of nature'.[66] Given the nature of the crisis, it is difficult to take the state government's promises to ensure uninterrupted power supply during the Games seriously.

Yet, as early as 2006, the then Cabinet secretary, B.K. Chaturvedi, had directed the Delhi government to put in place a financial incentive package for power companies to ensure precisely this: twenty-four-hour power during the Games.[67] As *Business Standard* reported, Delhi's power supply was aimed to be doubled over four years 'in a bid to prevent any shortage of power during the Commonwealth Games in

2010'. Delhi was slated to receive an additional supply of 3,970 MW by September 2010, over and above its 2006 supply of 3,500 MW.[68] Shortly before the power crisis of 2009 engulfed Dikshit's government, a note from her chief secretary's office laid out her ambitious agenda of power reform ahead of the Games:

> To lend a new direction and to accelerate the process of power reforms in order to make Delhi a power-surplus state, [the] government is taking all initiatives to improve the power supply in Delhi. Reforms are being all inclusive and contain new projects in the fields of generation, transmission and distribution to ensure twenty-four-hour uninterrupted power supply to the citizens of Delhi. New power projects have been planned to meet the power demand of Delhi, especially during [the] Commonwealth Games.[69]

The new generation projects being initiated specially for the Games are the Rs 8,000-crore Indira Gandhi Super Thermal Power Project (3 × 500 MW) at Jhajjar, Haryana; the Rs 5,200-crore, 1,500-MW Pragati-III Combined Cycle Gas Turbine Project at Bawana; and the 750-MW (nominal capacity) Pragati-III CCGT Project at Bamnauli in south-west Delhi.[70] Additionally, the Union Ministry of Power told the Parliament that five other power projects were in place to meet demands, 'especially during the Commonwealth Games'.[71] They were to generate 5,980 MW of power, 4,630 MW of which would come to Delhi.[72]

Why build so many power stations? According to figures released by the Delhi government, the current power demand in Delhi is 2,900 MW. This is slated to go up to 4,500 MW during the Commonwealth Games. In contrast, in early 2009, Delhi was getting only 3,297 MW (1,280 MW from its own stations and 2,017 MW from a central sector generating station). The government estimated that the new power stations would be able to provide an additional 4,350 MW of electricity, giving Delhi an estimated surplus of 3,147 MW by 2010.[73] The numbers look good but writing these lines in the middle of the great power crisis of 2009, it is difficult to be optimistic. Could it all really be so simple? Are the solutions to all our problems so near at hand? For Delhi's sake, we hope so.

Table 3.5: New PPAs Signed to Augment Power Supply by 2010[74]

S.No.	Name of the Project	Executing Agency	Installed Capacity (in MW)	Delhi's Share (in MW)
1.	Kahalgaon Stage – II	NTPC	1,000	81
2.	Damodar Valley Project (DVC) Agreement signed on 24 August			400
	Initial from existing project			100
	Chandrapur Unit # 7	DVC	250	130
	Chandrapur Unit # 8	DVC	250	170
3.	RAPPV and VI	NPC	440	55
4.	Sewa – II HEP	NHPC	120	10
5.	Koldam HEP	NTPC	800	75
6.	Dadri (Th.) Stage–II Unit – I & II	NTPC	980	760
7.	Barh	NTPC	1,980	88
8.	Koteshwar (SJVNL)	SJVNL	400	29
9.	Aravali Project in Haryana	NTPC	1,500	750
10.	Pragati Phase–II (Bawana Project)	PPCL	1,500	750
11.	Uri – II	NHPC	240	19
12.	Chamera – III (NHPC)	NHPC	230	37

A harried Sheila Dikshit was asked the same question by the *Times of India* at the height of the 2009 crisis. As the city sweated, the chief minister was asked if, given the current power situation, Delhi was ready for the Commonwealth Games. Delineating that 'outages of 8–10 hours cannot be tolerated' she answered:

> We already have our plans in place for the Games. There will be two dedicated plants for the Games, Bawana and Jhajjar, which will become operational from March–April 2010. Around 3,000–4,000 MW of power will be made available. Work on the Bamnauli plant is also on, although it will not be ready in time for the Games.[75]

At the heart of her plans are agreements signed by outside suppliers to augment Delhi's power supply for the Games as Table 3.5 details.

Two of the biggest problems in Delhi, though, are breakdowns and transmissions losses. As part of its reform process, therefore, the Delhi government also instituted several projects for improving power distribution by way of creating new sub-stations, overhauling and upgrading of old sub-stations, installation of increased capacity transformers, installation of new grids, augmentation of existing capacities of transformers, etc. (Tables 3.6 and 3.7) As the chief secretary's note optimistically put it, 'These measures will improve the overall power scenario and citizens of Delhi can be assured of uninterrupted, 24× 7 power supply.'[76]

Of course, Delhi needs the extra power. In 2009, it was only the weather gods who bailed out the city's power suppliers with unexpected rains.[77] However, to go from depending on the benevolence of Indra to providing twenty-four-hour power is a tall task indeed.

Dirty Flows the Yamuna: A City and Its Water

The Yamuna may be Delhi's lifeline and part of the holy trinity of rivers in the Hindu pantheon, but that does not change the fact that it is also the repository of much of the city's raw sewage. The problem is particularly acute between the Wazirabad barrage and Okhla, where seventeen storm drains emptying into the river have turned into conduits for sewage and garbage. While city authorities have been working on several schemes to clean up the river, the

Table 3.6: Transmission Projects[78]

S.No.	Name of Project	Estimated Cost (in lakhs)
1.	Maharani Bagh – 8 No. 220 KV Bays	3,859.24
2.	Masjid Moth – 220/33KV S/ Stn.	2,289.00
3.	Ridge Valley – 220 KV GIS	8,620.00
4.	IGI Airport – 220 KV GIS	12,033.00
5.	Electric Lane – 220/33 KV GIS	7,718.00
6.	Trauma Centre AIIMS – 220/33 KV GIS	7,855.00
7.	Ridge Valley to Naraina – S/C U/G	4,961.00
8.	Bamnauli to Mehrauli – LILO at IGI	17,750.00
9.	Maharani Bagh to Masjid Moth – D/C U/G	14,350.00
10.	Maharani Bagh to Electric Lane – D/C U/G	14,190.00
11.	Ridge Valley to Trauma Centre (AIIMS) – D/C U/G	9,200.00
12.	Maharani Bagh to Trauma Centre (AIIMS) – D/C U/G	16,333.00
13.	G.T. – Aug. of 1 × 100 MVA to 160 MVA	1,165.48

Cost: Rs 1170 Crore (approx)

Commonwealth Games have, expectedly, given new impetus to these efforts. The irrigation and flood department has begun constructing boundary walls along major drains to prevent garbage dumping. So has the MCD for the drains under its charge.

Delhi State Industrial and Infrastructure Development Corporation (DSIIDC) has already set up ten common effluent treatment plants (CETP) to cater to the city's industrial waste before it gets dumped into the Yamuna. The Delhi Jal Board has been instructed to ensure that untreated sewage flows into the drains and interceptor sewers are being laid, with provision for sewage treatment plants (STPs) in villages and unauthorized colonies.[79] Despite this, Sheila Dikshit has made it clear that expecting a clean Yamuna by 2010 is a tall order. 'It cannot happen by 2010,' she has said. 'I have studied Thames, Seine, Rhine and all of them took seven to eight years to get clean and the Yamuna is not even a perennial river.'[80]

It is clear that the Yamuna may take years to clean up, if at all. But the state of the city's water supply is, perhaps, not so gloomy. Delhi is an ever-expanding city, bursting at its seams and maintaining adequate water supply has become a major challenge. The existing availability of water

Table 3.7: Distribution Projects/New Grids[81]

S.No.	Name of the Project	Scheduled date of Completion
1.	Sonia Vihar Karawal Nagar	March 2010
2.	Integrated Flight Complex Pkt-C Gazipur	March 2011
3.	Mandawali Fazalpur	March 2012
4.	Akshardham	March 2010
5.	Puspvihar	March 2009
6.	Sainik Farm	March 2010
7.	West of JNU	March 2010
8.	Institutional Area Vasant Kunj	March 2010
9.	West End Green	March 2010
10.	Media Centre Jasola	March 2010
11.	X,Y-Block Okhla Phase-II	March 2010
12.	Rohini Sector 24	Completed and Commissioned
13.	Shalimar Bagh Facility Centre	Completed and Commissioned
14.	Ghevra Savada	2008–09
15.	Delhi University 33 KV grid	2009–10
16.	Bhlaswa 66 KV grid	2009–10
17.	Bawana 220 KV	2009–10
18.	Kirti Nagar 33 KV	2009–10
19.	Naraina 220 KV	2009–10
20.	Pitam Pura	2010–11
21.	Rohini District Centre-1 66 KV	2010–11
22.	Rohini Sector 28	2010–11
23.	Bawana DSIDC grid 1 & 3	2010–11
24.	Bawana DSIDC grid 2	–
25.	DCM Bara Hindu Rao	–
26.	Rohini District Centre-2	–
27.	Rohini Sector 26	–
28.	Bawana DSIDC grid 8 & 9	–
29.	Narela IFC	–
30.	Dhirpur 66 KV	–
31.	Wazirpur 33 KV	–
32.	Narela B2 66 KV	–

from all sources is 790 MGD, which is expected to go up to 945 MGD at the time of Commonwealth Games.[82] In 1982, the water situation was prioritized; the Ganga–Yamuna link was completed, providing

Delhi with an additional 15 million gallons of water a day.[83] In 2010, like in the power sector, the Delhi government has taken several steps to meet the additional water requirements. The construction of a parallel canal from Munak in Haryana to the Haiderpur water treatment plant was nearing completion at the time of writing in early 2009. This is expected to save 80 MGD of water out of Delhi's allotted share which was being wasted through seepage losses.

Similarly, the Renuka dam is an important new plan. The lack of an upstream storage facility on the Yamuna is partly responsible for Delhi's water problems. The Renuka dam is one of the three planned upstream storage projects that will provide the city with an additional 275 MGD. At the time of writing, the forest clearance was in the process of being sought.[84]

THE ORPHANS OF 1982 AND THE PROBLEM WITH THE COMMONWEALTH MANIA

For a chief minister who won a record third term on a development platform, the Commonwealth Games have been a godsend. It has given Sheila Dikshit the elusive password to Manmohan Singh's purse strings. No wonder the organizing committee has got complete cooperation from the Delhi government at every step. When questioned about the severe problems hindering the progress of the Games infrastructure, the organizing committee's director general made it clear that every time they ran into trouble, they would run to the chief minister:

> We have a very fine working relationship with the Delhi government. That is a boon … And that is because the chairman of the organizing committee who is a politician, Member of Parliament, [Suresh Kalmadi] he has extremely strong cordial relationship with Ms Sheila Dikshit, chief minister of Delhi. That sorts out many, many problems. Then, for Mr Kalmadi's team – which is me and my colleagues here [sic] – that warmth, trust feeds into our relationship with the bureaucracy of Delhi. Thirdly, for the chief minister of Delhi, this is a project as close to her heart, as important as it is to the organizing committee. In fact, it is the 2010 platform on which a lot of development work for Delhi is going to happen. And to be honest, the chief minister will be as much a face of the Games as Mr Kalmadi will be. More than anybody

else, these two individuals will be the face of the Commonwealth Games. So we have no problem whatsoever in dealing with the Delhi government. A lot of the major part of the activity or responsibility that we have discharged or obligations are being happily been taken over by the Delhi government ...[sic][85]

On this account, Suresh Kalmadi and Sheila Dikshit sound like the eternal *bhai-behen* of Hindi cinema. As one senior government official told us, their cordiality – combined with the fact that the Delhi government's stakes are so high – has sometimes led to the state government even stepping in to support the organizing committee on projects that it has already provided funds for.

It needs to be mentioned that many of the schemes outlined in this chapter are much needed and would not have been possible without the Games. As V.K. Verma points out, 'It's a win-win game. By doing this they are giving a helping hand to the organizing committee but all the legacy advantage goes to the Delhi government. And we have been able to import about 2,000 air-conditioned low-floor buses ... in normal times, no government would end up spending that kind of money.'[86]

Taking a step back from the rhetoric of a resurgent India, it is sobering to remember that as far as resource allocation goes, Delhi was already privileged, even before the Games.[87] Serious doubts remain about many of the projects. Many of these questions have been raised before and it is best to reproduce here the pointed riposte by Amita Baviskar:

...The Commonwealth (CW) Games are her [Sheila Dikshit's] show, her grand vision to make Delhi a 'world-class city', words that have been repeated so often that they have become Harry Potter-esque incantations, charms endowed with magical powers. Say 'world class' and you conjure up a gleaming cityscape of skyscrapers, fast-flowing traffic, and neon-lit branded shops and restaurants, with unlimited power and water. The Games offer an opportunity to fast forward into this future ...

The JN Stadium has also remained underused for the last twenty-five years. When was the last time you went to watch something there? Probably never. But you will be happy to learn that another Rs 1,250 crore

[1 crore = 10 million] of our money will now be spent to renovate this and other existing venues. And then, after a couple of weeks of use in October 2010, they will again relapse into comatose concreteness. If this has been the sorry fate of our last big building spree, why are we building four new air-conditioned stadiums? Why are we spending more crores on buildings that are destined to be dinosaurs from the day they are conceived? Is this the best way to use public money? Or is this the best way to line builders' pockets? A spanking-new stadium at the IG complex; another one in the Yamuna Sports Complex near Anand Vihar; one more at the Thyagaraj Complex near INA market; and another one at Siri Fort. Each one of these will swallow up precious open space and saddle us with a bigger tax burden. Another stadium will be built at the JN Stadium venue but, mercifully, it will be a less expensive open-air one. According to the Delhi Games website, this one will 'provide a lasting legacy for the sport of lawn bowls'. Yeah, that's what this city really needs, lawn bowls ...[88]

Armed with the new lawn bowls stadium, how the rest of the world sees Delhi has suddenly become paramount.

As the private developers make merry, what about the city's underclass, the majority of the denizens of this city who may not be pretty enough for this new vision? We have already heard of the bamboo curtains being erected to shield visitors from the city's poor. As one report points out, as many as 350 slum clusters housing nearly 3 lakh people have been demolished in Delhi over the past five years. 'Only about one-third of these families have been resettled. The rest have been abandoned to their fates. Sure, not all evictions in the city are for the Games, but even when they are, it's not mentioned for fear of creating a controversy,' says K.V. Krishnan of the Delhi Shramik Sangathan, an organization that campaigns for land ownership rights of slum dwellers.[89] Another activist points out that 'evicted families are either living on the streets or relocated to sites as far as 40 km from their work. To retain their jobs in the city, they join the ranks of Delhi's homeless.' As Paramjeet Kaur from ActionAid asks, 'Why can't the authorities allocate a fraction of these resources to find space for public housing and shelters for the homeless who are making an immense contribution to the city's development through their labour?'[90]

Delhi also recently announced a ban on rickshaws in the walled old city of Shajahanbad and a ban on street-food vendors and hawkers on all major south Delhi roads. According to one critical account of the city:

> The poor have become both extra visible and invisible at the same time; their visibility is a source of concern, but their marginalization and the causes for it are sidelined. Certain built environments associated with the poor, their modes of employment, indeed their very presence in the city, must literally stay out of sight as new flyovers and expressways allow the non-poor to move from one enclosed bubble to another without having to encounter the city they drive through. This changing set of values means that many urban residents are no longer urban citizens.[91]

Delhi's middle class may applaud the development drive but surely they can stop and realize that 'not everyone is sharing in the excitement. There are many in the city for whom the event marks an uncertain future, who are counting down to the day their houses will be demolished and their livelihoods destroyed'.[92] With honourable exceptions, there is little documentation of the slum removals in the mainstream media. An account in *Tehelka* notes that many of those evicted for the 2010 Games have been relocated to as far as Sawdaghevra in the west and Bawana in the north.

Perhaps we should not be surprised by the complete lack of empathy with the displaced – and remember they are being displaced for a twelve-day sporting event. Slum clearance has always had the support of the middle class. Historically, these policies have been built 'on the logic of erasure, designed to wipe out the ugly and sordid face of the metropolis – the cramped and overpopulated "*jhuggi-jhonpri* clusters" and the "inner-city slums". These were the aspects of Delhi that offended the eyes and noses of respectable middle-class citizens who did not want to see them ... and who certainly did not wish to preserve their memory'. The authors of Delhi's Master Plan also saw these 'ugly hutments', as 'filthy shacks' that 'pox-mark practically every part of the city', located in 'forsaken and unsanitary places'.[93] The Commonwealth mania simply allows a free run to these inbuilt attitudes. It is tempting to see what is happening as a kind of 'internal colonialism', a colonialism led by the urban rich where displacement and dispossession continue to be justified and legitimized in the name of development and progress.[94]

In 2004, government officials violently evacuated more than 150,000 people, residing in Yamuna Pushta colony, as part of a plan to develop the 100-acre strip on the banks of the Yamuna into a promenade for residents and tourists.[95] They were resettled in the newly created colony of Bawana and though government officials claim that they were adequately compensated, a study in 2008 blew the lid off that claim, documenting the terrible state of affairs in the Bawana settlement.[96] Ironically, a significant proportion of Pushta residents were brought to Delhi by contractors to build the infrastructure for the 1982 Asian Games.[97] Now they have been displaced again by another mega Games.

Their stories are being repeated again and 'few will survive to tell them; most will just disappear into the vast swathes of this country like so many did after the Games of 1982'.[98] If only they could be included in this new 'world class' city the chief minister is so gung-ho about.

4 | MEGA CITIES, MEGA EVENTS

LEGACIES FROM OTHER CITIES

Mega sporting events are intimately connected – for better or for worse – with the future of great cities. This is why, in October 2009, right in the middle of a high-stakes Afghan policy review and a contentious health policy logjam that may well define his presidency, Barack Obama flew down to Copenhagen to campaign for Chicago to host the Olympic Games. This is also why Brazil's President Lula de Silva proclaimed that that he 'could now die in peace' after Rio won its 2016 Olympics bid. As Emma Tarlo points out, urban spaces are structured as much through a succession of historical events at a national level as through local politics and urban planning:

> On the one hand, it is often historic events which create the political environment in which urban plans become realities. On the other hand, historic events often disfigure urban plans and this occurs with such regularity that in the final analysis it is tempting to perceive them less as impediments to urban development than as hidden agents of urban development itself.[1]

We have seen how the Commonwealth Games are changing Delhi. Now let us see how similar mega sporting events have changed other global cities. The Commonwealth Games have meant different things to different cities. The concept of the Games has often struggled for self-justification, given the seeming irrelevance of the larger Commonwealth idea but every event on such a scale has left a long-term imprint in political, social or urban terms. This chapter focuses on the historical meaning of the Commonwealth Games for host cities, turning the pages of history to put Delhi 2010 in perspective. It also provides snapshots of the profound urban impact of such mega events, using examples from Olympic Games cities. This comparison of legacies is pertinent because one of Delhi's long-term objectives is also to use the Commonwealth Games as a springboard for a future Olympic bid.

Robert Scott, chairman of Manchester's 2000 Olympic bid, aptly summed up the terrible anxiety for hosting such events, comparing it to the rigours of the Olympian marathon: 'It is a commonly held view that the toughest Olympic event is the marathon ... [However] there is another Olympic event which makes the marathon look gentle. It has only a handful of competitors, lasts many years, is fought out in every continent of the world, and ends with the presentation of just one medal.' As P.R. Emery suggests, for upwardly mobile cities, the hosting of the summer Olympic Games represents the ultimate marketing initiative, where state leaders make a case to stake a claim to the 'premier division of the global urban hierarchy'.[2] The general point is also valid for second-order events like the Commonwealth Games, which also often serve as stepping stones for upgradation to Olympic level – like in the case of Beijing and Seoul after their successful hosting of the Asian Games.

Using sport to fast-track urban development is a well-established phenomenon, with the hosting of mega sports events being looked upon as a prestige project. The 1984 Los Angeles Olympic Games, with a profit of 215 million GBP,[3] and the 1992 Barcelona Games, which resulted in unprecedented urban regeneration are cases in point. Yet, such initiatives may often end up all wrong as had happened in Montreal in 1976 or more recently in Sydney at the turn of the millennium.

The relationship between bid cities and mega sporting events has always been complex. For example, the slogan, 'We want bread, not circuses', raised by Toronto inhabitants, derailed the city's Olympic bid in 1996. Men and women from the city, smarting under the terrible financial toll of the 1976 Olympics on Montreal, were opposed to it from the very beginning. Montreal had been a sporting spectacle which resulted in a loss of GBP 692 million,[4] and Toronto's activists turned it into a popular movement questioning the prudence behind the mounting of an Olympic bid. Montreal was no exception. Four years prior to Montreal, Munich sustained a loss of GBP 178 million in hosting the summer Olympic Games.

The questions then are: Do mega sports events contribute significantly to host city development and do they provide an opportunity for urban regeneration? And, will Beijing, having spent a mammoth $42 billion, for example, benefit from hosting the Games in the long run? Will the facilities constructed for staging the Games turn into white elephants in the not-too-distant future or can they be harnessed for the welfare of the city's inhabitants? Obviously, the answers vary, depending on where you ask the question. But there's little doubt that once most mega events are over, the organizers are faced with questions like what would happen to the newly constructed stadiums in future, whether the money spent would prove to be a prudent investment and, how the investment will impact the ordinary taxpayer in the country.

A look at the experience of some of the Olympic and Commonwealth Games host cities makes clear the fraught relationship between development of the city and the impact of hosting premier sports competitions. Let us turn now to the specific experience of the Commonwealth Games cities.

MAHATHIR'S MALAYSIA: KUALA LUMPUR, 1998

Delhi is only the second Asian city to host the Commonwealth Games, after Kuala Lumpur. Within the literature on the Commonwealth Games, Kuala Lumpur has provoked much debate about what a sports event of this magnitude could do to urban and economic regeneration in the context of a troubled polity. In that sense, the 16th Commonwealth Games in Kuala Lumpur may be looked upon as a watershed in the history of these games.

Once conceived as the 'friendly games' to contest the growing clout of the Olympics and to offer support to the idea of Empire, the Commonwealth Games, in the course of time, did the exact opposite of what it had originally set out to achieve. In principle, the Games were and are meant to keep the Commonwealth together and foster a bond of healthy competition. In reality, it ended up dividing the Commonwealth along the North – South axis or along the developed centre/underdeveloped periphery model. It is instructive that only once in its eighty-year-old history have the

Games been held in an Asian country. Between them, Australia, Canada, New Zealand and the UK have organized these Games on sixteen occasions. Developing countries have only hosted it twice: Jamaica in 1966 and Malaysia in 1998.

By the late 1980s, though, it was clear that confining the Games within the former White dominions was killing it. The Commonwealth Games is the third-largest international event of its kind – after the Olympics and the Soccer World Cup – but audience size was disproportionately low, and sagging. The Olympics reinvented itself with savvy marketing in Los Angeles as an attractive vehicle for advertisers but the Commonwealth Games was moving towards irrelevance. It was confirmed, therefore, at the 1991 Commonwealth Heads of Government Meeting (CHOGM) in Harare that the Games must spread if the Commonwealth was to be strengthened.[5]

Somewhat like Indira Gandhi, who approached the 1982 Asian Games as an opportunity to showcase a new India after the Emergency,[6] Mahathir Mohammed of Malaysia looked upon the hosting of the Commonwealth Games as an opportunity to showcase 'a sophisticated, model Muslim state' before the world. He used the Games as a propaganda tool for his government. With these twin aims in mind, the Malaysian state spared no pains in making the Games a success. Despite being in the throes of a severe economic crisis, Malaysia spent a whopping $555 million for the 6,000 athletes. For the Malaysians, as Janis Van Der Westhuizen suggests, KL 1998 'represented the biggest, the best and the most lavish showcase they have ever staged'. The scale of spending becomes clear when we note that Bangkok, host to the 1998 Asian Games, spent only $42.3 million for 10,000-plus athletes, 'far less than 50 per cent of what Malaysia budgeted for just over half as many participants'.[7]

Malaysia first announced its intentions at the Auckland meeting of the Commonwealth Games Federation in 1990. The bid was formally placed through the Malaysian Olympic Council at the General Assembly of the Commonwealth Games Federation in Malta in April 1991. In the bid, the Malaysians aggressively played up the fact that Australia, the only other bidder, had already hosted the Games on three previous occasions and that the Games had never before been held in Asia. Discrimination against developing economies was the central tenet in the Malaysian bid.

Despite the politically correct nature of the Malaysian bid, KL did not have it easy. Adelaide put up a strong challenge, ultimately losing out twenty-five to forty in the final vote. KL, by including team sports like cricket[8] – a passion in many former British colonies – had already done much to secure the votes of some of its neighbours. A visit to New Delhi by the Malaysian minister for youth and sports and by the president of the Malaysian Olympic Committee in 1991 ensured that Malaysia received strong Indian support for its candidature.

As with most host cities, the Malaysian initiative was based on a series of calculations. The Games, it was hoped, would give tourism, both international and domestic, a significant boost. So much so that Malaysia wanted to use the Games to catapult itself into being the premier gateway to Asia, replacing Singapore. Inspired by this objective, Kuala Lumpur was provided with Asia's biggest airport at a cost of RM 9 billion, an overhead rail transit system and also a much improved ground transport network. Other associated industries too received a boost. Hotel rooms went up from 16,000 to 20,000 and a light rail system was soon put in place. All of these initiatives fed into Mahathir's efforts of projecting Malaysia 'as the "new voice" for the Third world … and the Commonwealth Games could be seen as a direct extension of Malaysian foreign policy'.[9] Also, as Van Der Westhuizen states:

> Being able to snatch the Games from a Commonwealth in which there was nothing 'common about its wealth' on behalf of the developing members, or the *Bumiputera* countries of the world, represented the Malay state writ large across the globe, with clear implications for constructed notions of Malaysian identity.[10]

Put simply, the Games were used as an opportunity for Malaysian foreign policy. There is, again, a loose parallel here with the way Delhi hosted the first Asian Games of 1951 to pursue pan-Asian leadership. We have detailed the intriguing story of that Asiad and its complex interplay with the Nehruvian world view elsewhere[11] but the difference here was the way the entire might and the resources of the state were put at the service of the Games.

The successful staging of the Games also offered the Malaysian elite an opportunity for internal political mobilization. The ruling dispensation, led by Mahathir, used the aura created by the Games to clamp down on the dissidents led by then deputy prime minister, Anwar Ibrahim, culminating in his arrest a day before the closing ceremony. The Opposition, for its part, used the opportunity to draw attention to the growing authoritarianism within Malaysia, claiming that the Mahathir regime had lost credibility and had degenerated into a dictatorship of the worst kind. Anwar Ibrahim even led a march of 30,000 supporters to the national mosque and demanded Mahathir's resignation hours before the closing ceremony.[12]

Mahathir, on the other hand, appeared unperturbed by the unrest gathering steam and went on to assert, soon after Anwar's arrest, that his party stood to sweep the general elections if voting was conducted at the time. Even within an ambience of growing disaffection, spurred by the escalating economic crisis, Mahathir was confident of holding on to power, riding on the successful staging of the Commonwealth Games. Not without reason did he declare that KL 1998 was 'the first Games to receive unprecedented government support at every level'. As one of his senior diplomats noted:

> Although the costs of hosting the Games are considerable, these are far outweighed by the benefits of ten days of global free publicity. Looked at in this light, the visual images of Malaysia portrayed on countless television screens will provide viewers with a vivid perspective of Malaysia's multicultural character.[13]

The political imperative to put Malaysia on the map was clearly the driving motive.

COMMONWEALTH GAMES IN HISTORY: THE ROAD FROM HAMILTON

1930: Women, Empire and the Games

If KL 1998 best demonstrates the close proximity between sport, national identity and religion, Hamilton 1930, the venue for the inaugural British Empire/Commonwealth Games, remains a standout example of sport being used as a vehicle for women's emancipation and as one of the first tools to ensure gender parity.

Prior to the first British Empire Games, Count Baillet-Latour, president of the International Olympic Committee, and also chief guest at Hamilton, had spearheaded the removal of women from all track and field competitions in the Olympic Games. At Hamilton, however, there was strong support for allowing women's track and field events to continue — support which yielded results in London four years later. Such vocal support in the presence of the IOC president was hailed as a major marker of difference between the Olympics, which prioritized sports competition above all else, and the British Empire Games, which lay emphasis on healthy rivalry and social integration. In fact, Count Baillet-Latour, as is evident from a report in the *Toronto Star*, refused to attend any of the women's competitions (swimming and diving) held at the Civic Stadium. When asked to comment on the issue of women's participation, Baillet-Latour, gave a rather bizarre explanation for his belief in removing women's track and field events from all forms of sports competition: 'Women in Europe are not of the same standard as your girls on this continent and I do not think for that reason it was a wise move to retain them on the Olympic programs of the future.'[14]

When questioned if he was in favour of women holding their separate Olympiad, the IOC president replied in the negative.

That Hamilton went against the IOC diktat and called for women's participation in the future editions of the Empire Games was made much of in the contemporary Canadian press. On the one hand, this was seen as the Empire Games charting out its own separate identity against the Olympics; on the other, it was an attempt to hail the principles of ethics and fair play, which lay at the heart of what has been called the imperial Games ethic and the British self-image of the Empire. Even within its limited context, Hamilton set an example for the gender battles that were to follow, and tradition that the Olympics would ultimately not be able to ignore.

Another issue, which hogged much limelight during the first British Empire Games was the issue of revenue generation and spending, especially as the Western world was still in the throes of the worst economic depression it had ever known till then. Financing a team to Hamilton, as Katharine Moore suggests, was the primary concern for most of the participating countries and it was not until subsidies were announced by the organizers that confirmations were received from the far-flung corners of the Empire.[15] This was made possible by the solid financial backing afforded by the Hamilton City Council.

Responding to the call of M.M. (Bobby) Robinson, the founding father of the British Empire Games, the Council, in 1930, sanctioned $5000 for operating costs. It also agreed to pitch in with a grant of $25,000, as and when it became necessary.[16] Accordingly, when the amateur athletic union of Australia reluctantly decided to stay away from the Hamilton competition in January 1930, citing financial considerations, the Hamilton organizers immediately came up with the offer of a $5000 subsidy towards team expenses that helped change the Australian decision.[17] New Zealand and South Africa, too, were paid substantial subsidies and the monies, in both cases, were 'gratefully accepted'. Hamilton's total spending in ensuring participation was a whopping $33,000, which was almost a third of the total revenue figure estimated at approximately $111,000.

In the ultimate analysis, the Hamilton organizing committee was left with a loss of $4000, which was considered minimal, given the hugely successful public relations exercise the inaugural games had been. Tourism had received a boost and the city was also gifted $8800 worth of equipment, 'which was incorporated into the parks and playgrounds around the city'.[18]

The Hamilton committee's awarding of subsidy to the participating teams, Moore argues, 'set precedents which have survived in the Games since 1930 ... The offer of a travel subsidy made the crucial difference in Australia agreeing to attend the Games, and this gesture was encouraged by the (Commonwealth Games) Federation to be a permanent feature of future celebrations. The provision of free accommodation for the athletes and officials was another major financial undertaking for the organizers, and proved to be a forerunner of the first Olympic Village in 1932.'[19]

To put this in perspective, Delhi is now providing free economy-class air tickets to all Commonwealth Games Associations (CGAs), with travel grants for at least twenty members each.[20] It is also providing free business–class travel for presidents and secretary generals of all CGAs and executive committee members of the CGF, apart from free accommodation for athletes and team officials in the Village. In addition, senior members of the CGF are to be housed in deluxe five–star hotels, with chauffeur–driven cars, translators and escorts. This is apart from the guarantee of a free entry to India for all accredited athletes and delegates,[21] along with a free trip to the Taj.[22] The antecedents of this policy go back to that first subsidy in Hamilton.

But back to the Canadian story. Hamilton became a useful vehicle for showcasing Canadian national identity, within the context of the then British Empire. This is how an account of the opening ceremony in the *Toronto Star* chose to describe it:

> Four hundred athletes from the British Empire, the first coming together of its kind in history paraded here before a big crowd this afternoon to open the British Empire Games … The stands were crowded, making the pageant of opening a vibrant ceremony as they greeted the incoming contingents with their cheers. Newfoundland's eight men in claret blazers, piped with white, had the honor, as representatives of the oldest colony, of leading the long procession. As they marched round the track they got a big hand.[23]

1934: Disappointment in London

Originally awarded to South Africa, the 1934 Games were subsequently moved to London. With the country gradually emerging from the clutches of the Great Depression, the Games were looked upon as an opportunity to reassert London's greatness at the world stage. Accordingly, the organizers left no stone unturned in making the opening ceremony a grand celebration of the virtues of the Empire. The scale of celebration is evident from the following report in the *Times of India*:

> Twenty years ago the dominions gathered round the mother country swearing loyalty at the time of war. Today six hundred athletes from sixteen dominions collected in England in friendly rivalry and swore

allegiance to the King Emperor in the name of sport. The opening of the British Empire Games at the White City was an impressive ceremony.[24]

Fifty thousand pigeons, valued at over GBP 200,000 were released and more than 40,000 spectators, the biggest crowd at the White City since the 1908 Olympics, witnessed the festivities.[25]

The contemporary reader cannot but be drawn to the myriad meanings and ironies of that name: White City. The break-up of the participants makes for interesting reading. Out of a total of 600 athletes, the colonies sent a handful of token representatives but the numbers were largely made up by large contingents from England and Canada. Canada, with 114 athletes, outnumbered all of the other overseas teams at a ratio of 4:1. Scotland sent a team of sixty but Wales had sent in only a dozen athletes. British Guyana had two, Australia twelve, Rhodesia six and Hong Kong a couple of representatives. Northern Ireland, Bermuda and Jamaica sent half-a-dozen athletes each and Newfoundland had sent only four. Britain had the largest representation, going up to almost 150, making up the grand total of 600.[26]

While the opening ceremony was a success, the organization of the Games left much to be desired and ultimately left London with a tainted legacy. The Canadians, among all teams, had a terrible time in London. As reported by the *Toronto Star*, it took more than five minutes to put a telephone call through from the hotel and sometimes the wait to put the call through could go beyond fifteen minutes. 'Meals without liquids were served and no tea at luncheon and coffee in the drawing room, no laundry facilities and six pence extra for a glass of milk or three pence for cream for your coffee.' The athletes desperately wished the competition to end.[27]

The Canadians also reported that they were made to walk from the underground at Wood Lane to the Wembley Stadium, an ordeal that left most of the athletes exhausted before formal training started. At the stadium, the organizers refused to open the nearest gate and those seeking training had to walk almost half a mile to the gate that was left open and another half a mile back to the dressing room. 'But the height was reached when the English officials suggested that it would be a good thing for the Canadians to walk to Wembley from their hotel near Hyde Park in London West. That finished it for the Canadians for they never let up until they got the nearer gate opened right next to the dressing rooms.'[28]

However, at the end of the Games, the Canadian manager, M.M. Robinson, tried to downplay the lack of facilities, suggesting that the Canadians had had a good time in London and were sorry to leave England.[29] This was essential to ensure that the Games went on and that the Empire, under pressure from nationalist movements in a series of colonies in the global south, continued to prosper.

Summing up the London experience, Vernon Morgan, bronze medalist in the first Games at Hamilton, stated: 'Somehow they (London) did not seem to have made a tremendous impact in spite of the fact that the competing nations had been boosted to sixteen and the competitors more than doubled to the region of 600.'[30]

1938–50: Success in the Antipodes

Following London, which was a failed experiment for some, Sydney 1938 was a mixed bag. Right from the opening ceremony, witnessed by over 25,000 people, spectator interest continued to support the Games till the very end, with the closing ceremony playing host to a crowd of over 30,000.[31] However, the number of nations competing dropped to fifteen and the competitors were down by a hundred. At the same time, it has been said that this was the beginning of the upsurge of sport in Australia in other games as well as those contested in the Empire Games. They were so shocked by their mediocre performance that they were shaken into activity. As Morgan writes, 'They went on to produce the athlete of the Games, the speedy girl sprinter long jumper Decima Norman who won five gold medals ... '[32]

The limited impetus gained at Sydney was soon lost as the 1942 Games, awarded to Canada, were cancelled on account of the Second World War. It is worth noting, however, that the Canadians, while initially agreeing to host the Games in 1942, were keen to give up their right if a colony, which hadn't yet hosted the Games, expressed interest in doing so.[33] This was a sign that the Games were proving difficult to sustain and the twelve-year break between 1938 and 1950, when the Games moved to Auckland, was in fact a blessing in disguise.

At Auckland, all seats for the opening ceremony at the Eden Park Oval were sold days in advance and not a single seat was left for the swimming and diving events, held at the Olympic pool. Such enthusiasm inspired hope that the construction costs of more than GBP 70,000 could be recovered.[34]

Auckland struck a chord with its easy *hospitality*. As reported in the *Toronto Star*, 'The enthusiasm shown by the citizens of Auckland has been tremendous and their hospitality equally as great. Not a single New Zealander wants any Canadian, Nigerian or Ceylonese, whatever color or creed, to put his hand in his pocket or her purse. Never was this great friendship among the countries of the Commonwealth more amply demonstrated.'[35] That Auckland was a major success is evident from the following description:

> Though some of the Canadian sports writers poked fun at the antiquated Victorian city of Auckland, these were great games. Though the competing nations had dropped to 12, there was a new record in the number of competitors with nearly 700. New records were set in the matter of spectators and the games were a thundering success from every angle. They started a new era in Empire Games, which subsequent host cities have happily followed. They were such a happy, friendly Games that none left without a tear in his eye and there never will be a finer closing ceremony than that at which the soul stirring Maori song of farewell *Now is the hour* was the glorious climax.[36]

In Auckland, for the first time in British Empire Games history, not all medals were won by the major nations. There was a first-ever gold for Fiji, with Mataika Tuicakau winning the shot put to the great delight of the huge crowd; and also for Ceylon, with Duncan White winning the 440-metre hurdles.

Continuing with the list of firsts, it was the first-ever occasion in international sporting history that a sports reporter, Larry Saunders of Christchurch, trailed the marathon runners in a cycle. The reporter, drenched in sweat, came to the press box just before eventual winner Holden entered the stadium, to 'tell the tale of the dramatic race'.[37]

With the success of the Auckland competition, organizing the Games also regained some of its attractiveness. This is evident from the fact that four Canadian cities – Toronto, Vancouver, Montreal and Hamilton – were in the running to host the 1954 Games. The decision, which was in the hands of the Empire Games Association of Canada, was a tricky one, which needed to weigh in the offers from the various centres and also weigh what each was willing to put forward.[38]

Up and Down to the 1980s

Eventually, the 1954 Games were awarded to Vancouver, which ended up having a terrible experience with organizing the event. With just days for the Games to begin, the organizing committee was facing a deficit of more than CAD 125,000 with all channels of fundraising exhausted. The situation was such that V. Stanley Smith, chairman of the British Empire Games Committee, said that he would have to beg, borrow or steal to pull the Games out of a hole despite government or city grants of more than CAD 1,350,000.[39]

Total expenditure for hosting the Games, Smith suggested, accrued to CAD 2,700,000. This included CAD 1,900,000 capital outlay and CAD 800,000 for Games operations. Construction of the new BEG Stadium, cycling bowl and swimming pool consumed a large chunk of the organizational budget. Total income from ticket sales, grants, television rights and concessions amounted to CAD 2,600,000. 'Then, Smith and the finance committee members hope to put the Games in the black by getting personal donations.'[40]

Word that the Vancouver Games weren't in great shape got round and the British and Australian press commented harshly on the disorganization. Reacting to such criticism, Smith declared that there was bound to be a certain amount of 'orderly disorder when we have over 1,000 athletes, managers and newspapermen suddenly descend on us'.[41]

Ultimately, however, Vancouver recovered to stage a fairly successful competition. For the first time, twenty-four nations took part and the number of athletes had risen to nearly 800. In one of the most startling races of all time, the 'Miracle Mile', as it is now called, the first six to finish beat the old Games record. It was also of significance that Pakistan won her first-ever Commonwealth Games gold at Vancouver, with Iqbal finishing first in the hammer-throw.

Compared to Vancouver 1954, Wales 1958 was a spectacular success. This was more so because Wales received no official subsidy or financial gift towards the cost of hosting these Games. Thus, Wales started with an initial handicap from which both Vancouver 1954 and Perth 1962 were relieved. (Vancouver began its organizing work with the backing of CAD 600,000 and Perth was gifted an initial subsidy of AUD 1,250,000.) Wales set forth with an overdraft, backed only by a guarantee of GBP 22,000. To complicate matters, cost of organizing continued to rise and by early 1956 it was evident that the final figure would be no less than GBP 250,000. This was attributed to a significant increase in the number of competitors – 800 at Vancouver to about 1,500 at Wales – and the accompanying costs of travel that the organizing committee had to subsidize. In trying to provide for the travel and hospitality of 1,500 athletes, Wales eventually ended up spending well over GBP 100,000.[42]

That the organizers returned a record surplus of GBP 37,000 speaks volumes for the spectacular public support for the Games. The revenue earned from ticket sales exceeded expectations and Wales also ended up earning a lot of revenue from unexpected quarters. For example, the commemorative souvenir published on the occasion raked in an unprecedented GBP 29,000 net profit for the organizing committee.[43]

A series of fundraising events organized in the months preceding the Games contributed GBP 41,000.[44] Among the major events staged to raise funds, a show jumping event was organized at Ninian Park and a polo match played, which the HRH Duke of Edinburgh not only attended but played in himself, adding enormously to its financial success. Also, sales from the three special commemorative stamps yielded considerable revenue, making the Wales Games one of the most successful ever.

The manner in which the Games came to be organized in Wales draws attention to the deep-rooted foundation of the Empire Games. The idea of the Games in Wales was first mooted when the Welsh team returned home from Sydney in early 1938, performing well despite handicaps in training facilities and infrastructure. In October of that year, Sir Robert Webber first mooted the idea of Wales playing host to the Games and 1946 was set as the target year.

However, with the Second World War playing spoilsport, the idea was once again revived in 1950, when, at the annual general meeting of the British Empire and Commonwealth Games Council for Wales, it was urged that efforts should be undertaken to build the membership and finances of the council with a view to hosting the Games in 1958.[45] In the same year, Ceylon, which had shown an interest in hosting the 1958 Games, decided that there wasn't sufficient time left for them to adequately prepare to host the spectacle. By September 1951, Nigeria and Singapore had come forward, but there was still some way to go for both of them before they placed their claims. This encouraged the British Empire and Commonwealth Games Council for Wales to actively press the Welsh case, assuming the Games would place Wales on the map of the Empire like never before.

In July 1952, with the field left clear by the withdrawal of Nigeria and Singapore, Lord Aberdare, president of the Wales Council, declared that his country would formally put forward a bid to host the 1958 Games. Once public, the lord mayor of Cardiff immediately pledged his support and that of his parliamentary committee and soon a detailed organizational plan had evolved. Finally, at the Vancouver Games of 1954, a bid was put forward. Australia seconded the motion and, by a unanimous vote, Wales was confirmed as the host country for the VIth Games in 1958.[46]

The spectacular success of the VIth Games was driven home by the Queen in her message at the closing ceremony: 'The British Empire and Commonwealth Games ... have made this a memorable year for the principality. I have decided to mark it further by an act which will, I hope, give as much pleasure to Welshmen as it does to me. I intend to create my son Charles, Prince of Wales today...'[47]

The Australians, thus, had something to live up to when they accepted the 1962 Games for Perth. However, they were handicapped by the absence of the South Africans, no longer in the Empire or the Commonwealth; the Indians and the Nigerians. Despite such troubles, Perth 1962 picked up from where Wales had left off. Despite the heat, a crowd of over 50,000 gathered to witness the opening ceremony at the $2,240,000 Perry Lakes Stadium,[48] which was finally demolished in 2008. The Games witnessed unprecedented activity in the Western Australian capital with construction work happening throughout the city. Hotels and dining facilities were improved to cater to the 1,000-plus athletes from thirty-five participating countries. It is interesting to note that the Commonwealth Games Federation vetoed a motion that suggested the deletion of the word 'Empire' from the Games. It was unanimously agreed that the Games would continue to be called the British Empire and Commonwealth Games.[49]

Another major decision taken at Perth was to award the 1966 Games to the Caribbean island of Jamaica. This was the first time the Games had been awarded to a developing country and while there were serious apprehensions about Jamaica's ability to host an international event, it was looked upon as a serious step forward to democratize the Games in an era of decolonization. With New Delhi withdrawing its candidature, Jamaica had emerged as the front-runner, with Kingston playing host to the Games in 1966.

Jamaica 1966, as Bruce Kidd has argued, was imbued with political significance. During the Games, Caribbean leaders Norman Manley and Grantley Adams called for a united Caribbean, and thoughts of a powerful CARICOM suddenly looked feasible. Huge crowds attended the political rallies in the centre of Kingston, rallies which were jointly addressed by political leaders from Jamaica and Barbados. Kidd vividly remembers the occasion: 'It was mobilization through sport at its best. There was hope all round that political barriers would finally be overcome and the Commonwealth Games would mark a new beginning in the history of the Caribbean. As an athlete, it was a historic moment and the true potential of sport, as one that helps transcend barriers, was clearly evident.'[50]

That such ambitions weren't fulfilled impacted upon the image of the Games in the longer term. At the time of the event, however, the entire Caribbean stood united behind Jamaica in what was the biggest sports spectacle ever to be staged in the Caribbean. The opening and closing ceremonies were held at the National Stadium, which was built as a monument to commemorate Jamaican independence in 1962. The National Stadium played host to all track events, cycling and the semifinals and finals of the boxing competition. Besides the stadium, the most beautiful section of the island's southern coast was redesigned as the cycling course for the 120-mile road cycle race, which ran along the harbour and seashore for many miles. Finally, the Games Village was situated at the University of West Indies, six miles from downtown Kingston and three-and-a-half miles from the National Stadium.

In Jamaica, much care was taken to design the medals awarded to athletes. Also, all participating athletes and officials were presented with a commemorative medal produced in gold and bronze. The medals awarded to the winners were conceived by Herbert Macdonald and depicted the statue of a Jamaican runner with the grandstand of the stadium in the background on one side. The statue was actually placed in front of the stadium and was also used in a design for a postage stamp, which was released on the occasion. The reverse side of the victory medal showed the established design of the Games Federation, which was the crown of St. Edward surrounded by an unbroken chain of lines representing the 'Chain of Friendship' of Commonwealth countries. Engraved alongside were the title of the organization with the venue and year. The commemorative medal was also designed by Macdonald and was similar on the reverse side to the victory medal and carried, on the obverse side, the arms of the City of Kingston.[51]

In trying to stand up to world scrutiny, Jamaica spent huge amounts in staging the Commonwealth Games, an act that left a serious scar on the country's exchequer. Nowhere was this more evident than during the opening and closing ceremonies, which were planned as a showcasing of Jamaican culture.[52]

The cost-intensive nature of the Games was once again the focus in Edinburgh four years later. Days before the start of the Edinburgh Games, there were numerous reports questioning the expenses incurred during the hosting of the Games and their impact on the ordinary taxpayer. As reported in the *Toronto Star*, even Edinburgh councillors were not all convinced about the Games and many thought that the huge spending wasn't justified. However, ticket sales were at a premium and by the second day of the Games, $491,675 worth of tickets had already been sold. By the end of the Games, the ticket sales target of $625,000 had been easily achieved, evident from an interview given by the Games financial secretary, Thomas Tait:[53]

> Edinburgh's taxpayers had spent $4,620,000 on the main stadium at Meadowbank and the city paid for the $4,000,000 pool. The city also coughed up thousands on a velodrome. Critics pointed out that there weren't many cyclists in Edinburgh and people questioned the utility of the facility after the Games were over. Eventually, most of the operating cost of $1,380,000 was paid for from public subscription, gate receipts and sale of television rights. Tourism, it is evident from the records, received a major boost. All of the 200 hotels and 600 guest houses were fully booked and 300 visitors a day, three times the normal average, arrived in Edinburgh during the Games. Tourist inquiries at the Waverley Railway Station doubled and shops in and around Princess Street, Edinburgh's main shopping district, did brisk business throughout the two weeks of the Games.[54]

Finally, Edinburgh finished off in style with a novel closing ceremony that highlighted the theme of the 'friendly Games'. Unlike the conventional norm in closing ceremonies, Edinburgh clubbed athletes of particular sporting disciplines rather than on the basis of nationalities.[55] This was especially significant given the heightened political consciousness and apprehension over apartheid seriously impacting sporting events across the world. The Commonwealth Games was no exception. In fact, the Edmonton Games organizers in 1978 had to spend a lot of time in trying to ensure that the Games weren't the site of a black African-led boycott, a subject dealt with in the following chapter. Sport realpolitik, it was evident, was much in vogue.

Edmonton 1978, coming right after the disastrous Montreal Olympics campaign, was a bigger challenge for the organizers than most other Games in the past. It was important that the Games had a plus balance sheet and that the taxpayers did not have to bear the brunt of the spending. It was also important for the organizers to demonstrate to the world that the Commonwealth, as an institution, had not lost relevance.

The organizers, to the great relief of political leaders from across the Commonwealth, were successful. A capacity crowd of 45,000 plus cheered the 1,900 athletes from the forty-six participating countries as they entered Edmonton's new Commonwealth Stadium.[56] Thousands of blue, red and white balloons filled the sky as the Queen declared the Games open. Special efforts were made at community integration, and operation costs, a major issue at Montreal, were kept at a minimum. This tradition of trying to ensure that the Games provided the Commonwealth with a renewed justification continued at Brisbane in 1982, amidst a growing chorus that the Games had lost the status it once had.

Reporting from Brisbane, Wayne Parrish summed up the deep existential crisis at the heart of the Games:

> At best the Commonwealth Games are a spectacle more rooted in tradition than reality, at worst a superfluous reminder of a long ago arena when Britannia ruled the waves. In 1982 the Commonwealth Games is a fragile affiliation of countries, which have escaped the bosom of mother England and show no inclination to return. The only real bond is a linguistic one … In itself perhaps this is not sufficient reason to question the concept and future of the Games but taken together with several other factors, it will have a lot of people doing precisely that over the next four years … Perhaps significantly there has not been talk of the next Games here that you usually hear at the close of an Olympics. For the record, they are in Edinburgh in 1986. They'll be the XIII Games. One only hopes that isn't unlucky XIII, as in last.[57]

The debate over the relevance of the Games continued in Edinburgh. In fact, it gathered steam because the world swimming championships, where the standard of competition was much higher, were scheduled to be held just three weeks after the Games. The Canadians, among all the participating teams, were most eloquent in outlining how seriously they were taking the Commonwealth Games. Trevor Tiffany, head of the Swimming Federation of Canada, emphasized the Canadian perspective in an interview: 'Athletes focus on world championships. I keep telling them that it's as if there aren't any world championships this year. That's how important the Commonwealth Games are.'[58] He went on to emphasize that the Canadian sports budget was dependant on the showing in the Commonwealth Games and the Canadian media covered the Games widely.

Despite such an assertion, the Games were increasingly losing currency as a quality sports competition, as is evident from some of the performances at Brisbane and Edinburgh. At Brisbane in 1982, the 1500 metres women's gold medallist from Britain was a staggering 16 seconds off the world record, drawing attention to the standard of competition in the Commonwealth Games. At the same games, Kirsty Mcdermott of Wales won the women's 800 metres with a timing of 2.01.23 seconds, slower than what Dixie Willis, who gave her the medal, had clocked in 1961.[59]

To add to the growing cloud around the Games, the Edinburgh organizers lost GBP 4 million, while the Auckland Games in 1990 lost double that amount.

Trying to Carve a New Niche: Victoria 1994 to Melbourne 2006

Knowing it was impossible for the Commonwealth athletes to match the standard of the world championships or the Olympics, the Commonwealth Games Federation decided to think fresh and innovate, so that the Commonwealth Games were able to carve out their separate identity. With this view, athletes with disabilities were invited to take part in the Victoria Games of 1994, a decision that sparked a major controversy midway into the Games.

At Victoria, the Australian Chef de Mission Arthur Turnstall sparked off a major controversy when he called the inclusion of disabled athletes an 'embarrassment'. Failing to understand the significance of the act and unable to appreciate the effort put in by the athletes, he declared, 'I do not believe they should be integrated with the Commonwealth Games. I can tell you it's an embarrassment for those people and for the athletes in the village.'[60] Though he did a double turn thereafter and offered an unconditional apology, he soon found himself in the eye of a storm with stinging criticism coming his way. His statement once again encouraged debate over whether the Games themselves were turning out to be white elephants with little significance, a debate that assumed centre stage at Manchester in 2002 and during Melbourne 2006.

The XVIIth Games at Manchester, it can be surmised in hindsight, gave the Commonwealth Games a new lease of life. The

Manchester Games resulted in the creation of 6,300 permanent jobs of which 2,900 were in the Manchester area alone. As is evident from a cost-and-benefit analysis conducted at the end of the Games, the rate of employment creation placed Manchester 2002 on par with the rate of return for economic benefits achieved by Olympic host cities like Seoul and Barcelona. In financial terms, for every GBP 1 million of public investment, there was a value addition of GBP 2.7 million. The report went on to suggest:

> ... the operating costs of the Games were also well within budget, with ticket sales exceeding targets and with TV rights, sponsorship and licensing on or above target. Over GBP 25 million of sponsorship was secured, with nearly GBP 15 million in cash and GBP 11 million in kind. As a result, the surplus remaining in the Games contingency fund was returned to funding partners.[61]

Other benefits arising out of Manchester included the development of significant business opportunities in East Manchester, including a regional retail centre, a four-star hotel, offices and new housing developments supporting up to 3,800 jobs. The Games led to the establishment of a new ASDA/Walmart superstore, which resulted in the creation of some 800 new jobs. Hotel occupancy rates in the city were at their best ever, with the number of rooms sold in July 2002 (57,689) being the highest in history. Moreover, 300,000 new visitors have visited the city every year since the Games, spending approximately GBP 18 million.[62]

While not being able to emulate Manchester in terms of the scale of success, Melbourne 2006 turned out to be much better than originally anticipated. At Melbourne, 4,500 athletes from seventy-one nations competed. Along with the athletes, 1,500 team officials, 1,200 technical officials and 3,100 media representatives made up the Games. Sixteen different sports were contested for, using sixty-one competition venues, of which fifty-five were located within the Greater Melbourne area and six were located in the region.[63]

A KPMG (a global network of professional firms providing audit, tax and advisory services) study conducted on the impact of the Melbourne Games revealed that Victoria expected to reap a

$1.6 billion growth in the Gross State Product over the next twenty years. Following up on the report, Justin Madden, the minister for the Commonwealth Games, argued:

> The MCG and MSAC have been redeveloped, the new William Barak Bridge now links the city to the Melbourne and Olympic Park precinct, residents are moving into our newest inner city suburb Parkville Gardens, large numbers of the 15,000 trained-up volunteers are assisting with local community groups and events, and over a million trees have been planted ... The Games was declared the best ever, was delivered $50 million under budget and provided an outstanding boost to the Victorian economy.[64]

The report also revealed that almost 13,600 full-time jobs were created because of the Games.

Tourism to Victoria received a significant boost with 60,000 interstate and 57,000 international tourists travelling to Melbourne during, immediately before and after the Games. According to the KPMG study, these tourists contributed about AUD 252 million of new money to the economy, resulting in a lower than expected overall Games expenditure of around AUD 2.9 billion.[65]

JACKPOT OR BURDEN: OLYMPICS AND HOST CITY DEVELOPMENT

In terms of the direct urban impact of sporting events, there is more recorded evidence from the Olympic Games, simply because of the greater importance and focus attached to them. The direct correlation between host cities and Olympic Games, as Adrian Pitts and Hanwen Liao have documented, can be traced back to the building of the White City Olympic Stadium in London in 1908. Yet, until the Second World War:

> ... provision of sports venues and athlete villages dominated Olympic preparation and the impact of the Games on the wider urban infrastructure was limited. It was not until 1960 that the dormant forces for large-scale development began to reveal themselves. From the 1960 Rome Olympics onwards, the Games began to have many far-reaching consequences on the local

built environment—particularly in line with the needs of urban expansion in the 1960s and 1970s, of inner city regeneration in the 1980s and 1990s and of sustainable urban form in the current decade.[66]

Before we travel back in history and analyse the impact of summer Olympics on host cities, it is of interest to take into account the debates over the 2008 Beijing Summer Games.

The Beijing Games, as Chinese scholar Xu Guoqui had suggested, was for his country a moment of 'crisis' in the Chinese sense of the word – a moment of mixed danger and unlimited opportunity. It was an opportunity to restore China's national greatness by erasing the scars inflicted by a century of humiliation by the West and then Japan, and to replace it with spectacular sporting achievements.[67]

Medals in the Games were the immediate aspiration but world dominance was the ultimate intent. There is little doubt that with the Chinese ruling the medal table, or the gold-medal count more specifically, the Americans will leave no stone unturned before the next Olympics to regain their lost position. The US, as Olympic experts have argued, will pump in billions into its athletic programmes despite the meltdown in preparation for the 2012 London Games.

The fight for supremacy between the US and China goes back several years. So much so that when the Chinese submitted a bid to the International Olympic Committee for the right to host the 2000 Games, the *New York Times* wrote, 'The city in question is Beijing in the year 2000, but the answer is Berlin 1936. The history of the modern Olympics is too short and the world is too small to forget murder.' And even when China won the rights to host the 2008 Games, Zbigniew Brzezinski, former US national security advisor, declared, 'The Olympics may be a triumph for China, but by intensifying the pressures for change, the Games are quite unlikely to be a triumph for China's waning communism. In fact, the Games may accelerate its fading.'[68]

Evidently, the Chinese government used Beijing 2008 to play up Chinese nationalism. Most student volunteers at the Games – wearing baseball caps and 'Good Luck Beijing' T-shirts – were charged up with patriotic sentiment and the dominant slogan on the streets of Beijing was: 'We are determined to win.'[69] Beijing 2008 demonstrated, more than ever before, that sport realpolitik was not dead.

There's little doubt that, in scale, the Beijing Olympics stands unparalleled. This is best understood in comparative terms. While the Greeks staged a successful Olympics at Athens in 2004 with a budget of $15 billion, it was only a third of what the Chinese put into the Games. Again, London isn't expected to put in more than GBP 15 billion, especially with the effects of the meltdown still casting their shadows on the British economy.

Even the unrest over Tibet was dealt with effectively by the organizers of the Beijing Olympics; except for the occasional critical report, the international media, too, was impressed with the organizational ability of the Chinese and labelled the Beijing Games as a watershed event in the history of the Games.

In Beijing, the show began at the first point of contact – the airport. A chic new Terminal 3, designed by leading British architect Norman Foster, awaited visitors. The terminal, covering an area of 14 million square feet, cost an approximate $3.5 billion. With a completely revamped subway system, new highways and thousands of volunteers, Beijing was all dressed up for the Games weeks before the spectacle began.

While there's little doubt that London 2012 or Rio 2016 will find it exceedingly difficult to match the perfect show put on by the Chinese government, it is also of interest to note that Beijing's organizers have already started feeling the heat over how to properly utilize the facilities built for the Games. On 1 February 2009, Chinese news agency Xinhua reported that the area around the massive Bird's Nest Stadium is to be turned into a shopping and entertainment complex in three to five years. The stadium, the news report went on to state, had not been used since the end of the Games. 'Paint is already peeling off in certain areas, and the only visitors these days are tourists who pay about $7 to walk on the stadium floor and browse a pricey souvenir shop.'[70]

The news report ended with the grim assertion that the stadium, 'a symbol of China's rising power and confidence ... may never recoup its hefty construction cost, particularly amid a global economic slump'.[71]

Growing criticism that the $450-million stadium is fast turning into a white elephant has forced the authorities to convert the stadium into a mall full of shops and entertainment outlets. The only event organized at the 91,000-capacity stadium in 2009 was Puccini's Opera, *Turondot*, held on 8 August to mark the first anniversary of the Olympics opening ceremony. To add to the stadium's woes, it has no permanent tenant after Beijing's top soccer club, Guo'an, backed out of a deal to play in the arena.

In contrast to Beijing, Athens 2004 appears minuscule. The Greek Games that staggered on the periphery of catastrophe before they began eventually did much for Greek national pride and determination. From an organizational perspective, the tumultuous build-up before Athens, it appears in hindsight, was not so bad after all. With news of under-preparedness emanating from all over, the world had braced itself for chaos on the eve of the Games. Everybody knew it would be rough. Since elections were held in Greece just months before the Games began and resulted in a change in government at the centre, problems were only natural. However, the final result was in no way disastrous. Athens did well to stand up to the scrutiny of the world, and the IOC and the Olympic world was relieved that the country managed to pull through without much trouble. With a reasonable budget allowing for modest new constructions, the Athens legacy isn't negative. Harnessing the facilities in the long term remains a challenge, but chances are that the 2004 Games will go down in Greek history as a successful experiment which helped bring about substantial urban revitalization. In fact, Athens continues to successfully use the newly-built metro and tram networks, and the numerous restored archaeological sites and museums have added to Athens' aura as a world heritage site. Finally, the transformation of the 530-hectare brownfield site at the obsolete Hellinikon Airport into Europe's largest park for sports and recreational use has served Athens well since the Games in 2004.[72]

Sydney, on the other hand, personifies the negative impact that mega events can have on host cities. The Sydney Olympic Park, once a symbol of Australian pride, which housed Olympic athletes in 2000, now stands derelict. In fact, getting to the Park – some twenty-five kilometres from the city's business district – is an ordeal, involving driving down Paramatta Road for almost an hour.[73] The link between Darwin Harbour, the Sydney CBD and Paramatta was not accomplished and the ordinary taxpayers continue to bear the brunt of this investment, while real estate prices in Sydney continue to be high despite the meltdown. Even as a tourist attraction, the Sydney Olympic Park has little currency. With no proper transportation to channel tourists to the site, the Park remains an example of how things can go wrong while trying to use sport as a module for urban regeneration.

If Sydney resulted in gargantuan spending with little post-Olympic usage, the centennial Games in Atlanta were severely criticized for the lack of adequate investment in building of infrastructure and poor transport facilities. The numerous problems prompted the *Observer* newspaper to describe Atlanta as a city in 'complete chaos'[74] during the Games. In fact, it can be suggested that the Atlanta Games were jinxed to start with.

The trouble began from the time the Americans landed in Greece to take the Olympic flame back to Atlanta. The Greeks refused the give the Americans the flame and argued that the hosts had devalued the flame and its significance. Greek nationalists criticized American attempts at commercializing the Games and their dislike of the visiting American delegation created a war-like situation in Olympia. A back-up flame was readied in Paris and current secretary of state, Hilary Clinton, then in Greece to accept the flame on behalf of the United States Olympic Committee had to use all her diplomatic skills to diffuse the situation.[75] Atlanta failed to recover from this poor start and is still regarded as one of the worst organized Summer Games in history. The expected boost to tourism never happened, jobs weren't generated for the economically underprivileged and by the time the Games finally started, most projects geared at the Games appeared to be non-starters. The desire to use the profits to develop the disadvantaged sections of the city's communities and to bring about integration had been replaced by the urge to ensure that the mega event did not end up rendering the organizers bankrupt.

Barcelona 1992, however, is the exact opposite. With careful planning and excellent implementation, the city serves as a perfect model of what the Olympics can do if facilities constructed for the Games are properly harnessed for the city's development. The underlying philosophy of the Barcelona Olympic Project, as Miguel Moragas suggests, was to 'ensure that the Games were decentralized. The idea of concentrating all installations in an Olympic park – as had been the case in Seoul – was rejected. Barcelona decided to share the games with as many subsidiary host cities as possible.'[76]

In Barcelona, four primary sites were selected for Olympic activity. The already established precinct of the Montjuic, which had a stadium built way back in 1936 and a swimming pool built in 1972, played host to the opening and closing ceremonies. The other existing sports precinct harnessed for Olympic activity was that of the Diagonal, which has the largest concentration of private sports facilities in the city. Poblenou – an area full of derelict warehouses and unused railway facilities, which resulted in a disconnect between the beach and city – was, as Liao and Pitts argue, integrated with the city and the area was revitalized with 'stylish apartments, a new sewage system, a new ring road, a new marina (Olympic harbour) and other amenities along the 5.2 kilometre barrier – free coastal strip'. Two other areas that were developed for the Olympics were the Parc de Mar and the Vall d'Hebron with a view to maximizing public access to sport in and around the city.[77]

Not only does every tourist who visits Barcelona visit these facilities, it is also well documented that the Games Village contributed significantly to solving the housing problem that plagued the city in the 1980s. Even the stadium, which hosted the opening ceremony in 1992, has since served as a home to the RCD Espaniol team, which ensures its regular use.

Barcelona, despite Moragas' claim, had partly followed the model of urban regeneration around the Olympics, initiated at Seoul in 1988. Seoul – which had a tumultuous time leading up to the Games in view of the change of guard in Korea on Games eve – managed, for the first time in history, to successfully harness the Games, to address environmental concerns. Since then, environmental issues have always received importance and even occupied centre stage in Sydney when the Games themselves were christened the 'Green Games'. In Seoul, the organizers successfully redeveloped areas of low-quality housing and ensured integration between the city's central business district and the slums, which occupied a vast land mass south of the Han River. The organizers took over the slum, helped relocate the existing dwellers to better community housing and developed a sixty-acre sports complex and a sixty-three-acre Athletes Village on the site.[78]

If Seoul marked a new phase in trying to use sport for reasons of urban regeneration, Los Angeles, by making a profit of GBP 215 million from organizing the Olympics, marked yet another watershed in Olympic history. Unlike in recent years, Los Angeles was the only candidate city in 1984 and the lessons from Munich and Montreal had seriously impacted upon national/city intentions to host the world's biggest sporting spectacle. The LA Games, unlike all the competitions preceding it, were almost entirely privately funded and marked a new era in Olympic organization. From selling the rights to be a torchbearer for USD 3,000,[79] the organizers left no stone unturned in making sure that the Games ended in a surplus. Also, with twenty-four of the thirty-one venues already in existence, Los Angeles had a marked advantage over others in trying to reach its designated goal.

Before Los Angeles, as mentioned earlier, Olympic organization was in total disarray. Montreal was a disaster in Canadian history and the city needed almost three decades to pay off the debt incurred in 1976. Munich 1972, too, wasn't an organizational success. With a $200-million loss to go with the political violence, Munich had not done much to inspire confidence among future bidders.

The long- or medium-term impact of a major international sporting event on host societies varies based on the context. As Renaud Donnedieu de Valises, French minister of culture, has argued, 'Each Olympic city has had appropriate pride in its national, regional and urban traditions and roots, while at the same time it has shared a common global Olympic heritage of creativity, innovation and positive purpose.'[80]

The interlink between hosting Olympic Games and urban regeneration is likely to be strengthened in London come the 30th Olympiad in 2012.

THE FUTURE

Echoing the concerns of Delhi 2010, the question of national pride is uppermost on the minds of the 2012 Olympics Games organizers in London. This is especially so after the spectacular success of Beijing. As documented by Gavin Poynter and Iain Mercury: 'On 29 January 2008, the House of Commons Culture, Media and Sport Committee met to discuss London 2012 with Tessa Jowell, the government minister with responsibility for the Games and London. The committee was questioning government ministers, civil servants and 2012 officers for the fourth time about the Games in a little over three months.' The committee's primary concern was/is the escalating cost of the Games, an interest that was stirred by government announcements in March 2007 that the cost of the Games was set to rise from an initial estimate of GBP 2.4 billion to a revised budget of GBP 9.3 billion. 'The additional money was to be raised through a further commitment by government of GBP 6 billion (including GBP 2.2 billion from the national lottery, of which GBP 675 million was extra funding). The revised costs were driven by several factors including the rising price of land remediation, the increased allocation to contingency, tax (the imposition of VAT) and the rising costs of security. To address this cost problem, government and the Mayor of London, committed in November 2007, to the sale of Park land post-2012 to offset any deficits that might arise from the event not covering its costs.'[81]

Despite agreeing to spend much more than was initially anticipated, London might still fall short of achieving its objectives. With the legacy of the Games being linked to challenging the underlying social and economic problems of east London – the skills deficit, lack of jobs, unequal access to healthcare and the lack of available and affordable housing for local people – only time will tell if London 2012 results in the scale of urban regeneration that is being envisaged.

Such doubts arise because prospective host cities have, to make their bids more fashionable, started incorporating social goals into the bids, not taking into account the responsibilities associated with implementing such large-scale projects. To quote Poynter and Mercury once more:

The bids are designed to win the competition, the reconciliation of aspirations set down in the candidate file with the financial framework required to deliver them really commences after the winning city is announced. The potential gap between aspiration and reality is filled, according to IOC regulations, by guarantees underwritten by the host city and national governments. The bidding process itself creates the capacity for the confusion of direct and non-direct event-related investment – the former being expenditure related to putting the event on and the latter being the investment in infrastructure that may strengthen the bid but not be attributable to meeting its direct costs.[82]

There are eerie echoes here of the gaps between the bid and the reality of Delhi 2010.

From the experiences of the multiple host cities described in the course of this chapter, it is evident that the relationship between host city development and mega sporting events will continue to depend on the city's ability to market itself as a key tourism destination following the event, and also on its ability to harness the facilities constructed for the Games for its residents. This requires the opening up of new tourist markets and sustaining them over time. Spurred by such intentions, Glasgow, the Commonwealth host city for 2014, has already embarked on projects of community integration and urban regeneration. It is too early to tell whether such projects will result in a positive legacy in Scotland.

As for Delhi 2010, the question is whether it can shrug off its exceptionally troubled prehistory and turn the Games into a new take-off point. Only time will tell.

5 | GAMES OF EMPIRE, 1930-1947

On an unusually clear October morning, Buckingham Palace threw open its gates to India like never before. Surrounded with the grace of kathak and the boisterous sounds of bhangra on a specially constructed stage at the Palace grounds, Queen Elizabeth II handed over the Games baton to President Pratibha Patil. Making a special effort to keep aside the controversies and the discords of the past, Suresh Kalmadi and Mike Fennell appeared together for the cameras. And like a champion winning a World Cup, Sports Minister M.S. Gill held aloft the baton in triumph. The Queen's staff took special pains to impress upon the Indian media that President Patil was only the seventh state guest since 1998 to stay in the Windsor Castle and that the Queen herself emphasized the importance of the strategic partnership between the two countries at the banquet. It was British pageantry at its best. Keen Indian observers were impressed but found a special irony in the slickly planned ceremony. Writing in the *Hindu*, Vidya Subrahmaniyam asked:

> ... really, what was the iron discipline and fussing all about? The UK was an ageing, declining power, hit by recession and looking somehow to hold its place in the comity of nations. India was messy, the bulk of its people were desperately poor, and even the better-off exasperated with their disregard for rule. Yet in a world that measured a country's worth by its money, India, with its vast markets and a recession-time growth of 6.5 per cent, counted for more than the UK. And indeed, if the Queen made her Indian guest feel special, which she did by all accounts, it was in recognition of this truth ...
>
> ... Clearly it made business sense to court India. Yet there was also the UK public-media indifference to the Indian President's visit. As a rare English hack present at the Windsor ceremony remarked, 'It will take a while before the altered UK-India equation sinks in.'[1]

The British Empire is a distant memory in both countries. It is imagined differently: every time surveys talk of curry being Britain's national dish, Indian newspaper readers have to endure a plague of clichéd headlines like 'the Empire strikes back'. Conversely, Southall may seem spiritually closer to Punjabi Bagh than Hampstead Heath, but a certain kind of Raj nostalgia has remained a staple diet of the British reading public. India and England have long moved on but scratch the surface, and the past is always there.

The Commonwealth Games are intricately linked with geopolitics. They have always been a useful lens to understand the larger politics of what is now called the Commonwealth, they opened a window into the inner politics of the British Empire in the years before decolonization.

THE EMPIRE AND THE GAMES: POLITICS AND MEANINGS

The Commonwealth Games were established at the high noon of *Pax Britannica*. Canada was a central force in its creation; in the 1930s, the Canadians arguably saw the Games as a useful tool to assert their nationalism within the cultural and political framework of the British bond. Based on the assumption that sport was a crucial binding factor in the British Empire, the Games were designed as a source of considerable cultural power, conveying through their establishment and careful nurturing a moral and behavioural code to connect and unite the far-flung British territories in Asia, Africa, the Caribbean, North America, Oceania, and of course, the British Isles.

In most cases, these ties outlasted the achievement of independence by the former British dominions, colonies and protectorates and the formal end of the British Empire. Sporting legacies continue to culturally link the former British territories together in the form of the Commonwealth Games, the cricket and rugby World Cups and other major competitions. In fact, with the political Commonwealth continually searching for a new relevance, the Games are now arguably its strongest outward manifestation. It is likely to become an even more important tie in the decades ahead, as an increasing number of governments seek to host them and corporations look to sponsor them.

Once an extension of imperial cultural power, the Games were also meant, from the moment of inception, as an antidote to the hyper-nationalistic and hyper-commercialized global sporting spectacle of the Olympics. This is why they were tagged the 'the friendly Games'. The idea of the Games was constructed as an opposing pole to the hard-nosed competitiveness of the Olympics, as an alternative forum for Empire countries to strengthen goodwill and harmony using intense but healthy sports competition.

At the same time, the Commonwealth Games have always been fraught with tension and contradiction as they both celebrate the shared quest of sport and provide an arena for playing up national ambition. The Games have always had a special place within the history and ongoing development of the modern Commonwealth in the context of the larger social, political and demographic transformations of the former British Empire. By reconstructing the context and tracing the debates surrounding the origins of the Games, this chapter unravels the complex ways in which the Games have helped reflect and express cultural and political power, adaptation and resistance. It goes back to the origins and unravels the early history of the Games to provide perspective to its modern meanings.

The Games may be tagged 'friendly', but in essence, they have always been political. The ebb and flow of politics defined the engagement. In the early years, the Games were extremely important for predominantly white dominions like Canada and its sport leaders. Four Canadian cities have held the Games – Hamilton in 1930, Vancouver in 1954, Edmonton in 1978 and Victoria in 1994. In contrast, in the years before Independence, countries like India, which had a robust anti-colonial movement, saw the Games as far less significant when compared to the Olympics. So much so that the Games were hardly spoken of in Indian sporting circles in the 1920s and 1930s even though these were the years when the great Indian hockey teams were wowing the playgrounds of the Olympics. The reason, as subsequent sections detail, is that Indian sport in those years was inspired by a singular ambition: strengthening the nationalist impulse.

In dominions like Canada and Australia, the desire was to strengthen the informal bonds with the Empire while retaining complete autonomy. Autonomy was already a fact of life in these dominions and therefore the Games took on a different meaning. In countries such as India, where the stranglehold of the Empire had a different connotation, the intention was to first appropriate and subsequently indigenize 'Empire' sports for purposes of resistance. This process of appropriation and subsequent subversion of 'Empire' sports in India can be traced back to the late nineteenth century.[2] The need to assert aggressive Indianness on the sporting field remained integral to India's sporting culture in the heyday of nationalism. The possibility of using sport for other diplomatic manoeuvres was a strictly postcolonial phenomenon. In fact, the Austro-Canadian reaction to imperial sport was simply the opposite of the Indian retort to the Games. One need only compare the varied responses to the Commonwealth Games to see this great chasm in views within the countries of the Empire. In doing so, the historian ends up with the same theme – nationalism – asserting itself in completely inverse ways across the globe.

What do these dissimilar reactions, played out in contexts grossly dissimilar, say about the politics of Empire? Why did Canadian and Indian contexts necessitate the adoption of disparate reactions to the Empire Games? If sport is in fact a metaphor (and in some cases a metonym) for war, then the Empire Games, tagged friendly from the start, were simply not considered a priority in India. Canada and Australia on the other hand, having acquired dominion status and virtual independence, had no need for 'war minus the shooting'. In India, prowess in sport wasn't enough. Accomplishments had to be measured against a more difficult scale, one that would mark a symbolic but highly significant nationalist victory against the ruling colonial state.

To substantiate the point: even when India won gold medals in field hockey in the Olympic Games in the years 1928–36, hockey could never rival cricket in colonial India.[3] This is because Britain refused to participate in Olympic hockey contests in the years 1928–36, knowing that the Indians were favourites to win the gold. This is especially interesting because Britain had won the Olympic gold in field hockey in 1904 and 1920, the only years when hockey was played before 1928, and years when India did not participate. Absence of competition against the colonizer, it can be argued, relegated hockey to a rung lower than cricket in the Indian sporting hierarchy.[4]

By the same token, it can be asserted that the Empire Games, opposed to the demonstration of aggressive nationalist sentiment from the outset, wasn't of utmost importance in colonial India. Rather, success at bilateral cricket contests against English teams or winning at the Olympic stage, which helped showcase a strong India to the world, were deemed far more potent. The 'absence' of an aggressive nationalist impulse on the playing field played a part in relegating the Empire Games to the status of an also-ran in the colonial Indian sportscape. Also, this could not but be otherwise at a time when the Congress and the nationalist movement remained ideologically opposed to the idea of the Commonwealth itself.

Things began to change with Independence. Post-1947, the chance to compete in the Games on an equal footing perhaps did much to persuade Prime Minister Nehru to keep India in the Commonwealth, a diplomatic manoeuvre deconstructed in detail in the following chapter. Suffice it to say that following independence in 1947, the Games became far more relevant to India than other smaller regional competitions. They became linked to India's larger self-image of being a major Asian power.[5] The next chapter fleshes out this evolution. For now, let us travel back to 1930.

ORIGINS AND PREHISTORY

The Commonwealth Games, formerly British Empire Games, were established in 1930 following 'a decade of fundamental economic and political change within the Empire. During the 1920s, the trend away from formal political control in dominions like Australia, Canada and South Africa was increasingly obvious and can be linked to the rise of informal influences. The founding of the British Empire Games in 1930 may be seen as a prominent example of this shift in emphasis.'[6]

Despite its formal establishment in 1930, the idea of the Empire Games had been in circulation for almost four decades. The original idea is credited to F.S. Ashley Cooper of Great Britain who wrote to the *Times* London in 1891, proposing the establishment of a Pan-Britannic festival to celebrate the virtues of the Empire. Cooper was relying on the fundamental assumption that sport was 'a most pervasive and enduring theme in the history of British imperialism. The central feature of its power is the subconscious influence it has exerted in both colonial and postcolonial conditions.'[7] 'Considered by the colonizers to carry with it a series of moral lessons, regarding hard work and perseverance, about team loyalty and obedience to authority and, indeed, involving concepts of correct physical development and "manliness"',[8] a sports festival was deemed the best means to informally bind the Empire in a period of turmoil.

The festival idea was in circulation for three years, 1891–1894, but lost currency once Baron Pierre de Coubertin revived the idea of the modern Olympic Games.[9] The Olympic idea – more pervasive and widespread from the start – found instant takers in Europe and elsewhere and Cooper's idea was gradually relegated to the back burner. As Katharine Moore argues, 'The desire for a family contest may have still been strong but there could be no disputing the fact that De Coubertin's plans had become reality, and the various countries of the Empire continued to participate individually in the Olympic Games.'[10] It was only after the London Games of 1908, which were marked by a growing degree of anti-American sentiment, that the festival idea witnessed a revival and the coronation of King George in 1911 witnessed the staging of a festival celebrating the culture, industrial progress and sporting achievements of the Empire.

It was during this festival that Richard Coombes of Australia appropriated the Empire Games idea with enthusiasm and suggested its establishment as a more regular gathering, bringing together all of the dominions, colonies and protectorates of the Empire. Supported by James Merrick of Canada, he also suggested that the Empire countries train together in London and then travel to Stockholm together for the 1912 Olympic Games. To quote Katharine Moore once again, 'A stronger leading role in sporting matters was beginning to emanate from the dominions ... the emerging role of the dominions was revealing itself, both in sport and politics, to be one of greater initiative and leadership.'[11]

The Empire Games idea gathered further strength in the 1920s, when a plan was mooted to set in opposition Empire athletes against the Americans, who had by then established a stranglehold over the Olympics. Unlike in the nineteenth century, when Britain was considered the epicentre of sporting achievement in the world, the balance of power had moved to the United States of America by the second decade of the twentieth century. The shift spurred a defensive reaction within the British Empire with calls for the establishment of a separate sports competition for Empire countries, one devoid of the excesses of competition and commercialization that were integral to the growing cult of the Olympics.

A GAMES OF ITS OWN: COMMONWEALTH VERSUS THE OLYMPICS

It was at the 1928 Olympic Games that the Canadian team manager, M.M. Robinson, tabled specific proposals for a celebration of Empire sport in 1930 at the Canadian city of Hamilton. Reporting on this meeting, the *Toronto Star* stated:

> Lord Desborough presided over the meeting at Stamford Bridge at which New Zealand, Australia, South Africa, India and Canada discussed the advisability of holding a series of British Empire Games every four years. P.J. Mulqueen and M.M. Robinson represented Canada. It was agreed the idea is excellent and Hamilton's application for the first Games in 1930 was approved and passed on for action by the permanent body when it is fully organized.[12]

At the meeting, steps were taken to form an Empire Games Federation, which was to present a united British front when matters of vital importance to athletes of the Empire were being discussed internationally. Interestingly, English sportsmen present at the meeting unhesitatingly declared that it was far easier to secure financial support for the Empire Games than for the Olympics.

The attendees also discussed the growing desperation to win a medal at the Olympics and condemned the cult of unhealthy competition encouraged by the Olympic organizers, something the Empire Games were decidedly intent on staying away from.[13] Finally, Robinson mentioned the financial backing of the city of Hamilton, which went a long way in carrying the British Empire Games to their successful beginning in August 1930.

That much care was taken to emphasize the distinctiveness of the Empire Games was evident from the official document drafted at the meeting:

> It will be designed on the Olympic model, both in general construction and its stern definition of the amateur. But the Games will be very different, free from both the excessive stimulus and the babel of the international stadium. They should be merrier and less stern, and will substitute the stimulus of a novel adventure for the pressure of international rivalry.[14]

It must also be noted that by the turn of the second decade of the twentieth century, the political context within the Empire was ripe for the Empire Games idea to move forward. Australia, New Zealand, South Africa and Canada had all gained self-government, and the statute of Westminster passed in 1931 had withdrawn the right of the British government to legislate on behalf of the dominions. To quote Moore once more:

> More formal political structures within the Empire were being replaced by less formal influences such as sport, and the establishment of the British Empire Games can be seen as an example of the 'informal Empire' at work ... Regular sporting contact was showing itself to be an increasingly unifying influence within the Empire, and the timing of the inauguration of the British Empire Games indicates a shift from formal to informal control.[15]

Add to this the impact of the Chanak incident in 1922 in Turkey, when Canada emerged as the first dominion to refuse to automatically stand by the remainder of the Empire in a serious emergency and it was apparent that a new age of Empire politics was at hand.

The position of the dominions vis-à-vis the metropole was defined by the Imperial Conference in 1926, which was a meeting of representatives from the dominions and the United Kingdom.

The changed relationship between the dominions and the UK was defined as follows: 'They are autonomous communities within the British Empire, equal in status, in no way subordinate to one another in any aspect of their domestic or external affairs, though united by a common allegiance to the Crown, and freely associated as members of the British Commonwealth of nations.'[16]

The meaning of the declaration was further elucidated at the next Imperial Conference in 1930, and the final legal steps taken to make it workable were drafted into the statute of Westminster in 1931. Also, the operation of the statute was made conditional for Australia, New Zealand and Newfoundland. The only obligation, binding in honour, not in law, on the dominions and the United Kingdom was that no unit of the Commonwealth was to negotiate with a non-Commonwealth nation without informing the other units and none could conclude a treaty which imposed obligations on another unit of the Commonwealth.[17]

On domestic matters, as mentioned earlier, the British government was forced to renounce rights of interference on issues of legislation passed by dominion parliaments. The only immediate link between the Crown and the dominions was the governor general, who, prior to 1926, was the representative of the Crown and also the British government. In the changed circumstances of the Empire, the governor general was solely the representative of the Crown and ceased to represent British interests, a high commissioner instead being sent to each dominion. In fact, with the disappearance of British Parliament sovereignty over the dominions, the Crown was the only remaining bond; the United Kingdom and the dominions united by the fact of the common allegiance they owed to it, by virtue of which they were all British subjects.

In sum, 'by 1930 the Empire was no longer the major force in the world, and the Games could be seen as one step towards re-establishing its sagging prestige'.[18] For all practical purposes, 'the Empire needed the British Empire Games in 1930, and the level of enthusiasm shown by both host and participants indicates the degree to which the idea was seen as a welcome salve for a damaged ego'.[19]

Amsterdam 1928: American Arrogance and Canadian Discontent

The brewing discord between the Americans and the Commonwealth nations came to a head at the Amsterdam Olympics, injecting much energy into the Empire Games plan. At Amsterdam, the Canadians felt discriminated against and were livid at the preferential treatment meted out to the Americans. Things came to a pass when the president of the Canadian Olympic Committee, P.J. Mulqueen, declared that the Canadians were seriously contemplating pulling out of the Los Angeles Games in 1932. More than the Games, the heightened tension between Canadian and American officials hogged media limelight in Canada and in the process helped generate a consensus for the British Empire Games.

Reflecting on the growing atmosphere of tension, Lou Marsh, reporting for the *Toronto Star* from Amsterdam declared, 'There is serious trouble certainly brewing between the Canadian and United States teams over Olympic matters and between the Canadian, representatives and the International Olympic Committee.'[20] The report went on to emphasize that the Americans had taken control of the Olympic movement, much to the chagrin of the Canadians, and the IOC had turned powerless in their presence. 'Last night I heard Bobby Robinson, manager of the Canadian team, tell Gustavus Kirby, president of the United States Amateur Athletic Union that Canada positively would not be represented at the next Olympic Games in the United States because of the treatment they had received here.'[21]

Finally, Marsh quoted P.J. Mulqueen who summed up Canadian discontent and the acute disappointment at the prevailing state of affairs:

> If Canada continues to get the rough ride we are getting here, it might help us to decide to drop out of Olympic competition and content ourselves with the British Empire Games. We have had nothing but the run around ever since we got here. The United States gets or takes what it wants.[22]

Mulqueen went on to accuse the IOC of practising double standards and regretted having spent $500,000 on bringing the Canadian team to Amsterdam. 'We are treated with the next thing to contempt. They give us badges which mean nothing and keep a brick wall between the United States and the officials when we want to lodge a complaint or enter a protest or anything for the welfare of our athletes. If we do not get on we are run off again.'[23]

Mulqueen found support in Robinson, the chief architect of the British Empire Games. He was forthright in declaring that he was tired and fed up of the Olympics and had it been in his power, he would never again send a Canadian team to an Olympiad. He was scathing in his criticism of the Americans, whom he chided for their lack of discipline and integrity. 'The rules and regulations mean nothing to them and they are powerful enough to get away with these breaches.'[24] He pointed out that the Americans disregarded the instructions regarding the use of the new stadium and had sprinters working out there when other nations were kept out. Robinson blamed such discriminatory practice on the tournament organizers and derided the American athletes for laughing at others for obeying the rules. 'The Yankee athletes who have no right to be out on the field until called for their events were out there acting as valets for their sprinters,'[25] he declared in frustration.

The Canadians weren't the only peeved lot of athletes in Amsterdam and many other Commonwealth nations made common cause with them. The following report published in the *Toronto Star* of 2 August 1928 clearly points to the growing alliance against American high-handedness:

> That the American Olympic team has dug its own grave with its own teeth is the general consensus of opinion of disgruntled coaches, officials and bystanders out on the floating hotel, President Roosevelt ... There may be something in it. This writer dined the other night with British and South African athletes and came away hungry, which was certainly not the case at the Roosevelt where the writer had thick soup, salmon and mayonnaise, roast long island gosling, potatoes and ice cream. 'I have never seen anything like it,' said a coach who added, 'Why, go up to the smoking room at 11 o'clock and you will see these fellows tearing into bologna sausage like a pack of animals ...'
>
> Patrick Walsh, manager of the American team, showed the writer a letter from the International Amateur Athletic Association turning

down his protest against the judge's decision awarding Fitzpatrick of Canada third and qualifying place over Cummings of the United States in the 200-metre semifinals. However, the jury might have had a guilty conscience for in the final of that event they awarded Scholz of the United States a tie with Kornig for third place, although everybody else seemed to think Scholz was fourth. Perhaps it is well they did for so far he is the only American to place one-two-three in any flat track event and it is being sold around Amsterdam that America will not win one more. The glee of the other nations over trimming America is obvious. When Percy Williams, the Canadian marvel, scored an Olympic double by winning the 200 meters, a German official ran across the field and kissed him.[26]

In fact, much was made of the fact that the British Empire representatives combined had given Williams a special felicitation at Amsterdam soon after he had completed his double. While this was a celebration of his feat, it was more a celebration of American defeat.[27] The Empire, it was apparent, was united against the common adversary and the start of the British Empire Games was a mere formality.

At a time when the world was raving about Williams and his incredible feat, the Americans, while conceding that he was the best and indeed better than their lot of sprinters, also came up with the excuse that the track used at Amsterdam wasn't up to the mark. They were rather blasé in declaring that there was not a single track in Europe that compared with their tracks back home and ascribed the failure of their sprinters to the inferior tracks on offer. Some of them even went on to deride Williams for his decision to join the University of Washington and suggested that his decision to move to the US had not met with any cheer in the country. 'There are enough fine athletes on the Pacific coast to keep up the intercollegiate championship in that section of the country,'[28] was the unanimous American refrain.

That these comments had driven a deep wedge between sports officials from the British Empire and the United States is also evident in the way events at Amsterdam were reported in the media. The rowing competition wasn't reported as one in which the world's top athletes were competing for honours. Rather, it was presented as a bilateral championship between the Empire athletes on the one hand and the American athletes on the other. The sporting world at Amsterdam, if the reportage is anything to go by, was divided into two blocs, the American and the Empire. It wasn't of much consequence if a British athlete was defeated by a Canadian or an Australian and such results were hardly given due coverage in the media. However, if the Commonwealth athletes managed to upset the fancied US team, such achievements were praised sky-high and plans for multiple felicitations in honour of the athlete were soon set in motion.

Commenting on the rowing competition, W.A. Hewitt, sports editor of the *Star* reported that the honours were split down the middle between the British Empire and the United States. In the single sculls, Australia won the title, beating the Americans; but in the double sculls, the Americans avenged the defeat, beating the Canadians fairly convincingly. While the 8-bar crew event resulted in a victory for the Americans over the English, in the four-oared race without coxswain the British crew from Cambridge University turned the tables on the Americans, winning a sensational race coming from behind.[29]

The final breach at Amsterdam occurred when the Canadians found out that the Americans had officials out on the field who acted as mediators between their athletes and the jury, the final arbitrating body in cases of on-field disputes. Canada, to their surprise and dismay, had no such official. Moreover, when the president of the Canadian Olympic Committee tried to draw the attention of the IOC to these cases of indiscretion, he was curtly told to take his place in the stands. He was once again told off when he protested against the use of a loose tape encouraging a false finish in one of the sprint events. The officiating IOC delegate from the United States, it was reported, shouted back at him in a loud voice, a behaviour for which he was never censured by the IOC top brass.[30]

The Canadians considered this incident to be an insult to their team and to Canada at large and had decided that the time had come to teach the Americans a lesson. More than anything else, the British Empire Games (BEG), it was evident, was the imperial answer to American domineering. A series of meetings were convened between

Empire officials and sports administrators and it was soon evident that the BEG had many takers across the world, making Robinson's task of spearheading the setting up that much easier. With the Canadians being the most vocal against unfair American assertiveness, it was only natural that Canada took the lead in giving the Empire its own Games in two years' time.

Canada Takes the Lead

Soon after the Amsterdam Games were over, the representatives of the Empire gathered in Canada at a convention organized to discuss issues of relevance to it. This was not only one of the largest-ever Commonwealth delegations to visit Canada but it also included representatives from Australia, South Africa, Southern Rhodesia, India, the Irish Free State and Malta, and the team was expected to be joined in Canada by delegates from New Zealand and Newfoundland.[31]

The stated reason for the convention was 'to confer with representatives of the Dominions and provincial parliaments in Canada on matters of common interest to the British Empire as a whole'.[32] Among the questions discussed were issues of trade within the Empire, issues of settlement and also the forthcoming British Empire Games at Hamilton in 1930. Structural changes within the Empire – like the proposed grant of complete self-government to India – was also deliberated upon at the convention. The keynote speech was delivered by the distinguished English statesman, Viscount Peel.[33]

This convention, a novel experiment of the Empire, was followed up within Canada by a series of felicitations for the country's Olympic champions, occasions that provided an opportunity for animated discussion on the outcome of the Amsterdam Games.

In one of these felicitations in Toronto, P.J. Mulqueen repeatedly emphasized the discriminatory treatment meted out to the Canadians, which had to be countered by extra effort put in by the athletes. 'Honestly when I sit down and ponder over just what our tiny little team of boys and girls did against the cream of the world I do not wonder that I am accused of running out upon the field and kissing Williams when he won his second championship and I do not mind admitting that I shed tears of joy when that smart little team of girls came down in front in the relay final and Ethel Catherwood won her championship and I was not the only one either.'[34]

The athletes too were all praise for the officials, who, they were unanimous, had done their best during times of adversity. The officials made it their business to ensure the Canadian athletes were not handed a raw deal, especially when disputed decisions were referred to arbitrators. Even if they weren't successful on occasions, the effort put in was commendable. The most commonly sighted case was that of Fanny Rosenfeldt who was unfairly relegated to second position when it was evident to all that she had touched the tape ahead of the American girl, Robinson. Soon after the verdict was announced the Canadian officials launched a formal protest, determined to draw attention to the fact that they were on their toes and would fight for the rights of their athletes. Mulqueen and his compatriots who saw Rosenfeldt finish the race from a position opposite the tape were convinced that she had touched the tape ahead of the American. They were justly outraged when Rosenfeldt was deprived of her championship title because of a bad decision. Mulqueen felt so strongly about it that he refused to discuss the details of the decision even after returning to Canada, while the other officials present made it a point to see that Rosenfeldt was felicitated in the exact same manner as the other gold-medal winners.

At the felicitation function in Toronto, 250,000 people had gathered to celebrate the winners and it was heartwarming for the officials to see that Rosenfeldt was singled out by the fans present. So much so that Rosenfeldt, unaccustomed to speaking in public, was literally pressured to speak in front of the microphone. '"Speech, speech, Fannie," shouted many voices as Rosenfeldt received her gift. "It was nice to get on in the Olympic," she replied, "nice to look forward to and mighty nice to get back. We all went into it as a team, and I am sure none went into it for individual honours."'[35]

Such celebration of Canadian nationalism, integral to every felicitation organized across the country, was at the root of the Canadian officials deciding to have a sports competition of their own, which was profoundly different in nature from the Olympics and was free from all the vices evident at Amsterdam. It was to be a celebration of Empire and a celebration of the virtues of sportsmanship, a spirit closely associated with the very ethos of the British Empire across the globe.

PLAYING IN THE EMPIRE'S IMAGE

Finally, forty years after the original proposal had been published in the London press, the British Empire Games were held at Hamilton, Canada. The event was a significant success from all standpoints. It was an organizational miracle because the General Council was only a few months old with no previous experience at organizing events. The Canadian organizers were similarly inexperienced and the dominions and colonies were handicapped both for time and possible expenditure.

Despite such shortcomings, the Games were a success with 400 athletes and 100 or more officials making it to Hamilton for the occasion. Interestingly, no winning points were awarded, drawing attention to the belief that participation mattered more than winning and, well before the Games concluded, it was decided that the event should be repeated every four years and that a British Empire Games Federation was an urgent necessity. J.F. Wadmore, secretary of the British Athletics team, was unanimously appointed secretary – treasurer of the interim federation and all of the other office bearers were confirmed in 1932 during the course of the meeting in which the federation was formally established.

That the Games had exceeded expectations was apparent when Bobby Robinson published this account in the *Hamilton Spectator.* 'During the organization period, a few of us had the opinion we would be able to put the British Empire Games over but few ever dreamed the Empire would rally so strongly. We had our moments of anxiety, but we always had a sensational ace in the hole, loyalty to the British Empire, and we felt that we could wave the good old flag and all would gather round.'[36]

Robinson repeatedly stressed the value of sportsmanship, best exemplified when New Zealand sprinter Alan Elliot, who false started twice and was hence disqualified, was given back his place in the starting line-up under pressure from the crowd, which believed it was only just that he be given a chance to compete. Though he finished third in his heat and was eliminated from the competition, his reinstatement in the starting line-up personified exactly what the Games stood for: fostering a healthy spirit of camaraderie among the world's best athletes.[37]

His views found resonance in the report of the Council for Great Britain, which concluded that the BEG had successfully brought together at Hamilton a diverse cross-section from around the world. This was proof that the informal connection of Empire was still strong enough – a realization that was interpreted as a significant boost to the fledgling imperial bond that aimed at uniting more than half the civilized world. The report went on to conclude that 'at Hamilton, where Britons alone were concerned, there was warmth of comradeship, a spirit of cordiality and even self-sacrifice which will assuredly bear fruit among those young men and women of the British race'.[38]

The following reports by British scribes, quoted with prominence in the *Hamilton Spectator*, best sum up the achievement of Robinson and the Canadians: 'For the first time, Canada, which has usually been regarded in this country as circulating within the American orbit, has cut herself loose and given a lead to the Empire that should inspire British sportsmen all round the globe.'[39] The second reporter declared, 'Even apart from the influence on imperial sport, the Empire Games have given the Dominion its finest advertisement for years.' Such reports ensured that Lord Willingdon, who declared at the opening ceremony that the, 'greatness of the Empire is owing to the fact that every citizen has inborn in him the love of games and sports',[40] was fully vindicated.

LOS ANGELES 1932: STRENGTHENING THE HAND

The growing tension between Empire countries and the United States was palpable once again at Los Angeles, during the 10th Olympiad. The sporting media did much to stimulate this rivalry, evident from the reportage of the events at which the Empire athletes defeated the Americans.

This is how the 800-metre race was described by the reporter of the *Toronto Star*:

How John Bull and a couple of his sons made uncle Sammy take it and like it up at the big cement rimmed saucer yesterday. Boy, what a spine-tingling thrill when an Englishman, a Canadian and a British Guianaian running for Canada cleaned the works for the cocky Sammies in the greatest event of the track program in this tenth Olympiad – the 800 meters final – and sent three Jacks to the triple mastheads on the victory tower!

And what sheer heart-throbbing ecstasy for the British-born in that mob of 45,000 people when the official band struck up that glorious old hymn of the British nation, *God save the king*, for the first time in this fearful orgy of record-shattering contests.

Just figure it all out – Hampson of England won it by a foot from Wilson of Canada, with Edwards of Canada third, three yards away and your uncle Sammie's boys didn't get a smell of it. The best they could do was to get Genung home fourth, Turner fifth and Cornbostel sixth … Do you wonder that the Canadian and English camps were bedlams of delirium? How John Bull's boys do like to take a fall out of Uncle Sammie's children?

Boy, what a whoop went up when those three Jacks, the big Union Jack for England and those two little Jacks in the upper corner of the red ensign for Canada, were hoisted on those victory flagpoles.[41]

Following the race, it wasn't surprising to note that journalists from the Empire assembled at Los Angeles called Hampson the best of all half-milers ever and Wilson as the best ever 800-metre runner to emerge out of North America. That Hampson was a much-respected professor from St. Alban's in Hertfordshire was made much of and it was argued that he was a model athlete who epitomized all that was worthy and desirable about the Empire.

INDIAN INDIFFERENCE AND THE BRITISH EMPIRE GAMES

In India, where dominion status or self-government hadn't yet been achieved and independence was still a far cry, the need to demonstrate a common bond with the Empire – the very essence of the BEG – was totally irrelevant. Rather, what was important in the 1920s, a period of intense nationalist activity, was to use sporting connections to assert an aggressive Indian identity, one that was capable of taking on the might of the Empire or stimulate the process of complete dissociation from it.

There is little doubt that the emergent Indian nationalism proved critical in influencing India's reaction to the British Empire Games. Indian nationalism in the early twentieth century was taking a firm shape under Mahatma Gandhi. It was, therefore, no surprise that an Indian sporting nationalism would assert itself at this time as well. In fact, the Gandhian call for civil disobedience clashed with the establishment of the Games and it was imperative that India would give it a miss. The 1920s turned out to be a critical period in shaping the Indian attitude to global sporting contests. While the Indians were all gung-ho about the Olympics, looking at it as a platform to showcase Indian prowess, they looked at the BEG as a stage that served interests contrary to theirs. In opting out of the BEG, they were trying to expose to the world the unfairness of the Empire.

Inevitably, emerging Indian nationalism found its expression in the sporting arena, eventually pushing the BEG into the margins of colonial Indian sporting life. It was during the 1920s that calls to set up an Indian Olympic Association were heard, and it was this decade that saw Indian patrons like the maharaja of Patiala take the lead in sending an Indian team to the Amsterdam Games of 1928.[42] The need to carve out an Indian sporting presence on the world stage, one that could stand independent of the Empire, grew out of the desire to challenge and dent British sporting supremacy.

Indian sports patrons, while working at setting up an organized sports structure in the country and demanding that India participate in the Olympics and the Western Asiatic Games, hardly ever mentioned the BEG. This, for the average Indian at least, was the Games of the British or the Australians or the Canadians. The process to give the BEG a cold shoulder gathered further steam once the Indians won their first Olympic gold in field hockey at Amsterdam. The Amsterdam triumph had been a spectacular follow-up to the successful Indian hockey tour of the UK, during which the Indians had defeated leading British sides with regularity. Field hockey, it was evident, had become the unequivocal Indian sport, and soon great pains were undertaken to protect its heritage. It was this desperate need to establish an 'Indian' sporting identity and to divest it of all connections with the ruling British state that led the Indians to give the first British Empire Games at Hamilton a miss.

It is almost certain, then, that the preference for the Olympics over the British Empire Games had much to do with nationalism. Humbling the British on the sporting field was an extremely popular topic in the Indian sporting media of the time. It was also very prominent in the minds of the Indian sporting patrons who, till the turn of the century, faced regular discrimination at the hands of the ruling British. Prohibiting Indians from entering British sporting clubs was a norm till the 1920s and was one of the central reasons that led to the establishment of the Cricket Club of India in 1937.[43]

What is most interesting about this desire to stay away from the British Empire Games is that it was aberrant. As emphasized at the start of this section, the 'colonial' Indian reaction to the sport of the Empire was simply the opposite of the reaction of the dominions to imperial sport. It was the British roots of the Empire Games that made it anathema to the Indians in an era of burgeoning Indian nationalism. On the other hand, in India, conditions of colonialism made it imperative for the nationalists to take up cricket as a way to compete with the ruling British. Bilateral cricket contests with England soon became politically charged and a victory was perceived as a significant nationalist triumph. The supposed lack of the competitive spirit, at the heart of the idea of the Empire Games, made sure that it had little attraction for the Indians in colonial India.

The gathering pace of Indian nationalism, coupled with the organization of the British Empire Games in 1930, a year of considerable turmoil in India's political history, meant that the Olympics would inevitably win the battle against the Empire Games in India. The general Indian apathy to the BEG was best borne out by the lack of protests when India, in yet another discriminatory gesture, wasn't offered a subsidy to participate in the inaugural edition of the Games, an offer that helped stimulate participation from Australia and New Zealand.[44] That a grant of financial subsidy to Australia and New Zealand wasn't even interpreted as an act of discrimination in

India demonstrates beyond doubt that the BEG just did not figure in the list of Indian priorities at the time.

India's peculiar dynamic with the BEG, it must be acknowledged, alludes to the fact that the story of Commonwealth engagement with the Empire Games was acutely political from the very beginning and provides historians of sport a unique prism to understand the workings of the Empire in a phase of intense political turmoil. In doing so, it also draws attention to the impact of the Indian nationalist movement on sport in the years immediately before Independence and shows that across historical contexts and timeframes, sport has played a critical role in shaping the modern Indian polity.

INDEX OF INDIAN APATHY: EMPIRE GAMES AND THE PRESS

The Indian attitude to the Games is best borne out by a comparative analysis of the media coverage in India and in some of the other Commonwealth nations. In Canada and the UK, the BEG was the central news item in August 1930, with entire pages dedicated to the Games in leading papers like the *Toronto Star* and the *Times*, London. In Australia, too, the Games attracted a lot of media attention. While the thrust was on reporting Australian performances, other issues like the formation of the Empire Games Federation, the spirit of friendly rivalry – the focal point of the Games discourse – were also deliberated upon in the media. The intensity of coverage left little doubt that the Empire Games was considered an issue of paramount importance in most nations across the Commonwealth.

Coverage of the Games in India, in comparison, was lukewarm at best. From a survey of leading newspapers,[45] it is evident that not all of them reported the Games on all days of play. Even when reports were published, they were more in the nature of summaries of results or small news items. Analytical articles about the Games and its future – how it was meant to strengthen the bonds of the Empire and how it was, in a way, a necessity under the circumstances – hardly ever found a mention.

During the entire duration of the inaugural British Empire Games, the formation of the Empire Games Federation was the only news item, besides results, reported in some detail by the *Times of India*. On 22 August 1930, the *Times of India* reported:

> The future of the Empire Games was assured at the first meeting of the Dominion delegates in the morning when it was unanimously agreed that the Games should be perpetuated. A draft constitution of the Empire Sports Federation was submitted and a sub-committee appointed to frame the concrete proposals for its scope and policy. The Federation's chief purpose will be to weld Britain and the Dominions together as a legislative force in international sport.[46]

This was followed-up by another report on 25 August, which declared:

> The Empire Sports Federation came into being today when the council of three appointed Mr Wadmore of England as Secretary with Headquarters in London. It has been decided to perpetuate the Empire Games, the second edition of which will be held in South Africa in 1934. The town has not yet been selected. New Zealand applied for 1938 but consideration was deferred. The delegations agreed to approach the respective governments for financial aid. Hopes were expressed that the question will be discussed at the Imperial conference in London in September.[47]

Two small news items of not even a column each were what the entire first edition of the BEG received in the *Times of India*, besides a regular 200-word summary of results. That the Indians weren't offered a subsidy when some of the other dominions were paid substantial sums to compete wasn't even mentioned in sections of the Indian press.

Things were hardly different four years later when India, for the first time, sent a small contingent to compete in the Games.

Most Indian newspapers wrapped up their London coverage by only publishing results and the occasional photograph of one of the Indian athletes taking part in the competition. With Anwar expected to do well in wrestling and Vernieux tipped to do well in the sprints, there was some interest in tracking them through the competition.[48] Once they were both defeated, coverage was restricted to a long list of 'day's results at the Games'.

In fact, the only report of depth was a criticism of the judgement that cost Indian wrestler Singh his place in the final. The report went on to suggest that it was impossible to ascertain how the judges came to their decision. The reporter had little doubt that the Indian was the better fighter and should have won on points: 'After six minutes Singh was definitely superior and after the interval Singh wrestled brilliantly.'[49]

Sydney 1938 was no different either. All pre–Games coverage was restricted to whether Janaki Dass, India's lone entry in cycling, would finally be allowed to travel to Sydney. While Dass had the backing of G.D. Sondhi, India's IOC member and secretary of the Indian Olympic Association, there was also strong opposition brewing against him from within the Association itself. Though Dass was able to compete at the Games with Sondhi sending him to Sydney on the recommendation of the Punjab Cycling Association, Sondhi ultimately had to tender his resignation for having violated the constitution of the Indian Olympic Association.[50] Much was subsequently made of the fact that Dass was out of the competition (injured) and had failed to achieve a podium finish. His style, too, came in for criticism when it was reported that, '[it] alternated between an unorthodox crouch and a bolt upright position, and in throwing up his head he lost control and crashed. He was carried off the track in a stretcher and removed to the hospital in Marrickville where it was ascertained that he was suffering from a slight concussion and minor abrasions on his head'.[51]

On most of the other days the only news published of the Empire Games was a list of results, an entry that hardly went beyond a single column insertion of 250 words or so. Clearly, even by 1938, India had not warmed up to the British Empire Games, which continued to be perceived as a British invention serving British/Empire interests only.

The growing intensity of the nationalist movement also did much to ensure that sporting nationalism was restricted to the Olympics, where the Indians had established a virtual monopoly over field hockey, and to bilateral cricket contests against the English. This reality is borne out by the fact that when Anthony De Mello published his chronicle of Indian sport in 1959, he hardly had a thing to say about the Empire Games. A crucial figure in the formation of the BCCI and the IOA, De Mello wrote entire chapters on India's cricket exploits and Indian performances at the Olympics. There was nothing in his book, though, that conveyed that the BEG was also a serious sports competition of the era.[52]

WHEN THE TABLES TURNED: APPROPRIATING THE COMMONWEALTH GAMES

The Indian reaction to the British Empire Games was inevitable in an era of hectic political activity back home. The very year the British Empire Games began, Winston Churchill had the following to say about India: 'To abandon India to the rule of the Brahmins would be an act of cruel and wicked negligence.' He went on to suggest that Indian Brahmins 'who mouth and patter the principles of Western liberalism are the same brahmins who deny the primary rights of existence to nearly sixty million of their own countrymen whom they call untouchable'.[53] This statement could not be treated in isolation, for, in 1929, Churchill, responding to the suggestion of granting dominion status to India, had labelled the idea 'not only fantastic in itself but criminally mischievous in its effects'. Over the next two years, as Ramachandra Guha writes: 'Churchill delivered dozens of speeches where he worked up, in most unsober form, the forces hostile to the winning of political independence by people with brown (or black) skins.'[54]

Churchill was not speaking in isolation. This was apparent from the British reaction towards the Motilal Nehru report that asked for dominion status for India in 1928. Nehru's report, the first constitution written only by Indians, conceived a dominion status for India within the Empire, akin to Australia, New Zealand and Canada. It was endorsed by the Congress party but rejected by more radical Indians who sought complete independence. The British government rejected this petition and, with British politicians treating India's demands with disdain, it was only logical for India to treat the British Empire Games with indifference.

The tables turned a decade-and-a-half later when India won independence in 1947. Soon after Independence, Jawaharlal Nehru insisted that India would only remain part of the Commonwealth if she was allowed to do so as a republic and without acknowledging the British sovereign as India's head of state. He suggested that the British head of state be given a separate identity as the head of the Commonwealth collective, one without any constitutional implications for India. It was a demand that was accepted after some deliberation. As J.N. Dixit argues:

> There was logic in India and other countries wishing to retain the British connection in the '50s and '60s. The political organization and state structures of all the non-White countries were rooted in institutions, procedures and laws inherited from British imperial rule. There was considerable dependence on England in technological, economic and defence supplies arrangements. Preferential trade arrangements and the special treatment accorded in higher education in England to young people from the Commonwealth countries was another factor that impelled the newly independent Asian and African countries to retain the British connection.[55]

Understandably, the Indian decision to stay in the Commonwealth significantly contributed to transforming the character of the British Empire Games, which were rechristened the 'British Empire and Commonwealth Games' in 1954. We turn to this phase of Nehruvian diplomacy and its impact on the Games in the next chapter.

CONCLUSION

The origin of the British Empire Games, as this chapter has attempted to demonstrate, was a matter of political exigency. Soon after the First World War, as historian John Kent has argued, the British state was put in an embarrassing position in which it had to depend on American aid to underwrite post-war convalescence, and at the same time try hard not to escalate economic dependence on the United States. At such a time, it was natural to turn to the comforts of the Empire.[56]

In trying to do so, the Empire had to come to terms with the changed conditions of imperial dominance across the dominions and colonies. The London Imperial Conference of 1926 was the first sign that Britain was keen to accept the changed conditions of Empire. In addition, the nationalist movements were applying pressure. On behalf of the Indian National Congress, Jawaharlal Nehru attended the International Congress Against Colonial Oppression at Brussels in 1927, which further pushed this agenda. This resulted in the Congress being accepted into the League of Nations as an associate member. Nehru was also elected one of the presidents of the Brussels conference along with other world figures like Albert Einstein, Madam Sun Yat-sen, Romain Rolland and others. He was later made a member of the executive council of the League.

After the 1926 Imperial conference, as Priya Jaikumar argues:

> The term Commonwealth began to replace the term Empire and the British state reoriented itself to a new political collective ... the British state hoped that reinvigorating the imperial market would assist Britain in counteracting its new rivals in trade (the United States) and ideology (Soviet Union). Rebelling colonies and nearly sovereign Dominions could still transform 'Little England' into 'Great Britain' if only Britain could appeal to the ideal of bilateralism in imperial affairs.[57]

The Empire Games were certainly a step in this direction. They were evidence that the Empire was moving 'from a posture of supremacy to concessions to the need for reciprocity in imperial relations'.[58]

Crucially, this change in imperial ideology was not uniformly applied to all of the Empire countries and wasn't all-encompassing in its scope. While it certainly offered more sops to the Western states like Canada, Australia and New Zealand, it hardly offered anything fundamentally different for countries like India.

Rather, the British attitude towards India hardened in the 1920s when confronted with Gandhian mass movements of non-cooperation and civil disobedience. The year of the first British Empire Games was also the year in which the Congress first announced its goal of complete independence and of Gandhi's epochal Dandi march. Attitudes towards colonies like India, it is evident from Churchill's terse statements about India and Indians, continued to be dogmatic and discriminatory. As a consequence, while the Empire Games were universally applauded in the West, they provoked a muted reaction in India, a ground reality that changed only after India achieved independence in 1947.

6 | 'MUTUAL BENEFIT ASSOCIATION'

THE COMMONWEALTH, INDIA AND NEHRUVIAN DIPLOMACY

'If one asks a well-informed Indian what is the content of the phrase [Head of Commonwealth], he is likely to answer: 'It means Nehru. The trusted leader says it is good, and therefore the people accept it.'

– H. Duncan Hall, December 1953[1]

WHO CARES ABOUT THE COMMONWEALTH?

Sixty-one years after the khaki-clad troops of the Somerset Light Infantry marched out from under the magnificent shadows of the Gateway of India, setting sail on a one-way ticket home, India is hosting the Commonwealth Games.[2] The Raj is long gone, yet India has made it a point of honour to bring home, and be party to, a sporting festival that is central to what Amitava Ghosh has called 'that particular memorialization of Empire that passes under the rubric of "the Commonwealth"'.[3] Why do we have to do it? Why has the Commonwealth connection endured for India? This, after all, is the country whose freedom struggle was seen as the torchbearer of anti-colonial struggles worldwide and whose independence very quickly led to the crumbling of the entire British Empire. Symbols are the very heartbeat of politics and the Commonwealth is an evocative symbol of the past. It is, therefore, important to explore why India is now a proud host of the Commonwealth Games.

The Games, after all, are now the most well-known publicity agent of the otherwise amorphous political Commonwealth. This is particularly true for the younger generations[4] and especially so for a country with one of the youngest populations in the world. The generation that Salman Rushdie hailed as 'midnight's children' has already entered the category of 'senior citizens' and half of India's population has no living memory of even Indira Gandhi, leave alone the Raj.[5] So we must come back to the question: why?

This book has so far unravelled the politics of sport, its interplay with the larger politics of Delhi and the origins of the Commonwealth Games. Now we must go back to the deeper intellectual question underpinning this entire business – that of the Commonwealth itself and its meaning for India. The Games cannot be seen in isolation from the larger context.

This chapter explains why India joined the Commonwealth; why, despite years of unremitting hostility by the Congress to the idea of an imperial association, independent India suddenly changed tack, with Jawaharlal Nehru forcing a reversal of the fundamental principles at the heart of the old Commonwealth and turning it into a motor for his ideas of an independent foreign policy.

Nehru's political beliefs were central to this; he was the man who single-handedly shaped and drove independent India's early diplomacy. So much so that by 1959 his biographer could declare that in 'no other state does one man dominate foreign policy as does Nehru in India'.[6] It was he, as hard-nosed a critic of British imperialism as there could be, who drove India into the Commonwealth. Nehru has often been accused of being too much of a romantic and too little of a strategist, in the realist sense. This judgement is now, at least in this case, increasingly at odds with the historical record. As a newly independent country, dealing with the trauma of the greatest mass migration in history, India needed a practical diplomacy that could help it stay the course at a time of great turmoil. This was not a compromise. As this chapter will show, Nehru changed the old rules of the Commonwealth to India's advantage.

India could have opted out of the Commonwealth but it chose to join, albeit on its own terms, as a republic, free from even a notional allegiance to the Queen. This was a development that overturned the old balance of power and one that had to be forced down the throats of the older White dominions. At one level, Nehru's Commonwealth gambit reflected his larger ideological understanding of history. At another level, it was also an audacious cold-blooded manoeuvre, worthy of a Bismarck in its intent and implementation. As Nehru put it, the Commonwealth 'has given us certain advantages [and no] liabilities in return'.[7]

Nehru only saw the Commonwealth as a practical forum for propagating the new Indian Republic on the world stage. He manipulated it to project Indian leadership of the emerging Third World – a move that was to foreshadow his later efforts with the Non-Aligned movement. Over and over again – on the Suez crisis, on Korea, on Vietnam and on China – Nehru used the Commonwealth forum to provide the rapier thrust to his independent take on the emerging power praxis of the Cold War, much to the indignation of the Americans and the British. Within the context of the Commonwealth, this policy was so successful that by 1974, one of its most critical historians could declare unequivocally: 'The key position [in the Commonwealth] ... was held by India. Its vast size and population and the highly articulate character of its leaders had given India special stature ... Nehru's policy of "non-alignment" was regarded as distinctive; when he spoke, men listened.'[8]

That non-alignment was ultimately doomed to failure is another matter. Within an organization that was created primarily to propagate the illusion of British pre-eminence in world affairs even after the end of its Empire, the success of India's subversive politics was a remarkable achievement.

A 'MOST IMPLACABLE' BRITISH 'ENEMY': NEHRU, COLONIAL INDIA AND THE COMMONWEALTH

By the early 1930s, the white settler dominions of Australia, Canada, South Africa and New Zealand had all become autonomous and Britain formed the modern Commonwealth as a means of keeping them and the other dependent territories within its ambit. The Commonwealth began essentially as an imperial association. Its formation in 1931 was preceded by gatherings that were known as colonial conferences in 1887, 1897 and 1902; imperial conferences in 1907 and 1911; imperial war conferences 1917 and 1918; the premiers' conference in 1921; and as imperial conferences in 1923 and 1926.[9] Britain's imperial reach was at its zenith and the nomenclature and the aims of what was known as the British Empire and Commonwealth of Nations were unambiguous. For the most ardent of British imperialists, the intellectual foundations of any such federation were simply built on furthering the 'expansion of England'.[10] People like Goldwin Smith, on the other hand, understood it in terms of a 'moral federation of the whole English-speaking race throughout the world'.[11] Whatever its predilection – political or cultural – it was rooted in colonial reality and Britain's self-image. So much so that one contemporary account in 1927 admiringly declared that the British Commonwealth of Nations 'appears to be a vaster and more powerful Empire than that of ancient Rome'.[12]

Such were the aims of the early Commonwealth. It is little wonder, then, that the Congress and Nehru were politically opposed to any such association during the halcyon days of the freedom struggle. Nehru, after all, was the man that Winston Churchill famously described in 1937 as the 'most implacable of the enemies of the British connection with India'.[13] Just a decade later, the same Nehru was to shepherd India into the Commonwealth; and the story of the turnaround in India's second-most towering personality of the time is fascinating.

As early as 1922, Lord Reading, the then viceroy had told the secretary of state for India that Nehru was 'fanatical in his hostility to the government'.[14] Nehru's political critique of Empire became sharper after a visit to Europe in 1926–27 and on his return to India, he 'became the champion of a passionate and defiant nationalism' beyond the then demands of the Indian National Congress.[15] It was Nehru who rejected dominion status as a goal and advocated complete independence for India. In 1929, two years before the creation of the modern Commonwealth, emphatically declaring that 'India is a nation on the march', Nehru delivered his most uncompromising anti-imperialistic speech yet at the Lahore session of the Congress. By the late 1930s, Nehru's 'alienation from the Raj seemed to have reached its highest pitch'. Writing to a friend, he recalled his father's description of the British government as 'the greatest terrorist organization'[16] and reiterated his assertion that real cooperation with the British was unthinkable for him till their rule ended. This was why Lord Irwin's private secretary, Emerson, for instance, said in 1937 that Nehru – 'intractable, uncompromising' – was 'more dangerous than Gandhi ever was'.[17]

By the late 1930s, Nehru was at the height of his powers as Gandhi's heir apparent and British irritation at his inflexibility, too, was on a high. Sample this comment from Viceroy Lord Linlithgow: 'It is a tragedy in many ways that we should have in so important a position a doctrinaire like Nehru with his amateur knowledge of foreign policies and of the international stage.'[18] He was portrayed, especially after the Quit India movement, by many Britishers as a 'Hamlet of Indian politics'.[19] Hamlet indeed! This Hamlet, in less than a decade, was to overturn the touchstone of the British Commonwealth and turn it into the playfield of his personal brand of global high politics.

EMBRACING THE COMMONWEALTH: INDIA'S 'LAST ENGLISHMAN' AND THE ART OF PRACTICALITY

Nehru may have been implacable in his opposition to foreign rule but his upbringing at Harrow and Cambridge had also given him a great deal of Englishness. Writing his autobiography in a British prison, he wrote frankly: 'Anger and resentment have often filled my mind at various happenings and yet as I sit here and look deep into my mind and heart, I do not find any anger against England or the English people ... They are as much victims of circumstances as we are.'[20] This, after all, was a man who would later tell John Galbraith that he 'was the last Englishman to rule India'.[21]

For Nehru, opposition to the British was an intellectual and ideological project, not a racial or personal one. As he wrote in 1933:

> This is not a conflict between India and England, much less it is one between the Indian people and the British people. The conflict is with a certain system called imperialism, which the British Government represents today in India and elsewhere ... If England changed her form and method of government and dropped all taint of imperialism from it, there would little difficulty in the two countries cooperating for a common purpose.[22]

This is a line of thinking that translated into practical politics as independence approached. As prime minister, Nehru accepted dominion status as part of Mountbatten's transfer of power package in 1947 and also agreed to join the Commonwealth, although only on his own terms. According to B.R. Nanda, the decision to remain in the Commonwealth brought with it certain in-built advantages in the transition period:

> … it softened the Tory Opposition in the British Parliament; it seemed a useful link with Pakistan even after the transfer of power; it could help retain the loyalty of British officers who had chosen to serve independent India in the defence services, and it could help to disarm the suspicions of the rulers of princely states and thus facilitate their integration into the Indian Union.[23]

Partly because of these reasons, by 1949, Nehru was convinced of the idea of the Commonwealth, as long as there was no compromise on Indian sovereignty. The Commonwealth now also had symbolic importance for Nehru. In 1949, he told the Canadian Parliament that after the bitter conflict between Indian nationalism and British imperialism, the Commonwealth showed the reconciliation between the two 'as an outstanding example of the peaceful solution of difficult problems'.[24]

The decision to join the Commonwealth was part of a deeper internationalist vein in Indian nationalist thinking. India's foreign policy, with Nehru at its head, was built on a certain kind of internationalism that sought to do away with old-style power politics.[25] A number of scholars have focussed attention on the legacy of the internationalist vein in Indian nationalism, its implications for the diplomacy of independent India and ultimately how this vision floundered in the face of global realpolitik. It is important to note also that this stemmed from the wellsprings of Gandhian thought. Gandhi did not see the freedom struggle as merely a step in throwing the British out of India, but as one towards a small international system, with states, equal in status, having the independence of withdrawing from such a Commonwealth should they wish to. As early as 1924, Gandhi argued: 'The better mind of the world desires not absolutely independent states working against one another, but a federation of friendly independent states.'[26] Even at the Round Table Conference he emphasized that the Congress contemplated a connection with the British, but one that was between equals.[27] This was typical Gandhian morality. As he put it, 'India's greatest glory will consist not in regarding Englishmen as her implacable enemies fit only to be turned out of India at the first available opportunity, but in turning them into friends and partners in a new commonwealth of nations.'[28]

Independent India, battling as it was with the misery of Partition and the birth pangs of freedom, wanted a voice in the world, an end to isolationism and a steadying influence in global affairs. No wonder then that in late 1947 and 1948 there was a '… gradual and discernible trend in Indian opinion away from isolationism and towards the maintenance of friendly associations which would not commit India to explicit policies but would enhance her influence in world affairs … In particular it was felt that friendly association with the Commonwealth might act as a steadying influence at a time when revolutionary forces within and without were challenging established authority.'[29]

The Commonwealth seemingly offered a ready-made platform and some easy advantages. The Constituent Assembly endorsed the decision with only one dissenting voice. Prior to this, though, Nehru also faced opposition from the Indian socialists and the communists and had to fight to secure Congress approval. Nehru used the argument of defence and stability to persuade his party colleagues.[30] Speaking in the Constituent Assembly, his justification for joining the Commonwealth was typical:

> We joined the Commonwealth obviously because we think it is beneficial to us and to certain causes in the world we wish to advance … The other countries of the Commonwealth wish us to remain there because they think it is beneficial to them. In the world today, where there are so many disruptive forces at work, where we are often at the verge of war, I think it is not a safe thing to encourage the break-up of any association that one has … It's better to keep a cooperative association going which may do good in this world rather than break it.[31]

For India, the Commonwealth clearly offered a 'half-way house between an impossible aloofness in international affairs and participation in the "Cold War" on the Anglo-American side'.[32] For Nehru, keeping India as an independent force was paramount and the Commonwealth was ideal because it provided consultations, not commitments, and discussions, without limiting free action. This was purely a practical arrangement.

Commonwealth membership also brought with it economic benefits. India, Pakistan and Ceylon gained substantially from the Colombo Plan, which started in 1950, and from other external sources. India received nearly GBP 200 million in loans and grants up to 1954. A further GBP 200 million was to be invested in the next two years.[33]

By the 1950s some analysts were optimistically arguing that the Commonwealth, once 'an Empire of power', now seemed to be on its way to becoming an 'Empire of commerce' and an 'area of culture'.[34] In 1967, for instance, as much as 85 per cent of bilateral aid from developed Commonwealth countries went to developing Commonwealth countries.[35] The Colombo Plan was followed by the Special Commonwealth African Assistance Plan, the Commonwealth Education Cooperation Scheme and the Commonwealth Caribbean Assistance Programme. There was clearly some truth in the argument that the Commonwealth's 'strength lies not in sentiment, not in constitutional ties, not in a common ethnic origin, but in its having become a mutual benefit association'.[36]

Nehru was pragmatic about this. He saw the Commonwealth merely as a 'meeting once or twice a year and occasional consultations' that could be put to India's use, and brought no harm.[37]

A CONSTITUTION AND A 'HYDROGEN BOMB': THE GREAT INDIAN CHALLENGE

As already mentioned, the modern Commonwealth was defined by the Statute of Westminster of 1931, with three defining characteristics: equality of status, freedom of association and common allegiance to the British crown.[38] The Crown link was critical to the self-image of the old Commonwealth but India presented a serious constitutional problem. While the older dominions were largely British and European in outlook, India was an ancient civilization proud of its own history. It was one thing to accept dominion status as a temporary measure to break the deadlock over transfer of power, another to do it permanently. Complete independence, with all its symbols, had been a non-negotiable tenet of Indian nationalism for nearly two decades. In January 1947, therefore, the Congress passed a resolution that India would be a sovereign, independent republic.

In the eyes of the Congress, republican status was the keystone, the only thing that would clear 'beyond all question or manner of doubt that India was a wholly independent nation'.[39] This was totally at odds with the rules of Commonwealth membership, which had never been open to a republic and required allegiance to the Crown. India forcefully pushed for a change in the status quo and the congress' Jaipur Resolution of 18 December 1948 spoke of a new vision of the Commonwealth:

> In view of the attainment of complete independence and the establishment of a Republic of India which will symbolize that independence, and give to India a status among the nations of the world that is her rightful due, her present association with the United Kingdom and the Commonwealth of Nations will necessarily have to change. India, however, desires to maintain all such links with other countries as do not come in the way of her freedom of action and independence, and the Congress would welcome her free association with independent nations of the Commonwealth for their common welfare and the promotion of world peace.[40]

This was a big challenge for the Commonwealth because when the Irish Republicans had suggested the same thing, they had been refused. The new Indian demand could only be met with a change in the criteria for Commonwealth membership and a compromise on the idea of the Crown as head of state, which had so far been the leitmotif of the Commonwealth.

The Commonwealth's prime ministers met in April 1949 with an Indian fait accompli to discuss. In the end, they had no option. As the first big country to be decolonized, India was central to the sustenance of the Commonwealth. It would set a pattern for the rest of the colonies and if it left, the Commonwealth itself would be doomed as a relic of the past. In the end, the prime ministers decided not to change the entry rules in general, but to make an exception for India. India would only have to acknowledge the Crown as a symbol of the Commonwealth federation, but this would have no bearing on Indian law, as it did in the other member countries. India would have no allegiance to the Crown and this was a major departure.[41]

There is a direct contrast with Ireland. When the Irish, in late 1948, started proceedings to repeal the Irish External Relations Act of 1936 in order to become a republic, Prime Minster Attlee immediately announced that Ireland would no longer be a member of the Commonwealth. Ireland became a republic on 18 April 1949. Just ten days later, the Commonwealth prime ministers announced that the Indian republic would remain a member.[42] What had been sacrilege in the past was now par for the course.[43]

It had been a tricky negotiation and the formula was worked out by Krishna Menon; B.N. Rau, constitutional advisor to the Indian government; Patrick Gordon-Walker, the secretary of state for Commonwealth Relations; and Clement Attlee.[44] When Nehru explained the London agreement to the Constituent Assembly, he was clear that this was a problem that could not have been left to the lawyers to solve; that at its heart this was a political question. He stressed that India would have 'nothing to do with any external authority', that it had not compromised its sovereignty and that the Crown had no function at all. He explained, 'I felt as I was conferring there in London that I had necessarily to stick completely and absolutely to the sovereignty and the independence of the Indian republic.'[45]

India had practical things to gain from remaining in the Commonwealth, as we have already seen. Some British romantics continued to harp on the metaphor of 'family' and sentiment as further reasons to add to the list of advantages that accrued from remaining in the Commonwealth. This was far from true in practical terms. Writing in 1959, Sir Ivor Jennings argued convincingly that sentiment played little part in the Indian decision. 'On the contrary ... *sentiment required that there had to be an express repudiation of allegiance to the Crown* ... India has to become a republic in order to maintain her self–respect and most of her leaders have used that phrase in defending her action.'[46]

Though the older Commonwealth members had virtually no choice but to accept India's insistence on becoming a republic and the junking of the notion of the Crown as a master symbol, this was seen as a tragedy in the old circles. Sample this 1955 critique by Duncan Hall:

> ...the adjustments required to accommodate in the Commonwealth the very different cultures of Asia and Africa involve a danger of weakening unity by the severing of bonds, or by weakening or destroying essential symbols ... An Indian republic has been grafted on the Commonwealth stock – not without cutting away of tissues of unity and a weakening of Commonwealth symbols. Yet time has shown that India's assumptions and symbols, ideas, policies and methods diverge widely from those of the Commonwealth. By conceding a republic, with present and future damage to itself, the Commonwealth gambled on the as yet doubtful chance that it might win India for the Commonwealth.
>
> The solution of an Indian Republic was met with great reluctance and misgiving by most of the Commonwealth prime ministers.[47]

Far from becoming a handmaiden of imperial politics, India was subverting its traditional tools to its own ends and on its own terms. The monarchy had been an article of faith for the old order: in Churchill's words, the 'mysterious' and 'magic' link that bound the Commonwealth,[48] and the Indian insistence on junking it as a symbol was met with some bizarre arguments. Ivor Jennings, for instance, argued in all seriousness that the 'Constitution of India can be wiped out by one hydrogen bomb: one can never wipe out the British Constitution because the Queen, or the Queen's successor can set up house in Carnarvon or Canberra, Edinburgh or Entebbe ...'[49] No wonder Nehru won his arguments with ease.

It wasn't in England alone that India was met with opposition. People like General Smuts, Gandhi's great South African opponent, argued in 1949 that the decision to keep India was a fatal mistake. The 1950s and 1960s saw a slew of articles and books written by woeful traditionalists who saw Indian membership as the death knell for the Commonwealth. Without the allegiance to the Crown, for these critics, it had 'become very difficult to see precisely what the Commonwealth really means and for what purpose it exists'.[50]

Membership for the Indian republic was meant to be an exception but it became the pattern for all. In the beginning, legal experts felt that this would not set a precedent but India was too big an elephant in the room. As Pakistan's prime minister, Liaqat Ali Khan, commented:

> The very doctrine of equality of members of the Commonwealth ... predicates that if any other member of the Commonwealth chooses henceforth to frame a Constitution for itself which involves an alteration of its relationship with the Crown, of a character similar to that which India has chosen to make, and decides, nevertheless, to continue its full membership of the Commonwealth on the same terms as have been accepted on behalf of India, it would be open to do so.[51]

A good example is what happened in Africa. Ghana became a republic in 1960, Tanganyika in 1962, Nigeria in 1963, followed by Kenya, Uganda and Malawi, to name a few.[52] By 1979, there were twenty-one postcolonial republics who were members of the Commonwealth.[53] India had opened the floodgates to a new kind of Commonwealth.

'ONE SWORD' OR POSTCOLONIAL PLAYGROUND: INDIA AND THE CHANGING BALANCE OF POWER

India was to be the torchbearer for decolonization and as the process unfolded across the world, it offered a constructive example to be followed. In this sense, Nicholas Mansergh has argued that Nehru was the real architect of the Commonwealth as a brand new experiment in international relations and a bridge between cultures.[54]

The traditionalists in the older dominions could whine all they liked about the way the world was changing but with the rise of the ex-colonies, the very nature of the Commonwealth was changing. By 1955, for instance, the total population of Pakistan (76 million) itself equalled the total white population of the Commonwealth. This was in addition to India's 250 million and Ceylon's 7 million.[55]

As such, it was also important to show that the Commonwealth was not a mere camouflage for British imperialism and that it was not just run from London. This was why the Commonwealth first came to Asia in January 1950 with the Foreign Ministers' Conference in Colombo, where Nehru emerged as its towering personality.[56] Nehru used Commonwealth meetings to propagate his vision of nationalism, racism, and the legacy of colonialism and 'the changing face of Asia' as he put it.

In an age where the Commonwealth's old powers were only really interested in the Cold War and the fight against communism, Nehru's independence and forthrightness was irritating for many of the older members. At the time of the Suez crisis in 1956, for instance, Nehru almost quit the Commonwealth to protest against the British action in Egypt and its decision to not even inform the other members before the invasion. Canada played a part in persuading him not to, because the Canadians understood Nehru and his notions of a liberal internationalism that could be pursued without taking sides in the superpower conflict.[57] The Suez was one of the Commonwealth's biggest crises and it clearly pitted the old order (except Canada) in opposition to the newer members led by Nehru.[58] For example, at the height of the crisis, Robert Menzies, the Australian prime minister, was constantly in touch with Anthony Eden, arguing at one stage that the Indian logic 'doesn't travel very far'.[59]

At the heart of the differences between the old Commonwealth and Nehru was a seminal intellectual divide. Robert Menzies, who symbolized the old order, viewed Nehru's non-alignment as 'foolish' and prejudicing the Western fight against communism.[60] More significantly, Menzies saw the Commonwealth as a 'precious family association',[61] as a spiritual continuation of the old Empire – a vision that was at odds with a 'multilateral, multi-racial association ... [that would be] a very useful piece of international machinery',[62] as envisaged by Nehru.

Nehru's hopes for the Commonwealth were in conflict with the traditional view held by the old order, which saw in the Commonwealth a vehicle to carry on the imperial signature of the British Empire, even in a world where decolonization was inevitable. The greatest among these old-timers was General Smuts, the man who Gandhi had first humbled with his satyagraha in South Africa. By the 1940s, he was prime minister of South Africa and widely being regarded as the 'father of the British Commonwealth of nations'. The famous Smuts memorandum of 1921, after all, had anticipated the declaration of the Imperial Conference of 1926 and the Statute of Westminster.[63] For people like Smuts, the Commonwealth was a link with an imperial past that contained all that was glorious and great about the British Empire. No wonder he called it 'this proudest political structure of time'.[64] He regarded it as a 'great power', like others,[65] falling in with the thinking of Menzies, who saw the Commonwealth as 'one sword'. For such imperial apologists, the key was the notion of a 'family' with Britain at the head – a master symbol; India's neutralism was seen as 'straying from the family circle'.[66] To such people, the Commonwealth was to be a new substitute for the Empire, with its nerve centre in London and the old bloc in the lead. For such an idea, Nehru's free thinking was anathema.

For Nehru, in contrast, the Commonwealth was also a forum to propagate India's independent vision, one that was bound to make the traditionalists unhappy. As the *National Herald* commented in 1956, 'Menzies does not seem happy over the presence in the Commonwealth ... of India [with its] own independent foreign policies.'[67] If the newspaper had added the South Africans and the British to the Australian Menzies, it would still have been accurate.

Starting with Indochina, the Indian stand created differences within the Commonwealth as early as during the Colombo meeting of foreign ministers in 1950. The older members supported the propping up of Emperor Bo Dai as a bulwark against communism in South-East Asia but the new ones were mindful of his imperialist backing. Nehru made it clear that India would not recognize any government till its independent authority was established over the whole area.[68] Nehru's foreign policy stance created tensions in the Commonwealth over the Suez crisis, the Korean aggression and the China question.

The common thread in all of this was a latent anti-Americanism. As a 1951 report put it:

The one Commonwealth country which displays ... an anti-American tendency is India. That may arise from the rather unreal suspicion of American materialism, Hollywood morals, and Chicago gangsters, which is voiced in Indian newspapers. There is also the feeling that the United States is a new imperialistic power which may use its dollars to control Asian peoples just after they have thrown off the yoke of the United Kingdom and other powers ... whatever the reason, a traveler finds in India more criticism of American policies and the American way of life than in any other Commonwealth country at the present time.[69]

With Korea at war, President Truman's indiscreet threats of using the atomic bomb on 30 November 1950 had raised Nehru's hackles and led to him dubbing it as 'evil incarnate'. At an international conference in Lucknow, there was actually talk of the Americans using the bomb against Asians, when they would not do so against whites or Europeans.[70] Soon enough, at the 1951 Prime Ministers' Conference, Nehru criticized US policy over China as 'unrealistic ... and lead[ing] towards war'. The ideal of Asian unity had been a central tenet of Indian nationalism[71] for years and he told the meeting that Asia did not see the war in terms of the division between communism and anti-communism and that the best defence against communism was to raise living standards.[72]

Nehru also linked the North Korean aggression with the admission of China to the UN, which he saw as the best and most inclusive way of dealing with China.[73] By 1949, India, the UK, Pakistan and Ceylon had recognized China but Canada, New Zealand, Australia and South Africa had not. India's position on China was to change after the Tibet aggression but this was still the height of Hindi–Cheeni *bhai-bhai*.

Nehru repeated his Asian line at the 1953 conference, where he argued that the 'simplification of our problems into fight of communism against anti-Communism was misleading. Asians have a different approach.'[74] This is a line of thinking that Nehru also followed through at Bandung, where he stated that India was neither communist nor anti-communist. He thought both were wrong and put the Cominform (Communist Information Bureau) in the same category as the South East Asia Treaty Organsation (SEATO) as being dangerous.[75] Little wonder then that the Commonwealth ruptured over SEATO in 1954, when Pakistan joined the pact, primarily as a means to take on India. Nehru saw US policy as neo-colonialism and considered Pakistan's arming as detrimental to the Kashmir issue. The SEATO divide came at a time when the French were taking a beating in Indochina and worries were mounting in Washington that once the French were ousted by communist forces, the dominoes would fall all over Asia. Washington and London, therefore, increasingly began calling for a NATO of the South. Nehru demurred, much to the chagrin of the Australians and the British. As he argued, 'Our participation ... would have meant giving up our basic policy of non-alignment ... its whole approach is wrong ... and may antagonize a great part of Asia.'[76]

The end result of all this was that by the 1960s, the Commonwealth had become a political battleground and British politicians, who had so far bent over backwards to assuage Commonwealth feelings, were no longer prepared to make sacrifices to it as a political ideal. The passage of the 1968 Commonwealth Immigrants Bill is a case in point.[77] Britain also decided to join the European Common Market, a decision which weakened the Commonwealth. The British disappointment was mirrored by Nehru's own. By now, world-weary and cynical, he was disillusioned with the Commonwealth as a political forum, calling it a 'tenuous and vague association'.[78]

'PAPER CONCEPTION' OR 'SMALL STATES FORUM': THE STRUCTURES OF THE COMMONWEALTH

Since the moment of India's joining, the Commonwealth has been a body searching for a purpose. It is strange that virtually all Commonwealth documents take pains to refer to the meaning of the Commonwealth, as if no one would take the organization seriously if it did not keep explaining itself. Often, the study of the Commonwealth has been propagated 'less by intellectual curiosity than by the desire to see it prosper' by the British who see it as a totem of their past.[79] Even in 1959, Hedley Bull argued, 'At each of the crises in the history of the Commonwealth, when the question is asked, "What purpose does it serve?", "What form shall it take?", the continued existence of the Commonwealth in its widest membership has been preferred to its serving any particular purpose or taking any particular form.'[80]

Even so, by 1965, the Commonwealth was being referred to as a 'dying patient badly in need of transfusion' or as Lord Casey called it, 'a paper conception, with little reality or practical usefulness'.[81] In fact, the 1964 Prime Ministers' Conference was being referred to as the last, by many. [82]

Partly, this is because of the vast and diverse nature of the body itself. As the *Economist* noted in 1964, for instance, the Prime Ministers' Conference that year consisted of 'a field marshal and a widow, a former male nurse ... winners of a Nobel Peace Prize and a Lenin Peace Prize ... a prince, an unbelted ex-earl and two other knights, and three "prison graduates" (there would be five if Mr Shastri and President Makarios had been able to come)'.[83] This was British derision of the new order at its sarcastic best, but it was also a reflection of the immense diversity of the Commonwealth and the varied nature of its constituent members.

In the absence of some institutionalization, centrifugal forces would quickly have eroded the little direction that the Commonwealth had, and this is why a Secretariat was created in London in 1965 and a Foundation in 1966. This is in addition to professional associations like the Commonwealth Parliamentary Union, which, founded in 1911, predates the Commonwealth itself.

The Secretariat approach is very different from La Francophonie, the parallel French organization of former French colonies, with most former French territories remaining linked to France through bilateral treaties. Commonwealth structures are much more loose, though Francophonie copied the Secretariat model in 1997, with Boutros Boutros-Ghali as its first secretary general.[84] A look at how the Commonwealth Secretariat's functions were defined gives a peek into the workings of the Commonwealth. The secretary general is authorized to prepare and circulate papers on international questions of common concern, provided they do not propagate any particular sectional or partisan points of view, contain no policy judgements or recommendations by the Secretariat and do not touch upon the internal affairs of a member country or disputes or serious differences between two or more member countries.[85] This was about as bland and non-functional as it gets, but the first secretary general, Arnold Smith, claimed in his memoirs that the Secretariat acted as an 'internal pressure group'. In his view, periodic heads of government meetings were valuable for the implanting of ideas and attitudes, though the quality of leaders varied.[86]

The balance of the Commonwealth shifted to the global South in the 1950s and 1960s, and the focus shifted to development as decolonization gathered pace. Until the late 1960s, Commonwealth members made up 10 to 15 per cent of the UN; by the 1970s they made up a quarter; and by the 1990s, a third. Looking at the major debates within the Commonwealth, in the 1960s, these were focussed on decolonization and development; in the 1970s/80s, on anti-apartheid; in the 1990s/2000s on issues of good governance; and are charting a trajectory in the 2010s on human development/security.[87]

The real usefulness of the Commonwealth has been in developmental issues and networking; and as a forum where small states get to play on an equal footing with the big boys. It may not matter much in the power sweepstakes, but as an Australian diplomat pointed out to us: where else would the president or prime minister of, say, Maldives or the Bahamas sit in a summit meeting every two years or so with nearly a hundred other heads of state and get to have his say too.[88] 'The Commonwealth has, indeed, become the premier small states forum.'[89] Small island states, for instance, account for more than half of its fifty-three members. By remaining in the Commonwealth, the former colonies conceded only a symbolic association to the British to secure their delusions of power and a 'dull[ing] of the sense of defeat' or even an assuaging of their 'guilt feelings', while securing conveniences, services and somewhat of an influence over British policy.[90] As the Commonwealth rightly claims, it is the 'only global organization in which small states can genuinely claim special consideration'.[91]

So, does anyone care about the Commonwealth at all? One criteria is attendance at meetings by heads of government. This declined from a peak of 90 per cent in 1944–55, to 84 per cent in 1956–65, to 73 per cent in 1966–77 – but the decline was not catastrophic.[92] Also, the average length of summits (about nine days) was more than that of the Non-Aligned Movement (NAM) or Organization of African Unity summits. Of course, the attendance could be explained by the tourism potential of London, but it is significant that countries who were members of both the Commonwealth and the NAM attended far more Commonwealth (70 per cent) meetings than NAM ones (56 per cent) in the same period.[93] Clearly, for many of the smaller countries, the Commonwealth remained an important international tool.

INDIA AND THE POLITICS OF THE COMMONWEALTH GAMES

What does the cut and thrust of India's international diplomacy have to do with the sweat and grime of professional sport? Actually, quite a lot. Nehru's support to the Commonwealth meant that India also embraced the idea of the Commonwealth Games. The Games predate the Commonwealth itself and they have now emerged as, perhaps, the most visible face of the Commonwealth. We have already seen the political disappointments in the association. What remains is the forum for developmental aid, cultural exchange and sport. The Games are managed by the autonomous CGF in London and the participants stretch beyond the Commonwealth member states – seventy-one in Melbourne (in comparison with fifty-three member states).[94]

The previous chapter has documented the lukewarm Indian response to the Games in the pre-independence period. Indian nationalism could not allow a ready embrace of an event that was linked to the idea of an imperium as long as India was a colony. In the 1934 Games, for instance, the athletes' oath, read out by England's athletics captain was a straight paean to the Empire: 'We declare that we are loyal subjects of His Majesty the King Emperor, and will take part in the British Empire Games in the spirit of true sportsmanship, recognizing the rules which govern them and desirous of participating in them for the honour of our Empire and the glory of sport.'[95]

No self-respecting Indian nationalist could associate with such a vision and this is why the Games did not pick up any traction in the Indian imagination.

With independence, and Nehru's acceptance of the Commonwealth, however, India changed tack. The Commonwealth Games emerged as an important item in the calendar of Indian sports.

As Table 6.1 indicates, the Games themselves changed character from the British Empire Games (1930–1950) to the British Empire and Commonwealth Games (1954–74) to the Commonwealth Games (1978–present). The change in nomenclature reflected the changes in the political nature of the Commonwealth itself. Independent India skipped the 1950 Games, which were still referred to as the Empire Games and only started participating from 1954, when the word 'Commonwealth' was added. After that, India has only missed two editions: 1962, because of the war with China, and 1985, because of the boycott over South Africa.

Indian participation has been far from token. The consistent haul of medals since 1958 is testimony to that. As the medals tally in Table 6.1 indicates, India remained a steady achiever between 1958 and 1990, but suddenly improved in Auckland, 1990, winning thirty-two medals. The real jump, however, occurred in Manchester when Indian athletes brought home sixty-nine medals. Melbourne saw a comparative dip, but it was still India's second-largest medal haul ever. The reasons for this change are beyond the scope of this chapter, because they are more to do with the larger ebbs and flows of Indian sport. It is enough to note, however, that Indian sport followed the larger trajectory of Indian politics in its engagement with the Commonwealth.

By the early 2000s, the Commonwealth Games had turned into the third-largest international event of its kind – after the Olympics and the Soccer World Cup. The problem, though, was that apart from garnering audiences in Australia, New Zealand, Canada and Britain, the Games failed to become a popular TV event elsewhere. This was reflected in lack of sponsorship and poor marketing potential for these Games.[96] Clearly, the Commonwealth Games had failed to catch the popular imagination in the erstwhile colonies. It was one thing to be part of the Commonwealth as an expedient exercise in power but quite another to actually share the imagination of its imperial past.

Part of the problem lay in the fact that the Games had never been hosted outside of the old white dominions, except on two occasions – Kingston in 1966 and Kuala Lumpur in 1998. In contrast, New Zealand and Australia had hosted the Games thrice, Britain four times and Canada five times.[97]

This became an important political issue and the Commonwealth Heads of Government Meeting (CHOGM) in Kuala Lumpur in 1989 expressed concern that the Games had to move to newer pastures if Commonwealth ties had to be strengthened. This was followed by the selection of an Asian chairperson to head the Commonwealth Games Federation for the first time in 1990, a decision reaffirmed at the 1991 CHOGM summit.[98] The Kuala Lumpur Games followed as a direct result.

Now it is Delhi's turn, with the Commonwealth Games Federation aiming to buy into the huge Indian market and New Delhi aiming to use the Games for its soft-power projection on the world stage, in a mini version of what Beijing did with the Olympics in 2008.

'GIGANTIC FARCE' OR SOMETHING MEANINGFUL?

In 2001, writer Amitava Ghosh returned a Commonwealth Literature Award from the Commonwealth Foundation, arguing that he did not agree with the very existence of such a category. 'Commonwealth literature', he argued, was 'not within the realities of the present day, nor within the possibilities of the future, but rather within a disputed aspect of the past.'[99] The Commonwealth's critics would say that he could have been talking of the Commonwealth itself. As early as 1950, even the Commonwealth's well-wishers like the historian Nicholas Mansergh had to, while explaining its existence, take recourse in the boast of Abbe Sieyes at the end of the French Revolution: '*I have survived*'.

That the Commonwealth had survived was achievement enough. We have seen how Nehru used the Commonwealth in the early years but politically it seemed to have outlived its usefulness with the end of decolonization. Countries like India used it for their own purposes while Britain continued using it as a fig-leaf to hide the end of its global pre-eminence. By the 1960s, it was clear that British writers were primarily responsible for keeping alive the myth of the Commonwealth as anything but a simple exercise in realist power play by its former colonies:

> The Commonwealth has become the great Utopia of British political writers and politicians. Here, in this community that nobody can

Table 6.1: India and the Commonwealth Games, 1934–2006 [100]

Year	Venue	Countries	Sports	Competitors	Officials	Indian medals
British Empire Games						
1930	Hamilton	11	6	400*	50*	**no Indian participation**
1934	London	16	6	500*	50*	1 bronze
1938	Sydney	15	7	464	43	–
1950	Auckland	12	9	590	73	**no Indian participation**
British Empire and Commonwealth Games						
1954	Vancouver	24	9	662	127	–
1958	Cardiff	35	9	1130	228	2 gold, 1 silver
1962	Perth	35	9	863	178	**no Indian participation**
1966	Kingston	34	9	1050	226	3 gold, 4 bronze, 3 silver
British Commonwealth Games						
1970	Edinburgh	42	9	1383	361	5 gold, 3 silver, 4 bronze
1974	Christchurch	39	9	1276	372	4 gold, 8 silver, 3 bronze
Commonwealth Games						
1978	Edmonton	46	10	1475	504	5 gold, 5 silver, 5 bronze
1982	Brisbane	45**	10	1583	571	5 gold, 8 silver, 3 bronze
1986	Edinburgh	26	10	1662	461	**no Indian participation**
1990	Auckland	55	10	2073	789	13 gold, 8 silver, 11 bronze
1994	Victoria	63	10	2557	914	6 gold, 11 silver, 7 bronze
1998	Kuala Lumpur	70	15	4600	1400	7 gold, 10 silver, 8 bronze
2002	Manchester	72	17	3679	2038	30 gold, 22 silver, 17 bronze
2006	Melbourne	71	16	4500	1200	22 gold, 17 silver, 10 bronze

*Estimated

**There is a discrepancy in the official report and the official website. The website mentions 46 countries as participants. We have gone by the figure of 45 listed in the official report.

define, Britain retains the leadership which she has lost in world affairs; and by grace of this position, she asserts her claim to be a world power and denies that she has become just an island off the north-west coast of Europe. What the British public needs just now is a succession of infants to point out the scantiness of the emperor's clothes.[101]

One of the most bizarre ironies to come out of this British romanticism was the fact that the Supreme Court of India had to actually rule in 1954 (in Madras vs C.G. Menon) that a nineteenth-century British law did not apply any more to India, because it referred to British dominions. Even though India had been independent for seven years, the Supreme Court was forced to pronounce this judgment because from the point of view of British courts, the old laws still applied – under the UK's India (Consequential Provisions) Act 1949 – which provided for the continued application of existing laws in relation to India![102] Delusion of lost grandeur has never been funnier.

A similar farce was played out in Pakistan. When Bills were submitted for Governor General Jinnah's signature, provisions were made for his signature in 'His Majesty's name'. Jinnah, however, proudly struck out these words, and the legal nitpickers brought in a lawsuit to establish whether his assent was valid or not, since technically he was only authorized to signed in His Majesty's name. Pakistan subsequently brought in legislation that removed all references to his 'His Majesty's name' while also deleting references to the Crown in Pakistani law. Some people, though, still argued that this 'legislation was in fact invalid because it had not received the royal assent'.[103] This perhaps explains why the *Economist* by 1964 was calling the Commonwealth 'the world's biggest experiment yet in sustained and creative historical humour'.[104] A British MP was more direct, calling it a 'gigantic farce'[105] founded on humbug.

Nehru had used the Commonwealth creatively for India's purposes but by the late 1960s, the political uses of such a fractious federation seemed to be a lost cause. South African apartheid, though, gave it a new reason to exist. As the next chapter will show, the Commonwealth – in large measure through the Commonwealth Games – emerged as the primary global community in the fight against apartheid in the 1970s and 1980s.[106] With the demise of the Cold War and apartheid, the Commonwealth needed a new raison d'être; and after the 1991 CHOGM at Harare, it transformed further into an advocacy coalition for good governance in the 1990s.[107]

Evidence of the Commonwealth's subsequent success lies in the fact that in 1995, after a special plea by Nelson Mandela, it admitted Mozambique – the first nation to join without any history of British rule. Cameroon followed, and there are now others with no history of connections with Britain wanting to join. The Commonwealth began as a 'decompression chamber' to ease the transition from colonialism but it has, over the years, reinvented itself into an intergovernmental organization, committed to small states, good governance and globalization – a 'network of networks', as it were.[108]

The Games have been integral to its public imagery and attained centre stage especially during the fight against apartheid in South Africa, to which we now turn.

7 | THE COMMONWEALTH, SPORT DIPLOMACY AND THE SOUTH AFRICAN BOYCOTT, 1961-1994

While trying to grapple with decolonization movements across the world, the Games were confronted with yet another challenge; perhaps the most significant one in their history. By the late 1950s, the Empire Games' organizers were forced to formulate policies to counter the growing menace of racially segregated sport furthered by the newly elected Nationalist Party in South Africa. Interestingly, mobilization over issues of discrimination in sport was not entirely new in Commonwealth Games history. The 1934 Games, initially allotted to Johannesburg, South Africa, had to be moved to London to avoid a political crisis over South Africa's evolving apartheid policy and its implications on visiting Commonwealth athletes and officials, especially those from developing countries that were engaged in movements of decolonization.[1] More than the realm of sports competition, where it was soon superseded by the Olympics and other world championships, it was in trying to resist the growing political ills through sport that the Games offered a voice to millions of peoples who were otherwise discriminated against in their home countries. It was in acts like these, actions that transcended the sporting barrier, that the Games found their real relevance.

The role of the Commonwealth Games Federation in defying apartheid assumes heightened significance because in this realm, more than anywhere else, it was the example of sport that led the way for world leaders to devise policies to counter racism. Until South Africa was banned from participating in the Commonwealth Games, and the Federation adopted a firm stand against racially segregated sport, politicians, especially in the white Commonwealth countries, did not hesitate in continuing their existing ties with that country. The idea of continuing business as usual with South Africa enjoyed considerable currency among many political leaders in countries like Britain, Australia and New Zealand. This also included support for sending sports teams to play against the white-only teams in South Africa. The question of sporting ties brought to the forefront many of the tensions within the Commonwealth, between its newly decolonized countries and the older members, and it became a powerful symbol of the global fight against apartheid. Once the South Africans were expelled from the Commonwealth in 1961 and banned from participating in the Commonwealth Games from 1962 onwards, the world was forced to take notice.

India played a central part in the diplomatic mobilization against South Africa. Apartheid, after all, was one of Nehru's biggest bugbears at the Commonwealth. For him, the Commonwealth could only exist on 'a strict adherence to ... racial equality [and] the policy of the South African government was not compatible with it'.[2] This was in sharp contrast to, say, Australia, which, at the time, saw any reference to domestic policy as inconsistent with the very idea of the Commonwealth. Australia's Robert Menzies, according to an Indian observer, 'was looked upon as South Africa's staunchest champion at Commonwealth gatherings ... favouring an inner club of the older white dominions, leaving new Asian and African members out in the cold'.[3]

For Nehru, on the other hand, apartheid and decolonization were inextricably linked, and more pressing than concerns in the West about the Cold War. In 1955, when he was still in his haloed period as a world statesman and volubly leading the anti-apartheid charge, a contemporary observer of the Commonwealth thoughtfully summarized his rationale: 'Mr Nehru believes that the people of Asia and Africa feel more deeply about events in South Africa and elsewhere than they do about communism and anti-communism. Racialism, he has suggested, may be more dangerous than any of the world's problems today.'[4]

Part of the problem was that the South African regime in the late 1950s was uneasy with decolonization in Africa. Particularly in West Africa, South Africa repeatedly argued for incorporating Basutoland, Swaziland and Bechuanaland in itself, instead of granting them independence.[5] South African rigidness on the question of race led to a concerted diplomatic offensive, culminating in a ban from the Commonwealth Games.

The International Olympic Committee followed suit and in 1963 adopted a proposal mooted by India. The proposal demanded that:

> The National Olympic Committee of South Africa must declare formally that it understands and submits to the spirit of the Olympic Charter ... It must also obtain from its Government before December 31, 1963, modification of its policy of racial discrimination in sport and competitions on its territory, failing which the South African National Olympic Committee will be forced to withdraw from the Olympic Games.[6]

However, it was soon evident that despite formal exclusion from the world's leading sports platforms – the Olympics and the Commonwealth Games – surreptitious sporting contacts with South Africa continued.

Bilateral sporting ties, especially with white Commonwealth dominions like New Zealand and Australia, continued to prosper, creating marked fissures in the growing anti-apartheid campaign, which demanded complete South African isolation. Attempts at trying to bring the intransigents into line dominated Games history for almost three decades. It was only in the early 1990s, with formal abolition of discriminatory policies in South Africa and its return to the international mainstream, did the CGF breathe easy.

This chapter documents the struggle against racially organized sport and argues that such close enmeshing of sports and politics, which hogged headlines across the world, catapulted the Commonwealth Games into a position of centrality in the global sporting hierarchy. As a South African analyst summed up in 1994:

> For those that argue that the Commonwealth is powerless, I have a simple answer as a South African. Look at what the Commonwealth did to us in the bad old days. The Commonwealth spawned the Frontline States, they invoked sanctions and helped sanctions spread like measles against us. They mobilized the UN and other organizations against the South African government. They lobbied the Congress in America. They were anything but powerless.[7]

The successful campaign against apartheid also helped counter the notion that sports boycotts have generally failed in achieving their goals and have more often than not gone against the interests of athletes who, as a result of the boycott, have lost out on opportunities to compete. As former Commonwealth Games champion and scholar–activist Bruce Kidd argues, 'Not all sports boycotts have ended in failure ... the black African nations have repeatedly used the boycott weapon to advance their campaign to bar the South African sports bodies which practice apartheid from international competition. In this, they have been remarkably successful.'[8] Sport emerged as the battering ram of the global campaign against South African apartheid.

APARTHEID AND THE SOUTH AFRICAN SPORTING CONTEXT

The history of racially segregated sport in South Africa can be traced back to the late nineteenth century. By the early twentieth century, whites-only sports organizations like the South African Cricket Association and South African Olympic Games Association had barred 'Africans' from representing South Africa at world meets. Discriminatory policies gathered steam in the 1930s, resulting in the shift of the second British Empire and Commonwealth Games to London. Subsequently, in 1946, a group of black South African weightlifters appealed to the British Amateur Weightlifters Association for recognition, urging them to exert pressure on their other South African counterparts. Responding to the appeal, Oscar State, secretary of the British Amateur Weightlifters Association declared:

> I had to wait until I placed the matter before our Central Council. They considered your request with sympathy but it is with regret that I have to inform you that we cannot bring any pressure on the South African Weightlifting Federation to force them to recognize you. Their rules, as with all national sporting associations in South Africa, will not permit mixed contests between white and coloured athletes. This is also a condition of the South African Olympic Council. Therefore, no coloured man could be chosen to represent South Africa in the international contests.[9]

Failing to elicit any response from international governing bodies of sport, including the Commonwealth Games Federation, black athletes, in the early 1940s, focussed on reforms within their local context, an effort stymied by the Nationalist Party government, which came to power in 1948.

Frustrated by conditions of discrimination, some coloured South Africans of fair skin tried to get into South African teams by passing themselves as white. As Sam Ramsamy has documented in his excellent treatise on South African sport, Smilee Moosa, a coloured man, managed to get into the all-white Berea Park football club. However, such concealments were soon found out and once Moosa's identity was exposed, he was instantly expelled from the club.[10]

Efforts at discrimination intensified in 1948 when the Nationalist Party assumed power. Noting that blacks and coloured men were trying to organize themselves to mount a concerted protest and, in 1955, had formed the Committee for International Recognition, the government, in 1956, promulgated a guideline which made it compulsory for whites and blacks to organize their sporting activities separately and banned all interracial sports competitions. In the same year, however, proponents of anti-racial sport won a minor victory when the mixed South African Table Tennis Board of Control was affiliated to the International Table Tennis Federation.[11]

Inspired by this victory and determined to take on the government, the South African Sports Association (SASA) was formed in 1958 with a specific brief to voice South African opinion before the Empire Games Association and the International Olympic Committee. The SASA won an important battle when South Africa was expelled from the Commonwealth in 1961, a task made easier by South Africa's turning into a republic. At home, however, their efforts at trying to ensure that blacks were granted membership of the Commonwealth Games Association or the South African Olympic Council came to nothing. It was then that SASA, together with a number of other coloured sports bodies and individual athletes, formed the South African Non-Racial Olympic Committee (SANROC) on 13 January 1963 in Johannesburg.[12]

While SANROC was advancing the cause of non-racial sport within South Africa and was successful in getting South Africa banned from participating in the Tokyo Olympics of 1964, the government at home was zealously continuing its policies of racial segregation. So much so that the minister of the interior, P.M.K. Le Roux, declared in Parliament on 8 February 1967: 'Precisely because it is our declared policy – the world knows it – we will not in this country allow competition between whites and non-whites on the playing fields.'[13]

Two years prior to this declaration in Parliament, in February 1965, the government had issued a proclamation under the guise of the Group Areas Act, which prohibited all interracial sports meets except by permit. In the few cases that permits were granted, the organizers were categorically told to separate audiences by race, with wire fences. Further, spectators had to use separate entrances and toilets during the course of the event.

While trying to fervently guard its policy of apartheid, the government was, on occasions, forced to grant concessions to demonstrate to the world that the South African situation was not as bad as it was made out to be in some quarters. These attempts, aimed at hoodwinking the world, were undertaken to regain admission into the Olympics and the Commonwealth Games fold. For example, in April 1967, the government offered to send a mixed team to the Olympics at Mexico in 1968.[14] What was left unmentioned, however, was that the athletes were to be chosen in separate trials for the races. The government also agreed that it wouldn't attempt to influence the composition of sports teams invited to tour South Africa. Again, left undisclosed was the fact that this was a contingency with the New Zealanders cancelling a rugby tour because the South Africans had declared that Maoris would not be allowed in the team.[15] The government reaction was also prompted by the United Nations General Assembly declaration in 1968, requesting all states and organizations 'to suspend cultural, educational, sporting and other exchanges with the racist regime and with organizations or institutions in South Africa which practise apartheid'.[16]

Things came to a head in 1970 when South Africa was finally expelled from the Olympic movement.[17] Soon after, it was also debarred from participating in most of the major world championships. In all, thirteen white South African sports federations had been expelled or suspended from international sports bodies in the course of one year and it was soon evident that South Africa's sporting contacts had been reduced to participation in tennis and golf and bilateral exchanges with a few countries in cricket and rugby. In tennis too, as Bruce Murray notes, while South Africa escaped expulsion from the International Lawn Tennis Federation, it was soon suspended from competing in the Davis Cup. South African national tennis championships were also ousted from the ATP circuit. 'Rugby alone survived the onslaught of the sports boycott. Despite organized opposition and protest within New Zealand, the All Blacks rugby tour of South Africa went ahead in 1970, with the inclusion of three Maoris and a Samoan in the touring party.'[18]

Cornered, the South African government tried to aggressively promote sporting contacts with a handful of Commonwealth nations like Australia, New Zealand, Canada and the United Kingdom. The government was encouraged to do so because political and diplomatic relations with some of these countries continued to be amicable in the 1950s and 1960s. The Canadian government, for example, as Donald Macintosh and Donna Greenhorn have argued, showed great reluctance in undertaking concrete economic, social or diplomatic measures against the South Africans. This was because Canada's economic relations with South Africa, 'although small in absolute terms, were, nevertheless, lucrative and weighted toward manufactured exports, a sector of the economy that was traditionally weak ... In addition, there remained in Canada some nasty elements of racial prejudice, perhaps best manifested in certain "legal disabilities" imposed on Asians in British Columbia. Although these were largely, if not entirely, eliminated in 1947, residual strains of racial prejudice still lingered in Canada. These had the effect of tempering Canadian criticism of South African policies during the period.'[19]

The British government, too, valued its trade links with South Africa. For instance, British Conservatives had, in 1970, decided to consider applications from certain types of firms to sell arms to South Africa. Not surprisingly, this controversial move was met with strong protests within the Commonwealth, including from India.[20] Afraid of losing the South African market, the British government was hesitant to impose its will on the British cricket establishment when the cricket board, despite growing international pressure, appeared determined to continue with the South African tour of England in 1970. That this tour was ultimately cancelled was a singular contribution of the Edinburgh Commonwealth Games of 1970, which ran the threat of being reduced to a white-only affair if the South African cricket tour to Britain had gone on.

D'OLIVERA TO EDINBURGH: CRICKET, THE GAMES AND COERCIVE DIPLOMACY

While there was no apparent connection between cricket and the Commonwealth Games, sports diplomacy resulted in the Games coming into close proximity with cricket in the years between 1968 and 1970. If the South African cricket tour of England in 1970 had not been cancelled, the Commonwealth Games could well have remained whites-only.[21] Commonwealth countries used the Games to bear pressure on the British government and the English Cricket Board to shun cricket relations with South Africa, which had continued uninterrupted during the 1950s and 1960s. That the English cricket establishment had little interest in the growing anti-apartheid campaign is evident from the following comment by Jack Bailey, assistant secretary of the MCC:

> The cricket world was strongly inclined to getting on with the game with South Africa – or anybody else – leaving politics to the politicians. It was, and always will be, an attitude of substance if your brief is the administration of your sport and the well-being of your sport and your penchant is loyalty to good, time-honored and loyal friends, and if you believe contact is more productive than isolation.[22]

Inspired by this mindset, the MCC was keen to carry on with its tour of South Africa in 1968, a tour that was ultimately cancelled because of the fiasco over the inclusion of coloured South African batsman, Basil D'Olivera. The D'Olivera affair, which hogged the limelight in the cricketing world between 1968 and 1970, contributed much to the souring of the relationship between the MCC (subsequently TCCB) and the South African Cricket Association (SACA).

The controversy started when the newly elected South African prime minister, Balthazar Johannes Vorster, communicated to the MCC that though his government was willing to send a mixed South African team to the Mexico Olympics in 1968, he was unwilling to allow Basil D'Olivera, a coloured South African domiciled in England, to play for the English against South Africa in South Africa. While it amounted to a blatant violation of his own policy of encouraging mixed sport, Vorster looked at D'Olivera's inclusion in the MCC team as an attempt by the anti-apartheid lobby to use sport to hurt South African political interests. Faced with such a threat, the MCC, which had included D'Olivera in the touring team when Tom Cartwright had withdrawn citing injury, had little option but to cancel the tour.

The cancellation was the logical culmination of a mounting protest movement led by Reverend David Sheppard and John Arlott. Sheppard and Arlott had earlier protested against the MCC's initial decision to leave out D'Olivera, labelling the decision as one based on political considerations.[23]

Once the tour to South Africa was cancelled due to the obstinacy of the South African premier, attention shifted to South Africa's forthcoming tour of England in 1970, a tour that the cricket establishments in both countries were determined should carry on. It is with this objective that two influential SACA representatives, Vice President Jack Cheetham and Arthur Coy, flew to London to hold meetings with the honchos of the MCC.[24] That they were largely successful was evident when the MCC declared its intentions to go ahead with the 1970 tour on grounds that mainstream public opinion favoured the continuation of the tour, which was economically a profitable proposition.

It was also argued that cancellation amounted to bowing down to blackmail by a minority fringe determined to politicize sport. The MCC was encouraged to take such a stand because it knew well that the government, despite opposing the move in principle, preferred to stay away from direct political intervention in sporting affairs. Such intervention was contrary to the oft-stated government policy of allowing sport to retain its autonomy. It could also have, perhaps, jeopardized existing trade relations with South Africa, which would have been detrimental to the British economy. The economy was still heavily dependent on the growing South African market, something that the government was well aware of, and which it knew could be lost in case of a direct intervention in sporting matters.[25]

Soon after the MCC intention was made public, the Commonwealth Games participants from Africa swung into action. Having realized that the Edinburgh Games were an opportunity to drive home their point, the Supreme Council for Sport in Africa (SCSA), as Bruce Murray has documented, threatened that a slew of African countries would boycott the Commonwealth Games scheduled for Edinburgh in July 1970 should the tour go ahead:

> Cricket was placed in the awkward position of seeming to sabotage the Commonwealth Games if it stubbornly proceeded with the tour, but that was likewise resented at Lord's as a crude attempt at political blackmail. As the Foreign and Commonwealth Office submitted in a note for the Cabinet, it could not be expected that the Cricket Council would back down in the face of the African threat: 'they would be criticized bitterly by their supporters for giving in to black blackmail after having held out against strong white pressures and threats.' The real challenge of the African boycott threat was to the government, and it was this that put the whole question of the South African tour on the Cabinet agenda.[26]

Getting the African Commonwealth countries to speak in one voice was SANROC, which was keen to enlist the support of the Asian bloc to strengthen its anti-apartheid campaign. In March 1970, two key SANROC members – Chris de Broglio and Wilfrid Brutus – attended the General Assembly of the Supreme Council for Sport in Africa in Cairo to lobby for action against the cricket tour. In what came as a major boost for SANROC's activities, the General Assembly agreed 'that no African team would attend the Games unless the MCC's decision to invite a South African cricket team was reversed'. However, this decision wasn't revealed to the world till 23 April, allowing the MCC to carry on with its preparations for the tour.

Once it was informed that the Commonwealth Games stood to lose all sheen if the threat wasn't taken seriously, the British government was forced to act.[27] Soon, it was seen exerting diplomatic pressure on the MCC to cancel the tour. SANROC's hand was strengthened when it received unequivocal support from Jamaica, Trinidad, Barbados and, most importantly, from India.

New Delhi, which had established itself as a key Commonwealth player by then, instructed all Indian cricketers playing in the county circuit not to play in any match involving a South African cricketer. The British government, it was later evident, would not have been unduly worried had the Indians not thrown their weight behind the 'Stop the Seventy Tour' campaign. Soon after the Indians had made known their intention of boycotting the Edinburgh Games, the British Commonwealth Games Federation, under duress, appealed to the Wilson government to intervene.

The Indian stand was followed in 1971 by the passing of a further resolution in the UN General Assembly, 2775 D (XXVI), asking sports organizations to uphold the anti-apartheid policies and strongly supporting the growing international campaign against racial discrimination in sports. 'Working in close cooperation with SANROC, the anti-apartheid movements, and the Supreme Council on Sport in Africa, the Special Committee (of the UN General Assembly) against apartheid publicized and denounced all sports exchanges with South Africa, encouraged groups demonstrating against apartheid teams and contacted governments and sports bodies to take action.'[28]

With the prospect of a North–South divide looming large, the government on 21 May 1970 asked the TCCB not to go ahead with the proposed tour. Encouraged by the cancellation of the tour and the success of their endeavour to bring the MCC to book, all of the Commonwealth countries sent in their delegations to Edinburgh in what ultimately turned out to be a spectacularly successful Games from the perspective of spreading the gospel of the 'friendly Games'.

As noted in Chapter 5, the Edinburgh Games, held just months after the cancellation of the MCC tour, finished off in style by introducing a novelty in the course of its closing ceremony. Rather than having the athletes march according to nationalities, which was and is the norm in closing ceremonies of most mega sports events, the Edinburgh organizers invited athletes participating in specific disciplines to march together as a demonstration of Commonwealth harmony. With the white athletes marching together with black and coloured athletes from across the world, it was the best symbolic demonstration of solidarity that sport could put together to strengthen the hands of the spreading anti-apartheid campaign.[29]

SPRINGBOKS, ALL BLACKS AND THE ROAD TO GLENEAGLES

The symbolism of Edinburgh, however, had little impact on racist policies in South Africa. This was evident when F.W. Warring, minister of sport and recreation, declared in Parliament on 12 May 1971 that 'the springbok colors are for white sportsmen only'.[30] The government's policy of promoting racial segregation in sport was reinforced by his successor Dr P.J. Koornhof, minister of sport and recreation in Parliament on 25 May 1973:

> Announcements in respect of certain points of departure relating to sport should therefore be seen as adjustments, development and progress without sacrifice of principles ... The interpretation of the sports policy should constantly be consistent with the country's fundamental policy of separate development. If this is not done, it is not only erroneous and meaningless, but also causes confusion.[31]

Holding firm, the government was determined to consolidate bilateral sporting ties with countries that had continued to defy international pressures and had refused to cut off all sporting engagements with South Africa. New Zealand, under Premier Robert Muldoon, was one such. In 1976, its rugby team toured South Africa at a time when world attention was focussed on the Montreal Olympics.

Though Canada, the hosts, had nothing to do with the tour, twenty-nine African nations, along with Guyana and Iraq, left Montreal just days before the Games to protest against the IOC's non-committal stand against the racist South African regime. While such action was widely criticized by the Western press, the boycott, as Bruce Kidd argues, achieved both immediate and long-term results. In a matter of days, international federations of track and field and soccer expelled South Africa.

Within the Commonwealth, the boycott stimulated the adoption of the 1977 Gleneagles Agreement between Commonwealth prime ministers, which made it a prerequisite for member states to 'combat the evil of apartheid by withholding any form of support for, and by taking every practical step to discourage contact or competition by their nationals with sporting organizations, teams or sportsmen from South Africa or any other country where sports are organized on the basis of race, colour or ethnic origin'.[32]

CANADIAN CHANGE: GLENEAGLES, TURMOIL AND EDMONTON 1978

The Montreal boycott served as a warning for the Canadian organizers of the 1978 Edmonton Commonwealth Games. A boycott along similar lines threatened to put the Edmonton Games in jeopardy at a time when the Canadian government had already spent a huge $12 million on capital costs.[33] It also ran the risk of adversely affecting the future of the Games as an institution that aimed to foster a spirit of friendly rivalry among athletes of the Commonwealth.

To compound problems, there was growing pressure from activist organizations demanding more concerted action against apartheid, which was so far lacking in Canada. All of these explain why Canada took a much stronger position against racially segregated sport in the lead up to the 1978 Commonwealth Games.

The principal task confronting the organizers was to get New Zealand to accept the majority stand on apartheid sport. That New Zealand, too, was willing to compromise was evident when, in October 1976, the Kiwi foreign minister, B.E. Talboys, declared in a statement that he expected all New Zealand sports bodies to seriously consider UN resolutions on apartheid sport before agreeing to further sporting ties with South Africa.[34] This came soon after a statement by the minister of state, Sir Keith Holyoake, discouraging sports bodies from sending teams to South Africa. As a follow-up to these statements, the New Zealand Rugby Union, in December 1976, refused an invitation to tour South Africa. This was despite the South African willingness to allow Maoris to be part of the team. The prime minister of New Zealand, Muldoon, congratulated them on the decision but, at the same time, refused to acknowledge that his government had moved away from its stance of non-interference. This was confusing because Muldoon had responded to a letter from Jean-Claude Ganga, secretary general of the SCSA, by 'indicating that his government supported the campaign against apartheid, and deploring the selection of any sports team on the basis of racial discrimination. Furthermore, Muldoon stated that he believed that significant contacts with racially selected teams from South Africa would no longer take place.'[35] The ostensible change in attitude appeared to work when the SCSA executive announced in January 1977 that it was against a boycott of the Edmonton Games. However, this decision was soon made contingent on New Zealand severing all sporting links with South Africa.

The situation was so grim that Commonwealth Secretary General Sridath Ramphal announced in June 1977 that unless the impasse was resolved soon, he was looking at the possibility of requesting the CGF to postpone or cancel the Edmonton Games. Soon after this announcement, Iona Campagnolo, Canada's fitness and amateur sports minister, issued a statement that emphasized Canada's determination to spearhead the movement for South African isolation. 'The government will, in the future, strongly discourage and, if necessary, take a very critical attitude in public towards any proposed sporting contact between Canadians and South Africans, whether federal funding is involved or not.'[36] While this statement wasn't backed by any real policy decision, the rhetoric did much to convince Commonwealth heads of government about Canada's commitment to the anti-apartheid policy.

CHOGM was taking place in London and, on the third day of deliberations, when the heads of government had retired for a one-day retreat to Gleneagles, Scotland, the issue of the Games boycott came to the fore. The outcome of these negotiations was a path-breaking draft that eventually came to be known as the Gleneagles Declaration of 1977. It was formally presented to the leaders when the meeting reconvened in London and was unanimously passed by all diplomats and heads of state present. The media release issued a day after the agreement declared that:

> The member countries of the Commonwealth, embracing peoples
> of diverse races, colours, languages and faiths, have long recognized

racial prejudice and discrimination as a dangerous sickness and an unmitigated evil and are pledged to use all their efforts to foster human dignity everywhere. At their London Meeting, Heads of Government reaffirmed that apartheid in sport, as in other fields, is an abomination and runs directly counter to ... Commonwealth Principles ...

They were conscious that sport is an important means of developing and fostering understanding between the people, and especially between the young people, of all countries. But, they were also aware that, quite apart from other factors, sporting contacts between their nationals and the nationals of countries practising apartheid in sport tend to encourage the belief (however unwarranted) that they are prepared to condone this abhorrent policy or are less than totally committed to the Principles embodied in their Singapore Declaration. Regretting past misunderstandings and difficulties and recognizing that these were partly the result of inadequate inter-governmental consultations, they agreed that they would seek to remedy this situation in the context of the increased level of understanding now achieved.

They reaffirmed their full support for the international campaign against apartheid and welcomed the efforts of the United Nations to reach universally accepted approaches to the question of sporting contacts within the framework of that campaign.[37]

The South African activist scholar and leader, Sam Ramsamy, later provided a most gripping ringside-view account of the lead up to the Gleneagles Agreement. We quote it here at length to convey some of the drama and the urgency of the diplomatic twists and turns that led up to the agreement:

Wednesday, 9 March 1977

The grapevine suggests we will see positive developments at the Commonwealth Heads of Government Meeting in June. CHOGM, at it is popularly known, will be held in London. This is encouraging.

It seems as though the Canadian Prime Minister, Pierre Trudeau, is pressing for the meeting to take a united stand against apartheid sport, and so persuade the African countries to compete at next year's 1978 Commonwealth Games in Edmonton. He wants to avoid a Montreal-style boycott.

We are now working hard behind the scenes, preparing draft statements, finding the words that would satisfy the African nations on the one hand and countries like Britain and New Zealand on the other. As always, this is a delicate balancing act.

A Springbok rugby tour of New Zealand is looming in a few years' time, and a right-wing New Zealand prime minister has recently been elected after campaigning in favour of the rugby tour, saying, 'I will personally attend the Test matches.'

As usual, Jeremy Pope, legal adviser at the Commonwealth Secretariat and a determined and exceptionally bright supporter of our cause, is playing an important role in preparing a draft document for the attention of Commonwealth Secretary General Sridath Ramphal.

Wednesday, 15 June 1977

At CHOGM meetings, it has become traditional for Heads of Government to take a day out of their formal meetings, and escape to a more relaxed environment. This time, they have escaped from London and decamped to Gleneagles in Scotland.

In these beautiful surroundings, they have finally approved a comprehensive declaration on apartheid sport.

We have received a document entitled the Commonwealth Statement on Apartheid Sport, although it is already being called the Gleneagles Agreement. It's pretty emphatic.

'Apartheid in sport, as in other fields, is an abomination,' it declares unequivocally, adding that sporting contact with South Africa represents tacit approval of apartheid.

The statement then concludes: 'The Head of Government specially welcomed the belief, unanimously expressed at their meeting, that there are unlikely to be future sporting contacts of any significance between Commonwealth countries, or their nationals, and South Africa while that country continues to pursue the detestable policy of apartheid. On the (sic) basis, and having regard to their commitments, they looked forward with satisfaction to the holding of the 1978 Commonwealth Games in Edmonton and to the continued strengthening of Commonwealth sport generally.'

Some of our allies, notably Abraham Ordia and the Nigerian delegation, felt the wording could have been stronger, and there is no doubt at we would have preferred a firm commitment to stop all sporting contact with South Africa, but I believed we had reached a reasonable compromise. It was worthwhile.

Apparently Ramphal orchestrated the whole affair with a touch of genius. New Zealand's Muldoon was the likely sticking point. After considering the strengths and personal relationships of the various leaders, Ramphal mandated Jamaica's prime minister, Michael Manley, to tell Muldoon he had no option but to go along with the document. Manley chose to do this in the hotel bar.

At least, the Commonwealth has taken a stand together. In some ways, a noose has been placed around the neck of apartheid sport. Our challenge in the coming months and years is to sustain our campaigns and, tug by tug, to tighten that noose.

The Gleneagles Agreement is a huge achievement for us. For the first, time an international governmental organization has signed up to our cause.[38]

In July 1977, as Macintosh and Greenhorn have written, the New Zealand Parliament approved the Gleneagles Declaration and Prime Minister Muldoon called upon all sports bodies to comply with the principles enshrined in the declaration. Such an announcement was cause for great relief for the organizers of the Edmonton Games and they were now confident of staving off the boycott threat.[39]

Not resting on their laurels, the organizers followed up the Gleneagles Declaration by undertaking a tour of Africa during the fall of 1977. Maury Van Vliet, president of the Edmonton Commonwealth Games Federation, met with representatives from all of the African Commonwealth countries and reinforced Canada's belief in the Gleneagles Declaration.[40]

Finally, the Games received a major shot in the arm when, in December 1977, the Canadian government announced a package to demonstrate its commitment against apartheid. The package asked for the cancellation of all government-funded commercial activities with, and urged immediate stoppage of all exports to, South Africa.[41] It also proposed new visa regulations for South Africans.

Previously, South Africans could enter Canada with just a valid passport, as was the norm for most Commonwealth citizens. However,

Prime Minister Pierre Elliot Trudeau was unwilling to seek Cabinet approval, knowing that a strong opposition was brewing against the government's proposed immigration policy. In July 1978, though, the federal government finally accepted the new immigration policies and disallowed visas for all South African athletes wanting to enter Canada to compete in sports meets or conventions. This decision, which ran counter to the government's earlier stand of not changing immigration rules, went a long way in securing the participation of the African Commonwealth countries at Edmonton.[42] Soon after the promulgation of the new immigration rules, eleven of the thirteen African commonwealth members confirmed their participation at the Games, a decision wholeheartedly welcomed by the organizers and the Commonwealth Games Federation.

The celebrations were somewhat spoilt when Nigeria, all of a sudden, announced its intention to boycott the Games and also started a clandestine campaign to ensure that other African nations reversed their decision to participate.[43] Because the Nigerian decision had come very late in the day, there was little time left to convince them to reverse the decision. Much to the relief of the organizers, Nigerian attempts at lobbying failed and all African nations except Nigeria, Uganda and Botswana were present in Edmonton for the opening ceremony of the Games.

BRISBANE 1982: NEW ZEALAND'S U-TURN AND A NEW CODE OF CONDUCT

The success of the Edmonton Games had little impact on the South African situation. This was best borne out when F.W. De Clerk, minister for sport and recreation, declared in Parliament within months of the Edmonton Games that 'the National Party reaffirms its well-known standpoints on sport as formulated in 1976 as general and fundamental guidelines to be pursued wherever practicable. Exceptional circumstances do not always permit of consistent implementation of the mentioned guidelines and it is recognized that special arrangements are justified in such circumstances. But necessary deviations must be guarded against, and exceptions must be dealt with in such a way that they do, in fact, prove the rule'.[44]

Canada may have changed sides on the South African question but trouble was brewing in New Zealand. The South African political establishment received a boost because the New Zealand government had, in a dramatic about turn following the Gleneagles Accord, declared that it wouldn't interfere in sporting matters and sports bodies were free to play against whoever they chose. Inspired by this attitude, six New Zealand sports bodies flouted the agreement and reiterated their commitment to sporting relations with South Africa.[45]

While such actions prompted Halt All Racist Tours (HART), an organization set up in 1969 in New Zealand to spearhead the anti-apartheid campaign, to mount a stinging criticism of these bodies, the government continued to be indifferent and refused to get the Gleneagles Accord ratified in Parliament.

All Blacks Again

In line with the New Zealand government's indifference, the New Zealand Rugby Federation, in late 1978, reversed a decision prohibiting six All Blacks players from playing in a festival tournament in Northern Transvaal.[46] Despite criticism from the Commonwealth secretary general, the proposed tour received a boost when newly appointed minister for Maori affairs, Ben Couch, supported it.

As this was shaping up to be the most violent breach of the Gleneagles Accord yet, HART, as Trevor Richards, leader, diplomat and member of the UN Secretariat argued, pledged an 'intensive international and national campaign' to check the visit. The only New Zealand government official opposing the visit, it appeared, was Foreign Minister B.E. Talboys, who, in January 1979, wrote to each of the six players, drawing their attention to New Zealand's support for the Gleneagles Accord.[47]

The pressure tactics failed. Eight All Blacks toured South Africa in March 1979 with former captain Brian Lochore travelling as manager. To add insult to injury, Lochore remarked on returning to New Zealand that substantial progress had been achieved in integrating South African sport and much of the credit for this improvement was due to the All Blacks tours of South Africa in 1970 and 1976.[48] This was the most blatant breach of the Gleneagles Accord and had occurred just months before the Commonwealth heads of state met in Lusaka.

At Lusaka, however, as Trevor Richards lamented, the CHOGM was hardly concerned with issues pertaining to sporting contacts and spent all their time deliberating on the deteriorating political situation in Zimbabwe.[49] Accordingly, though the 1979 Lusaka Declaration of the Commonwealth Prime Ministers on Racism and Racial Prejudice reaffirmed its faith in the Gleneagles Agreement, it did not pre-empt all Commonwealth ties with South Africa. As a result, in 1981, as Bruce Kidd argues, 'despite unprecedented pressure from the rest of the Commonwealth and the withdrawal of a finance ministers' conference scheduled for Wellington, the New Zealand government permitted a South African rugby tour to take place.'[50]

Soon after the tour, African countries issued a call to boycott the 1982 Brisbane Commonwealth Games unless New Zealand was banned from participating in the competition. New Zealand, it was apparent, had clearly emerged as the problem child with all other nations reinforcing their belief in the Gleneagles Accord and severing sporting ties with South Africa.

The New Symbolism of Gleneagles Policing

Understandably uneasy at such unpleasant developments, the Brisbane organizers convened a special meeting of the CGF's general assembly in London on 5 May 1982. At this meeting, a compromise was struck whereby New Zealand could participate in Brisbane since there was no procedure to pre-empt them from doing so but a 'policing mechanism for the Gleneagles agreement would soon be placed in the Federation's constitution'.[51] This policing mechanism took the form of a code of conduct, which was to henceforth govern the implementation of the Gleneagles Declaration, and which became the basis of African participation at Brisbane. It was ratified in Brisbane with only England, Nigeria and New Zealand abstaining during the voting.[52]

The new code of conduct, as Bruce Kidd has argued, was 'unprecedented in the scope of its undertaking'. It clearly laid out what constituted a breach in the Gleneagles Agreement for individual Commonwealth sportsmen, for Commonwealth sportsmen as members of teams and for Commonwealth sports administrators:

For Individual Commonwealth sportsmen: competing in a sports event in a country which practises apartheid or competing elsewhere in a sports event in which an individual from such a country is competing in a representative capacity for his country or sports body.

For Commonwealth sportsmen as members of teams: participating in a sports event which includes a team from a country which practises apartheid.

For Commonwealth sports administrators: planning or facilitating such competition or participation by Commonwealth sportsmen as noted above.[53]

It also called upon the national Commonwealth Games bodies to enforce Gleneagles, failing which strict action would be taken against them, and required member associations to prevent sporting contacts with South Africa or a country that practised apartheid even if such contact was taking place in a non-Commonwealth Games sport. In case member associations were found to condone such contacts, strict penalties could be imposed on them.[54]

The code meant that the Commonwealth Games Association of Canada, which had earlier contented itself with sending a team to the Games, was to now ensure that other sports governing bodies of Canada did not foster any sporting ties with any South African sports body or individual.

One result of the adoption of the code of conduct, as Bruce Kidd explained, was that it brought about a 'dramatic change in the symbolism of the Games. As the British Empire Games they were held together by the imperial connection and a common love of sport fostered by colonialism and overseas settlement. Now their effective basis is a united stance against apartheid and other forms of racism in sport. Under Article 11.6, the General Assembly may, by special resolution, 'with a view to ensuring that future Commonwealth Games are not impaired and where it is satisfied for good cause that there has been gross non-fulfilment of the objectives of the Gleneagles Declaration of 1977 by the action of a country in relation to its obligations under the Gleneagles Declaration or of its Commonwealth Games Association and such actions imperil the forthcoming Commonwealth Games, suspend the right to participate in future Commonwealth Games of that country's Commonwealth Games Association'.[55]

The code, in the immediate future at least, had a mixed impact. At Brisbane in 1982, all African nations participated and the Games did not suffer from any immediate threat of boycott. At the same time, however, the atmosphere was highly politically charged with the African nations determined to make their displeasure felt over New Zealand's participation. Security in Brisbane, contemporary reports mentioned, was tighter than ever and there were guards and checkpoints almost everywhere in the Games Village. Further, Queensland Premier Johannes Bjelke Petersen called in sixty members of the SAS, Super Australian Soldiers, to handle a potentially volatile situation.[56]

Ultimately, the Games passed without any incident and, in fact, witnessed great scenes of camaraderie between rival athletes, a fact extolled by the reporter of the *Toronto Star* who wrote:

> Take a stroll through the athletes' village and your cynical view of the world lifts for a while. A sprinter from England sits watching a concert and trading criticisms of the band with a shot putter from Guyana and a boxer from Nigeria. A Canadian discus thrower walks up and introduces herself to a group of Zimbabwe throwers and an animated discussion on technique ensues. Smiles are the order of the day. Elsewhere there may be hatred and prejudice, but in this small corner of the world there is only mutual respect. It's an artificial environment of course, one that will disappear in ten days. Even now, once outside, you recall it only vaguely as in a dream.[57]

Soon after Brisbane, the Commonwealth world was once again united against apartheid when the New Zealand Rugby Union threatened to undertake a tour of South Africa in 1985. This agitation is perceived as one of the climactic moments in the struggle against apartheid. The drama of the moment is best summed up in Sam Ramsamy's account published in 1985. Sam came close to selling his apartment to finance the campaign against the All Blacks tour and his blow-by-blow narration best sums up the urgency that animated the controversy. In his words:

Friday, 12 July 1985

> I received a telephone call around three o'clock this morning in London, just after lunch in Wellington, New Zealand. The conversation

lasted only a few minutes, after which Helga turned to me and blearily asked what was wrong.

'Not much, dear,' I said, 'the lawyers in New Zealand need NZ$1 million by this afternoon.'

'What are we going to do?' she asked, now sitting up, wide awake and alert to the crisis on the other side of the world.

'Well. We may have to use the flat as collateral,' I said.

Silence.

'OK,' she whispered, and we both went back to sleep.

The following situation had unfolded: the New Zealand rugby team was scheduled to tour South Africa in 1985, and we had sent our representative, Reverend Arnold Stofile, to New Zealand to try and dissuade officials and players from going ahead.

He worked hard and effectively, but the rugby authorities were determined to proceed and, upon his return to South Africa, he was promptly thrown into prison, indicating the degree of collusion that existed between Muldoon's New Zealand and apartheid South Africa.

As a last resort, two club players in Auckland, Phillip Recordon and Patrick Finnegan, used their legal knowledge to bring a court action against the New Zealand Rugby Football Union (NZRFU) on the grounds that they were acting contrary to its rules and constitution by accepting an invitation to tour South Africa.

The NZRFU constitution states that the Union must act in the best interests of the game and the two players claimed that they had a contract with the NZRFU that they were entitled to enforce.

The case was initially struck out by Chief Justice Sir Ronald Davison on the basis that Recordon and Finnegan were not of proper standing as members of the NZRFU. However, this ruling was in part overturned by the Court of Appeal and the case went to the High Court in Wellington to be heard by Mr Justice Casey.

Ted Thomas, a Queen's Counsel who was later a Court of Appeal Judge, headed the legal team. Jeremy Pope had helped to prepare the case and spoke to Ted every day, suggesting that he ask for an interim order to prevent the team from traveling on the following Monday.

However, this morning (London time) he told Jeremy that he could not apply, as it would bankrupt his clients. He had spoken to the NZRFU lawyers and they wanted a copper-bottom guarantee for $1 million.

The team would be leaving in three days' time, but the court would continue to hear the case through the weekend. Jeremy asked Ted to hold fire and not to abandon the idea of the interim order. 'Just give me twelve hours and let me see what I can do,' he said. Ted agreed.

It was at this point that Jeremy called me at three this morning, asking where we could find NZ$1 million in twelve hours.

'Well, Sam,' Jeremy said, 'there's only one solution that I can see, and that's for you to offer your Hampstead flat as a guarantee, but that's obviously a gamble for you and Helga and there's no certainty that the two players will win the case. This is making new law.'

I felt it needed to be done. We needed to stop the tour, and Helga agreed with me.

It all seemed pretty hairy, but Ted Thomas – more than surprised at the speed with which all this had been accomplished – said he would apply for the interim injunction first thing on Saturday morning.

If it is physically possible to go to sleep while holding one's breath, that is exactly what I achieved that night.

Saturday, 13 July 1985

It's five o'clock in the morning in London, mid-afternoon in New Zealand, and the telephone is ringing again. I recognize Ted Thomas's voice immediately and he tells me that Mr Justice Casey has just granted the interim injunction against the tour. It is the lead on the BBC World Service news bulletins; Jeremy and I can hardly believe we have managed to pull this off.

Thursday, 18 July 1985

I hear Ces Blazey, chairman of the NZRFU Council, interviewed on the radio and he says the NZRFU has cancelled all plans for a tour to South Africa, but adds there is now talk of the All Blacks wanting to tour as individuals, without the consent of their union.

Sunday, 21 July 1985

South Africa is first on the BBC TV news tonight. After protests in townships near Johannesburg and Cape Town, the State President, P.W. Botha, has declared a State of Emergency,

Tuesday, 23 July 1985.

We are told the New Zealand rugby players have met to discuss their options and finally decided to stay at home.

Their South African tour is cancelled. We have won.[58]

THE EDINBURGH BOYCOTT

Edmonton and Brisbane had avoided the boycotts. Edinburgh was not so lucky. With New Zealand falling in line, it was inevitable that Edinburgh 1986 would turn into a major show of strength for the anti-apartheid campaign. In fact, the agitation had turned significantly more aggressive in the interim and most Commonwealth nations threatened to boycott the Games in Scotland if Britain, the erstwhile mother country, did not impose economic sanctions against South Africa.

The organizers had the first whiff of the brewing boycott threat in May 1986, when a number of African nations announced their intention to boycott the Games if England, under Margaret Thatcher, held on to her policy of not imposing economic sanctions against South Africa. No fewer than thirty-two countries, from Africa, Asia and the Caribbean were planning to boycott the Games.

As Sam Ramsamy explained:

> The split has been prompted by Britain's refusal to impose sanctions against South Africa. Margaret Thatcher made her stand clear at a Commonwealth Heads of Government meeting in Lusaka, Zambia, thereby precipitating the boycott. Indeed Britain's intransigent attitude prompted Major General Henry Adefope, the Nigerian Foreign Minister, to announce his government would immediately retaliate by nationalizing the British Petroleum operations in Nigeria. Rightwing British newspapers have accused countries like Nigeria of being so wedded to a political agenda that they never had any intention of competing in Edinburgh. This is nonsense. The Nigerians have already spent more than US$ 1 million preparing their athletes for the Games.[59]

The threat turned real in early July when Nigeria, Uganda, Ghana, Tanzania and Kenya pulled out of the Games.[60] Ghana's boycott significantly weakened the Games field in boxing, while Kenya's withdrawal adversely affected the track and field competitions with Paul Kipkoegh and John Ngugi, ranked one and three in the 5000 metres, not competing.[61] Even the showpiece events, like the 100-metre sprint, were affected. Nigeria's Chidi Imoh, who finished second behind Canada's Ben Johnson at the Goodwill Games, and Nigeria's number-one ranked 400-metre runner Innocent Egbunike were also absent from Edinburgh, substantially weakening the fields in both these events.[62]

Compounding problems for the organizers, there was a distinct possibility of high-profile individual black athletes pulling out, demanding imposition of immediate sanctions against South Africa. Under fire, the organizers, on 13 July, expelled South African-born athletes Zola Budd and Annette Cowley from the Games. This expulsion, records indicate, was looked upon as a major success by the leaders of the anti-apartheid campaign. We refer back to Sam Ramasamy's diary to highlight how the campaigners pooled their efforts together:

Sunday, 13 July 1986

Zola Budd and Annette Cowley, a South African swimmer claiming to be British, have today been withdrawn from the English team to compete at the Commonwealth Games in Edinburgh. Another long SANROC campaign has yielded a positive result.

We have simply pointed out that neither Budd nor Cowley had spent the legally required number of days in Britain to sustain their qualification to compete the Games. Budd was effectively based in South Africa, and Cowley spent most of her time in the United States. Neither could be described as resident in the UK.

Our opponents repeatedly claim we are bullying these young girls, but this has never been personal. The fact is that high-profile South African athletes competing on the international stage under a flag of convenience represent a coup for apartheid.

Within our continuing campaign to isolate and eventually overcome apartheid in sport, we cannot stand by and allow such blatant abuses to go unchallenged; in the past few months, we have argued our case in a calm and rational manner.

This afternoon, I telephoned Sharad Rao, legal adviser to the Commonwealth Games Federation, and Jeremy Pope to thank them for their efforts in preparing our case.

In fact, people have been complaining that Jeremy spends too much time assisting SANROC, but the situation is under control. The Secretary-General of the Commonwealth, Sir Sridath Ramphal, is a strong supporter of our cause, and he has simply asked Jeremy to be more discreet in his antiapartheid activities.

Kader Asmal, a South African exile based in Ireland, has also played an important role in drawing up the legal documents relating to Budd and Cowley. This has been a team effort.

Tuesday, 15 July 1986

The controversy over Budd and Cowley is still rumbling on, with a few newspapers casting them as innocent victims and claiming we have attacked them just because they are white.

In a series of media interviews this afternoon, I have tried to set the record straight and make two points clear.

First, even their supporters accept that both Budd and Cowley would have eased the situation if they had publicly condemned the system of apartheid. Neither has been willing to do so.

Second, their case is often compared to that of Sidney Maree, a black South African middle-distance runner who settled in the USA and has been competing under the American flag. Critics ask why we pursue Budd, and leave Maree alone.

The difference is simple.

Our opposition to Budd lies in the fact that, by steadfastly refusing to denounce apartheid, she has allowed herself to become generally portrayed as a symbol of the system, and she has been unashamedly hailed as such inside South Africa.

As evident from the above account, the expulsion left the political class divided. While the left-wingers supported this step, right-wing politicians were critical and labelled the step as a cheap act in trying to prevent the boycott from spreading.[63]

That the African boycott had every chance of spreading was evident when India, on 14 July, declared its intention to stay away if things did not look up in Britain. True to its promise, the Indian government asked its 125-member contingent to delay their departure for Edinburgh.[64]

Following India's lead, Sierra Leone, Bahamas and Papua New Guinea joined the boycott squad on 17 July, adding to the organizers' woes.[65] Trinidad and Tobago, Zimbabwe and Jamaica followed suit. Announcing the Jamaican decision, Minister for Youth and Community Development Edmund Bartlett declared that the decision to pull out was a question of principle in keeping with the country's anti-apartheid stance.[66]

With the situation spiralling out of control, the British government decided to step in and, soon, the British high commissioner in Zimbabwe, Robert Martin, delivered individual letters from the British government to a series of front-line African leaders.[67] The letters, it was later revealed, had statements by Prime Minister Margaret Thatcher and British Foreign Secretary Geoffrey Howe, explaining the government's position on South Africa. Following the government's initiative in trying to salvage the Games, the front-line leaders intensified the offensive. This was evident when Zambian President Kenneth Kaunda declared that they had not yet discussed the issue of withdrawing from the Commonwealth: 'The Commonwealth is a very important organization. It is an organization that cuts across colour, religion and many other gulfs that separate mankind today. It will be very sad to lose that organization.' He went on to add: 'We have not decided to boycott the Games. What we have done is we have decided to ask Mrs Thatcher what she will do. The ball is back in her court. We will consider what she says as long as it is before the 24th of July.'[68]

Amidst growing opposition, the organizers received some support when the Canadians decided to join the competition and the mainstream Canadian media criticized the boycott arguing that such an action was a 'futile sacrifice of a lifetime of costly training by athletes and will do nothing to encourage an end to apartheid in South Africa'.[69] The Canadians, though, were in a minority.

The West African country of Gambia and seven other Caribbean states joined the boycott bandwagon on 19 July. Even Lesotho, a tiny kingdom landlocked by South Africa, decided to stay away from Edinburgh. Fearing a backlash from South Africa, Lesotho High Commissioner John Kolane stated in London that their decision had little to do with apartheid and was due to them not having athletes of the desired standard.[70]

With just days to go before the event, the organizers were eagerly waiting for the Indian decision. They were offered partial relief when an Indian foreign ministry spokesperson suggested that India was not planning to join the boycott if Margaret Thatcher promised to address the South African question at the London summit due in August. An Indian pullout, Canadian observers feared, 'would not only deal a mighty blow to the prestige and credibility of the Games, it will also have serious implications for the future of the Commonwealth group'.[71]

While the Canadian media was deeply divided over the apartheid issue, it was interesting that the government was holding firm. The manager of the Canadian team, Jim Daly, declared, 'We saw what effect the boycott had on the 1976 Olympics in Montreal. To be honest, the only way some of these countries would get their name in the papers is to boycott the Games.'[72] However, the official Canadian stand was considerably tempered after the prime minister's staff met officials of the external affairs ministry. It was decided that Foreign Minister Otto Jelinek would travel to Edinburgh and update the prime minister on the developing ground situation. The tempered stand was partly an outcome of the New Democratic Party declaration that it was in Canadian interests to withdraw from the Games. 'Participating in what could be an all-white Games would be damaging to the spirit of the Commonwealth. While we don't believe a boycott is an appropriate method to protest against British policy on sanctions against South Africa, we also believe it is wrong for Canada to participate in an all-white Games.'[73]

Cornered from all quarters, the Edinburgh organizers hit back warning that boycotting nations would be billed the equivalent of $4 million as cancellation fee. Robert Maxwell, chairman of the Games Organizing Committee, declared, 'You must hit them in the pocket. The boycotting governments have caused a great deal of inconvenience and loss.'[74] He concluded saying that the Games organizers would demand compensation from the British government if the Games ended with a negative balance sheet as a result of the boycotts. The organizers were now prepared to roll out the red carpet for any country willing to participate. The desperation showed when Games director Jack Hall declared very late in the day that 'any country can still enter competitors and I am quite prepared to put their names into the computer and enter them'.[75]

The Queen Vs Margaret Thatcher

By now it was clear that Edinburgh would be nothing like a 'friendly Games'. Adding a further twist in the tale, news broke of a rift between the Queen and the prime minister over the apartheid issue. On 22 July, a news report in the *London Times* by Simon Freeman mentioned that the growing boycott of the Commonwealth Games over Britain's stance on South Africa had led to widespread speculation in the country of a growing rift between the Queen and the prime minister. He somewhat intriguingly suggested that 'far from being a middle-aged grandmother who is most at ease when she is talking about horses or dogs, the Queen is an astute political infighter who is quite prepared to take on Downing Street when provoked'.[76] The report went on to predict that the Queen was determined to safeguard the interests of the Commonwealth and was determined not to allow her prime minister to destroy its fabric after having nurtured it for thirty long years through the tumultuous era of postcolonial resistance and the crisis over the Zimbabwe–Rhodesia civil war. It concluded with the words: 'The key to a successful working relationship between the British Prime Minister and the Queen appears to lie in their accepting or pretending to accept the Queen's view that she has responsibilities beyond the immediate interests of the government.'[77]

The depth of the Queen's feeling was best described by Arnold Smith, secretary general of the Commonwealth between 1965 and 1975: 'She believes that the Commonwealth helps reduce tension in the world. She believes the Commonwealth brings different regions and races closer together. She is wise and intelligent, a very considerable stateswoman who has more experience of international politics than any politician.'[78]

The Canadian Public Debate

Difference of opinion over apartheid had also spread far and wide within Canadian society, apparent from the many interesting letters to the editor received by the *Toronto Star*. Here are a few samples:

> Britain's obstinate refusal to employ economic sanctions against a cruel and racist South African regime threatens the breakup of the very organization that makes these Games possible. Boycotting the Games to impart this message to Britain's Prime Minister Margaret Thatcher may well help preserve these amateur events for the future ... The *Star* correspondent's recommendation to African athletes to stage temper tantrums on international television as an alternative to boycott is clearly infantile. The Commonwealth will not be saved by allowing protesters a few moments

of media time while the Center of the Commonwealth, Britain, does nothing effective to oppose one of the vile (sic) regimes in history.

– Thomas K. Bowers, Toronto

Western Attitudes Are Hypocrisy Personified

The attitude of the Western nations and of Canada to South Africa is hypocrisy personified. Assuredly we must condemn South Africa and all others for apartheid and every form of horrible discrimination. However, the black people in most African nations are just as restricted by current laws and roadblocks as those in South Africa and the vote in black Africa is a farce since opposition has been forbidden and black leaders have declared themselves Presidents for life.

– Henry Mathews, Toronto

Thatcher's Morality Ends with Economics

It is amazing to me that Margaret Thatcher can justify the British non-application of economic sanction on South Africa by pointing to the rise in unemployment it would create. Her personal level of morality extends only so far as economics – no thought to the thousands of lives which are destined to be lost violently when the revolution brings the walls tumbling down in that country. The US and British governments are only concerned with the possibility of an economic slowdown precipitated by the economic collapse of their South African ally. Imposing sanctions is by far the fastest and most moral way to ending apartheid. Economics is surely a lesser moral consideration.

– John M. Pope, London, Ontario

History Students Urge End to Business, Trade

We are concerned high school students who are attending summer school at Weston Collegiate Institute. In our Canadian history course, we discussed the issue of apartheid. We feel that Canadian corporations should stop dealing with South Africa. We want the Canadian government to pass a law prohibiting business and trade with South Africa. We believe imposing sanctions will help end apartheid and we would like to see Canada take a leading role in this process. Canada must act now! All people are equal. Racism everywhere must end now!

– Canadian history class, Grade 9, Weston Collegiate Institute, Weston[79]

The Edinburgh boycott, which finally resulted in thirty-two countries staying away from the 1986 Games, was one of the most effective sports boycotts in history. Its deep impact was evident when the IOC, in 1988, passed a declaration against 'apartheid in sport'. The declaration urged members of the Olympic Movement and also the sports federations of all countries to take action to ensure total isolation of any country or organization promoting apartheid in any manner or form.

Vijay Amritraj at the UN

From an Indian perspective, Delhi's stand against apartheid was best articulated by Vijay Amritraj in his speech before the United Nations special committee on apartheid on 6 May 1988. In his deliberation, Amritraj described his experiences of not having played the Davis Cup final in 1974 because India was drawn to play South Africa, the only time India had made it to the final during his tenure till then as player. This was partly a result of his commitment to anti-apartheid sport and partly a result of the government's determination to combat the growing threat of apartheid in the world. As Amritraj put it:

> Sport is big business now and not just a game any more and sportsmen and women must realize the world over that with fame and fortune come an incredible responsibility which may affect the lives of people in different countries. It is very easy to say 'let us keep sports out of politics', but practically that is just not possible in certain cases. There are some issues that we must support or oppose, because we must clearly understand in our minds that we are first human beings before being sportsmen or women … Over the years as a professional, I have been made several offers including vast sums of money to play exhibition matches in South Africa, which I have declined. I feel that every individual, important or unimportant, artist, diplomat, professional or sportsman, has a certain responsibility towards his fellow men and if I may add, hopefully, a conscience. It is thus up to each of us to contribute in our own way towards a better world – a world of equality, of dignity, of freedom.[80]

The united Commonwealth action against apartheid sport had an incredible impact and by the time of the next Games at Auckland in 1990, winds of change had started blowing in South Africa.

AUCKLAND: A NEW ERA

Auckland was far removed from Edinburgh. An unprecedented fifty-four nations were present at the Games. However, that is not to say that there were no scares in the days leading up to the spectacle. With a month or so left for the Games, a group of African nations expressed their displeasure over a proposed rebel English cricket tour of South Africa. It did not turn into a boycott threat because the British government was quick to act and supported a Commonwealth Games Federation resolution condemning the cricket tour.

During the Auckland Games, multiple resolutions were passed against South African apartheid and there was a lot of excitement over the impending release of Nelson Mandela, which marked a real high point in the anti-apartheid struggle.

The euphoria over Mandela's release was such that the Games were often relegated to the sports pages of newspapers with Mr Mandela's release occupying the front page headlines.[81] His historic return to freedom brought an end to three decades of a global campaign that found at least some of its most powerfully symbolic moments on the international sporting stage.

VICTORIA 1994: THE FINAL CHAPTER

Before the South Africans completed the full cycle of their return into the international sporting fold by participating at the 1994 Victoria Commonwealth Games, they had already participated in the 1992 Barcelona Olympics and the Cricket World Cup in Australia and New Zealand in the same year. In fact, it was India that played a dramatic role in South Africa's re-entry into the international sporting realm in 1991.

Though the BCCI had agreed in principle to support the motion for South Africa's re-entry, India's moving of the motion at the ICC was a last-minute decision. Supported by then BCCI President Madhavrao Scindia, Jagmohan Dalmiya moved the proposition for South Africa's readmission at the ICC annual meeting in June 1991. Pakistan seconded it, thus ending a long and agonizing wait outside the world sporting domain for the South Africans.

Soon after the Indian delegation championed the South African cause at the ICC, a friendship series between the two countries was organized in India, marking the first officially recognized South African foray into international sport since readmission. It was Pakistan's cancellation of a proposed tour of India that created room for the historic tour in November 1991. The tour was the culmination of a dramatic forty-eight hours of planning in Kolkata. As Geoff Dakin, president of the United Cricket Board of South Africa was to recall, 'We were in Calcutta on a goodwill visit when Jagmohan Dalmiya proposed this tour. We were, to put it mildly, thrilled. It was a long-cherished dream to tour the country of Mahatma Gandhi. We will never forget the reception we were accorded in Calcutta and at the Eden Gardens. It was special.'[82]

Though the South Africans returned to the world's biggest sporting stage in Barcelona in 1992, their participation at the 1994 Commonwealth Games in Victoria held special significance for the rainbow nation. As Sam Ramsamy put it, 'We are here with a bit more political liberation.'[83] At Victoria, the South Africans marched under a new flag and a new anthem was played every time a South African won a gold medal. The new anthem was a combination of the old African hymn *Die stem* and African liberation song *NKosi*.[84]

To demonstrate to the world that it was indeed a new South Africa, the flag bearer was 800-metre runner Hezekiel Sepeng. The team captain, Mariann Kriel, interestingly, was white. Addressing a press conference, Mleuki George, president of the South African Commonwealth Games Association, and Steve Tshwete, the new sports minister, turned emotional when asked what it felt like to be back. 'We would have died in prison if we did not have hope. We always had hope that one day our country would be free. We bring a strong message for reconciliation. Let bygones be bygones and we must build on the Ashes of the past for the future.'[85]

Of the 112-member South African contingent at Victoria, only seven were black (three boxers and four track athletes). However, Tshwete did not see a problem with such lopsidedness heavily weighed in favour of the whites. 'Very soon the South African team will reflect the demographics of our country, but we do not apologize for the composition of our team as it stands today.' He said that the dearth of blacks representing a nation where blacks far outnumbered the whites was due to the 'historic imbalances' imposed by the policy of apartheid. 'Certainly a situation where black athletes have been left out on the periphery is a situation that cannot be expected to change in four years.'[86] With time he has partially been proved right. Though most South African teams continue to have a white majority, the situation is far improved from what it was at Victoria in 1994.

SPORT AND POLITICS

South Africa's re-entry into the Games after a hiatus of thirty-six years brought to an end a long struggle against human rights violations, a process that harnessed sport for reasons of political and social mobilization, demonstrating the futility of the slogan: 'sports and politics do not mix'.

Though the South African problem was finally brought to a close at Victoria, the close proximity between sport and human rights have continued to dominate the Games, and chances are the situation will be no different come Delhi 2010. That Delhi is apprehensive of protests over issues of human rights violation was evident when Suresh Kalmadi justified the tight security in the capital on 17 April 2008 on the occasion of the Beijing Olympic torch relay arguing: 'We're hosting the Commonwealth Games in 2010. What if some nations want to boycott it citing our rights violation record in Kashmir?' Inherent in his statement was the fear that India might soon find itself confronted with unpleasant questions over the issue of human rights violations in Kashmir ahead of the 2010 Commonwealth Games. As Rohit Mahajan wrote in *Outlook*:

> Kalmadi wasn't speaking up for the world's downtrodden. He was merely cautioning those fanning the flames of trouble for the torch's truncated run in Delhi. His message: keep it quiet, for India has skeletons of its own in its cupboard. All of our rights groups, at home and abroad, agree – India's record on human rights is deplorable.'[87]

As we have said earlier, 'With the Commonwealth Games Village built by demolishing slums on the Yamuna riverbed and with the displaced slum dwellers not properly catered for, Delhi 2010 is a sure site for protests from civil rights groups and NGOs. While some are of the opinion that such protests will hinder Games preparations, a counter view is that only because of the Commonwealth Games will the poor and the displaced get a chance to be heard. To go a step further, more than the medals won or records broken, such actions using the sporting stage make major international sports events like the Commonwealth Games what they are: events that do much to promote inter-cultural communication and understanding.'[88] It is this potential of the Games that this book has repeatedly sought to highlight.

The struggle against apartheid was an acutely political one and provides a unique prism to understand the role played by the Games in the complex evolution of modern societies within the rubric of the Commonwealth. In that sense, the Commonwealth Games Federation, which has managed the Games for over three quarters of a century, has emerged as a composite meeting point of people, power and national interests – a global political arena with all its attendant intrigue, power machinations and high-stakes manoeuvring.

8 | BEIJING TO DELHI: INDIAN SPORT 2010

'The sob story is finally coming to an end. Things are falling into place. And now is the time to go for the kill. By 2016, India will be among the top twenty countries in the Olympic standings.'

– Randhir Singh, secretary general of the IOA,
1 February 2009[1]

THE FACE-SAVERS OF BEIJING

When Sir Dorabji Tata organized the first modern meet of Indian athletes with an eye on the 1920 Antwerp Olympic Games, he found that, despite running barefoot, their performance compared 'well with the times done in Europe or elsewhere'. Suitably impressed, Tata personally financed three of the best runners for Antwerp, a move that in his own words 'fired the ambition of the nationalist element in the city'.[2] Eighty-nine years after that windswept day in Pune, when Tata first dreamt of an individual Olympic gold for India, shooting prodigy Abhinav Bindra finally found the Holy Grail at the 2008 Beijing Games. As the Indian tricolour was hoisted in Beijing, the poise and pride on the bespectacled shooter's visage spoke to a billion Indians, becoming a leitmotif of gung-ho chest thumping in media commentaries and nationalist iconography. In a country undergoing a media revolution like no other – India now has more than fifty twenty-four-hour satellite TV news networks alone – the Beijing victory created an unprecedented national frenzy.[3] In a country of a billion, and a competitive media industry looking for new heroes and new stories, the lone gold medal was justification enough to spark off celebrations worthy of topping the medals tally.

For Indian sport, Beijing was looked upon as a watershed. It was much more than a sporting spectacle not just because India's performance at Beijing was its best ever at the Olympics but also because it heralded the promise of a new beginning for Indian sports. Bindra was not an aberration. His performance was followed by near-podium finishes in badminton, tennis and archery.[4] Just when it was turning out to be a tale of so near yet so far, Vijender Singh (bronze in boxing, 75 kg) and Sushil Kumar (bronze in wrestling, 66 kg, freestyle) ensured that the Indian tricolour went up twice more at Beijing. Their achievements, analysed for hours on television, turned them into national celebrities overnight. If the media catharsis that followed was any indication, for the first time, Olympic sports, apart from hockey, were at the centre stage of what could be termed as the national consciousness. It was an indication that decades of ill-treatment and neglect, which had reduced Olympic sport to a footnote in India, could just change.

At a time when the country was reeling under the impact of serial blasts in Gujarat and Karnataka, followed by the unprecedented carnage in Mumbai in November 2008, medal successes at the Olympics and subsequent international sports competitions like the Boxing World Championships in Moscow in December 2008[5] helped emphasize the point that, across contexts and timeframes, victories can catapult sport to the forefront of a nation's imagination. Three major themes emerged in the discourse that followed: renewed media focus on sport as a nationalist playing field, the promise of a new Indian Olympic culture and the fear that without systemic change in Indian sporting structures, this would be yet another false dawn.

For the first time in Indian sporting history, the media appropriated these accomplishments in a manner associated commonly with cricket. All of a sudden, Bindra was flooded by sponsorship offers that had long since been reserved for over-pampered cricket stars alone. A poll on Times Now, a leading English television news channel, revealed that the national religion of cricket had slid in the popularity charts. According to the survey, 53 per cent of sports fans in Chennai and 44 per cent in Kolkata were glued to the Olympics. In contrast, 41 per cent of sports fans in Chennai and 29 per cent in Kolkata watched the Indian cricket team in action against the Sri Lankans. In Mumbai, an amazing 64 per cent of the fans interviewed were unaware of the ongoing cricket series between India and Sri Lanka.[6]

The medal haul – by Indian standards – at Beijing, it seemed, had suddenly woken up the country to the significance of the Olympics as an event that Indians could win at as well. The medal winners appeared to satisfy a national yearning and, therefore, made a statement about the significance of sport in an era of escalating political turmoil. International sporting success, the victories demonstrated, held the promise of uniting Indians across the country. With some of India's greatest sporting achievements at the Olympics coming at a time when the nation was seeking answers to sudden terror attacks, their impact was all the more visible. In the days before the Olympic Games, most Indians were grappling with the political crisis at hand and were hardly concerned about what the small contingent of fifty-six could achieve in Beijing. So much so that Suresh Kalmadi had issued a statement asking sports fans not to expect miracles from the athletes.[7] Set against this backdrop of gloom and limited expectations, India's successes shone even brighter.

The success of the three Beijing winners was as much a testament to their own skills as it was a metaphor for the larger story of India. Arguably, they had shattered the grand narrative of failure that has characterized Indian sport, almost in the same manner that the emergence of the IT industry in the 1990s signified the end of the 'Hindu rate of growth' that defined the economy since the 1950s. Just as a Narayan Murthy or an Azim Premji – founders of the IT giants Infosys and Wipro – created the self-assurance for Indian business to act as a global player after decades of isolationism and the license–permit raj, so did the Beijing victories usher in a new era of self-confidence in sport. As John MacAloon argues, the Olympics are a 'crucible of symbolic force' into which the world pours its energies and a stage upon which, every four years, it plays 'out its hopes and its terrors'.[8] For every Indian, that terror always came in the form of a question: a billion people and no gold medal. Why? Beijing provided that answer.

The annals of Indian sports writing have been full of complaints about sporting failures for far too long. Analysts have blamed the system, the politicians who run it and have even questioned Indian genetics. Every four years, it has become a collective national ritual to blame everyone else when found wanting in the global mirror of the Olympics, only to move on and repeat the same exercise four years later. The Beijing athletes showed that it is possible to succeed in spite of the system. Late BJP leader Pramod Mahajan had once said half jokingly that the Indian IT and beauty industries rose to great heights only because the government did not realize their presence until they had already made a mark. Abhinav Bindra's success, too, followed a similar template, at least with respect to the national sporting superstructure. Born into affluence and provided with an indoor shooting range in his own home, he emerged as a child prodigy only to taste initial defeat at Sydney and Athens. He could as easily have given up, blamed the system and have been content with his World Championship and Commonwealth Games medals. But he persevered. It was a victory born out of the pain of loss and an iron will to succeed. Here, at last, was India's answer to those that point to the success of Surinam's Anthony Nesty or that of the Ethiopian runners, for that matter. It is indeed possible to succeed without access to government-sponsored sporting facilities. This is not to argue against creating efficient systems – that would be a terrible folly – but in sports there are moments when all it boils down to is self-belief.

As India hosts the Commonwealth Games in 2010, the question that confronts it after Beijing is simple: are we to finally witness the birth of a national sporting culture? Or will Indians clap their hands in glee and return to their daily dose of cricket once the euphoria has receded? The three medals won at Beijing and the lead-up to the Commonwealth Games could certainly be the catalyst to help correct years of frustration at the country's poor sporting performances. With various state governments promising to set up academies to promote boxing, wrestling and shooting, India did look poised in 2008 to have a sporting culture of its own. At the same time, it was important to keep these promises and remember amidst the euphoria of victory that at least fifteen corporate houses had turned down pleas to sponsor the Indian shooters before the Olympics. While the Beijing winners deserved the highest accolades – and corporate coffers had justly opened up for them – the true legacy of these victories depended much on whether money was finally made available to build the training superstructure for other athletes.

Delhi 2010 is an important pit stop in the journey of Indian sport. Lifting up Indian sport is one of its avowed aims. So where do we stand two years after Beijing? Does Randhir Singh's boast of putting India in the Olympic top twenty by 2015 have any basis at all? Or was it just spin? These are the questions this chapter explores.

THE MAKING OF A NATIONAL AUDIENCE

Beijing was no flash-in-the-pan success. Bindra, for instance, was only part of a phalanx of world-class Indian shooters that has emerged in the past decade. Beijing was his moment but each member of the Indian shooting team was capable of winning a medal.[9] Following on from Rajyavardhan Rathore's success at Athens, India, at the time of Beijing, had more than ten shooters in the world's top ten across disciplines, a first in the history of Indian sport. Similarly, Vijender Singh was part of a boxing team in which his compatriot Akhil, and not him, was tipped for a medal in the run-up to the Games. His defeat of the reigning world champion, Russian Sergei Vodopyanov, in the 54-kg pre-quarterfinal turned him into a national hero before he crashed out in the quarter finals, just like his nineteen-year-old roommate, Jitender Kumar, who fought valiantly despite ten stitches on his chin. This is the terrifying beauty of sport, its unpredictability. This is why we watch it – because it showcases all that is glorious and tragic about human nature; all that is uncertain and indescribable. The key for the future is to invest in having enough people at the top echelon of any sport, for one to click when the moment comes.

What has happened since Beijing? Can it be regarded as a true watershed or was it another false dawn? There are many in India who look longingly across the border at China's awe-inspiring sporting machine. The Chinese, too, have built their success by focussing on key sports initially – gymnastics, table tennis, badminton and athletics. India, however, cannot hope to replicate the Chinese model blindly. The organization of Indian sport is far too complicated and far too political to allow for a uniform approach like the Chinese or the East Europeans before them.[10] Like Indian democracy, Indian sport, too, has evolved its own unique model, distinct from everyone else. When the Kapil Dev-led team of underdogs won the Cricket World Cup in

1983, no one could have predicted that the surprise victory, coinciding with the television revolution, would ignite deeper processes that would ultimately turn India into the spiritual and financial heart of global cricket. The Beijing successes created another opportunity that, if harnessed, could well usher in a new era in Indian sport.

As Bindra grabbed gold and the boxers charged through the early rounds, for the first time, a national television audience, led on by a cheerleading media, focussed on Olympic sports. The fact that the entire boxing team had emerged from the small north Indian town of Bhiwani with few facilities or that Sushil Kumar had trained in Delhi's Chatrasal Stadium with rotting wrestling mats and twenty other wrestlers as roommates provided too irresistible a story of human triumph against all odds. The hype was such that even the Haryana chief minister turned up at Vijender's house to watch his semifinal bout. It was a televised photo opportunity for the politician but also an event that led government officials to build a new paved road overnight to show their boss that developmental schemes were working. Similarly, the Delhi chief minister immediately announced a huge cash award for Sushil Kumar and, at the time of writing, he was busy travelling to various international competitions with substantial government support coming his way.

When K.D. Jadhav won India's last wrestling medal at the Helsinki Olympics in 1952 the celebrations at home were extremely muted, restricted to the sports pages of newspapers, unlike the mega hype around Sushil Kumar and the new breed of Indian boxers. To compound Jadhav's agony, the political class gave the victorious hockey team of 1952 a tumultuous welcome in ceremonies across the country while he had to make do with a localized cavalcade of a hundred bullock carts from his native village. In 1952, hockey was a potent symbol of Indian nationalism and Jadhav, despite winning independent India's first individual Olympic medal, was left to ultimately die in poverty. He was forced to sell off his wife's jewels to build a modest cottage and won a posthumous Arjuna award only in 2001. In sharp contrast, governmental coffers opened up for the Kumars from Beijing. In a nation starved of sporting glory, the intense media focus on the Beijing battlers turned them into new national heroes. Clearly, the registers of iconicity had changed in the intervening years, with individual Olympic success becoming an important barometer of national triumph.

What explains the change? Let us be clear: this is not necessarily about some new-found love or understanding of sports. There is a marked disconnect between the hype about a resurgent India, which the Beijing boys supposedly represent, and the reality. On the morning of Sushil Kumar's bronze-medal-winning effort, most media outlets carried online stories saying he had 'crashed out' of the Olympics. There was even an undertone that he had somehow wasted his first round bye. Few, at least on television or in the immediate Internet discourse, remembered the repechage rule until the Jat from Najafgarh pleasantly shocked the nation with his marathon string of victories to clinch bronze.

As reporters struggled for epithets about a shining India, nothing characterized the madness better than the television scrum at Bhiwani. On the day of the two boxing quarterfinals, the squadron of satellite broadcast vans from various channels stationed at Jitender Kumar's village of Devsar shut shop and ran as soon as he lost. Their destination: Vijender's village of Kalua, 10 km away, in anticipation of his fight. With TV channels looking to maximize costly resources, this was partly understandable, but as one reporter on the spot pointed out: has Jitender's village suddenly ceased to be a symbol of the new resurgent India we are talking about simply because he lost? This, after all, was a twenty-year-old gallantly fighting the weight of history with ten stitches, but all that mattered it seemed was the ruthless logic of victory. The hype was about nationalism, pure and simple; and that tells us something for the future as India hopes to build on the successes of Beijing before Delhi 2010 or London 2012.

Television had certainly helped create a national public focussed on boxing, but with all of India glued to the gripping celebrations in Bhiwani, at least one TV editor was said to have gloated in private that the channels had turned the boxers into heroes. Nothing could be further from the truth.

The media went to Bhiwani and to the boxers because it needed their story. TV reporters, expecting awestruck country bumpkins, were received with a busy matter-of-factness in a town that is used to winning medals. It is just that it took an Olympic medal for the rest of India to wake up to it. Bhiwani today is home to at least 1500–2000 regular boxers and 20,000–25,000 active sportspersons. It alone has produced fourteen Arjuna awardees – India's highest award for sportspersons – and is part of an economy that thrives on local sportsmen making it to the sports quotas of the paramilitary forces, the army and the police.

LESSONS FROM BHIWANI: DEMYSTIFYING THE REVOLUTION

The Bhiwani Boxing Club's iconic coach Jagdish Singh is fond of saying 'Geedar ka shikar karna ho to sher se ladna seekho.' (If you want to hunt jackals, learn how to fight a lion.) Surprisingly enough, till 2008, Bhiwani was a rather insignificant presence on the Indian sporting map. Despite giving the country multiple Asian Games gold medallists and a slew of medals in other international boxing competitions, the nation hadn't trained its eyes on Bhiwani before Beijing 2008. A few startling days at the Olympics changed all of this. As Akhil Kumar punched his way past Sergei Vodopyanov after four gruelling rounds and Vijender Singh matched up to Emilio Correa in the semifinals, media persons swarmed to make every inch of Bhiwani their own. Apathy soon gave way to unending television glare and Bhiwani, from being a shantytown, suddenly turned into the cynosure of all attention.

Bhiwani had its first tryst with international sporting success in the 1960s when Hawa Singh won a gold at the 1966 Asian Games. He followed it up with another gold medal at the Bangkok Asian Games in 1970, giving rise to a boxing culture that has since flourished in this village on the Haryana–Rajasthan border. Despite such success on the international stage, no funding was directed towards developing a boxing culture. But that didn't dampen the gung-ho sporting spirit of the Bhiwani boxers, who continued to pursue their sporting dream.

Things hardly looked up in the 1970s and '80s. Consequently, a section of the youth left Bhiwani for neighbouring states in search of work and livelihood. This was their way of showing discontentment over the Central government's prolonged apathy. Things reached a climax during the 1980s and early 1990s amidst a growing sense of frustration and uncertainty as unemployment prevailed. Thousands of Bhiwani youths were left with two options – either to take up sport or fall prey to unemployment.[11]

In a desperate act to protect young children from future unemployment, most parents encouraged their wards to embrace sports. To encourage this effort, the Sports Authority of India (SAI) started a training school, giving Bhiwani its first organized sports facility. They were encouraged to do so by the achievements of Raj Kumar Sangwan who won golds at two Asian-level meets – at Bangkok in 1991 and at Tehran in 1994.

However, this solitary SAI facility did little to solve the problems of infrastructure. It was the Bhiwani Boxing Club, hardly a modern facility itself, which ultimately made a perceptible difference. The club, as it exists today, was thus described in the *Indian Express*:

> Tucked in a corner, almost hidden by fields, the yellow brick building is more a farm outhouse than a possible breeding centre of international sportspersons. If quaintness equaled success, the place would get top marks. And well, now it does … The Bhiwani Boxing Club is just that, two rooms and a shed. A peepul tree and a Shiva idol stand to the left outside the gate, a sagging volleyball netting graces the right flank. The blue iron gate is never locked and opens out to a small brick path lined with wild rose, hibiscus and other flower shrubs. There is one room with a bed and a television, one tiny toilet and a tinier storeroom for gloves and other equipment. Five punching bags hang next to the room, a huge mirror frames one wall, there is a basic weight-training machine on one side, and a new ring on the other.[12]

Problems of infrastructure were, however, more than counterbalanced by individual passion for boxing, as the turn of the century marked the arrival of a golden era of Bhiwani boxers in the national arena. Despite making a mark in almost every recognized competition, it was at Beijing 2008 that Bhiwani finally scripted an unparalleled success story.

The nodal boxing body of Bhiwani – the Bhiwani Boxing Club – was established in 2002 by current coach Jagdish Singh. As reported by the *Indian Express*:

Six years ago (in 2002), Singh, one of the many boxing coaches with the Sports Authority of India, decided the daily effort he was putting at the SAI centre in Bhiwani needed to be topped with something more. So, in a move that some would describe as whimsical, he got together his life's savings, took a bank loan, and set about realizing his dream of having his own boxing club. Singh the boxer could not go places but, as he says, he wanted to keep the faith his coaches had placed in him. He was also driven by the urge to put Bhiwani, the land of Asian gold medallist Hawa Singh, back on the boxing map. Singh has always had an eye for spotting talent and following an approach that focuses on dealing with the worst-case scenario, he trained a band of boxers who slowly began dominating the national scene. A diploma in coaching from Hungary, and tips collected from trips abroad ensures that the methodology does not get outdated.[13]

After almost seven years since its inception, the boxing club has finally spread its wings to the far-flung corners of the state through its policy of decentralization. In fact, Bhiwani's glittering track record (of producing as many as fifty sportspersons who have represented India in internationals competitions) can largely be attributed to the modus operandi of the nodal organization, which tried its best to promote a healthy sporting environment. There has been, of late, an abundance of talented Bhiwani boxers in Indian teams across various age groups.

For the people from one of the most remote and long-neglected Indian states, it was not an easy road to success. At the height of the turbulent days of economic stagnation, absence of lucrative non-governmental jobs had ensured that boxing could not become a full-time profession for the poor sports enthusiasts of the region where agriculture still forms the backbone of the economy. Lack of exposure and absence of recruiters acted against Bhiwani's boxers, while mainstream Indian sport remained unaware of their maturing skills.

At the turn of the millennium, a few self-made individuals training under the watchful eyes of Jagdish Singh finally broke all shackles to catapult Bhiwani to the national and subsequently international level. Akhil Kumar, for example, beat all odds to come out stronger from a career-threatening injury and made it to the Olympics quarterfinals.

He followed up his Olympic showing by winning a bronze medal at the world championships in Moscow in December 2008.

Akhil, media-savvy and courageous, has become the first real star of Indian boxing.[14] Following his example, a few others, including Olympic medallist Vijender Singh and Jitender Kumar, joined the fray. Interestingly, all present and past Bhiwani boxers were encouraged to take up the sport by their state predecessors or seniors. Inspired by the simple logic that a good showing at the national level is the best bet to securing a government job, a vast array of talented youngsters have now taken to boxing in Bhiwani. If boxing can spread its wings to the neighbouring villages, which are also torn by unemployment and economic stagnation, and can appropriate the majority of the youth within its fold, it may surely do the nation yeoman service. On the Haryana–Rajasthan border, where the options for the youth are almost limited to sport or unemployment in the absence of fertile agricultural land, boxing has emerged a saviour and, in the process, addressed apprehensions. It is this sentiment that finds echo in Jagdish Singh's words when speaking about his ever-growing number of trainees: 'Parents are keen to bring them here, knowing this is a future they can dream of. They plead with me to enrol their children. It's something they didn't get a chance to do, and they hope their children will stand up to the test and become known all over the country. Plus, now that they've seen the success stories, it's a reality they want to believe in.'[15]

THE PROBLEM: WE ARE LIKE THIS ONLY

While Bhiwani was suddenly the cynosure of all attention, it was important to remember that only a sustained effort at building infrastructure could ensure that Beijing wasn't an exception. In 2004, the ruling Bharatiya Janata Party (BJP) fooled itself into believing that five years of 8 per cent economic growth on paper had all but assured its victory. Sure of sweeping back to power, it overconfidently called a general election six months before time, ran a campaign focussed on the catchy tagline 'India Shining' and was duly voted out of power by the majority of Indians who had been left out of the success of the economic reforms. There is now a danger of a generic 'India Shining' kind of discourse subsuming the real achievements and the real resurgence of the Beijing athletes. The boxers have emerged from a town which goes sometimes for days without electricity, where the rains have made it impossible to drive a car faster than 5 km/hour on most roads and where most people had to rely on inverters to watch the home boys win. In such a setting, sport has emerged as a way out for many.[16] The real success of Bhiwani lies in the rock-solid confidence of the new generation of athletes and a nascent public–private partnership which allowed them to transcend a system used to mediocrity. They have not been content to merely repeat the past; and this is the new Indian spirit that needs to be celebrated.

However, in an atmosphere of optimism, caution is an urgent necessity. India's sporting structure is in dire need of an overhaul and three individual Olympic medals can only create a *possibility* for such a change to come about. Unless the government, sports administrators, the IOA, and, finally, the corporates come forward to embrace sport, Beijing 2008 will remain an aberration. Private efforts such as the Mittal Champions Trust and Olympic Gold Quest Foundation must contribute more towards Indian sport. Tough questions need to be asked. What happened, for instance, to the Indian Army's celebrated Mission Olympics and why can't it be integrated with the larger national effort?

While India celebrated Bhiwani for what it did to place boxing on the national map, it is time to replicate such achievements across the country. With boxing being a television-friendly sport and with twenty-four-hour television channels multiplying almost daily, the media will surely embrace boxing if properly marketed and managed. With such a systemic overhaul, India could start to expect more medals in boxing in the 2012 London Games, and Vijender's bronze could then have the significance of being more than an Olympic medal in the overall sporting context.

SORRY SAINA

It must be asserted that India, at the time of writing at least, has failed to take advantage of the fertile conditions created by Beijing. This grim reality was driven home when the nation's best medal hope, Saina Nehwal, suggested that, contrary to expectations, India would struggle to win more than one medal at the 2012 Olympics in London. Nehwal, who has played brilliantly in the super series competitions and has risen to the position of world number three, even winning the Indonesian Open in June 2009 and three straight titles in June–July 2010, was of the opinion that winning medals at Olympics would not be easy. 'Many people are saying that we will come back with ten medals and so on. But I think we are not going to win more than one from the next Olympics,'[17] was her candid confession.

This was startling because India now has a handful of players who have made it to the top fifty in several categories in world badminton. Nehwal, currently India's best bet for the upcoming Commonwealth Games, trailed off with the following lament: 'A lot of cricket is happening … nobody wants to take it (badminton) up professionally. It is not easy to be ranked number eight or nine. A lot of sacrifices have to be made and still not many are ready to do that. So maybe once in ten years we will have a Saina Nehwal.'[18]

That Nehwal is right is evident from a comparative analysis of media coverage of cricket and badminton in March–April 2009. In these months, leading lights of world badminton were in India to participate at the Indian Open tournament in Hyderabad. Around the same time, the Indian cricket team was playing New Zealand for a bilateral series in New Zealand. Even on the day of the Indian Open finals, coverage of the competition was relegated to the lower half of most sports pages across the country when items about India's preparation for the third Test of the series in New Zealand were given eight-column banner headlines.[19]

The same story was repeated at the time of the World Badminton Championships in Hyderabad in August 2009. Even this premier competition, which had sporting heroes like Olympic champion Lin Dan participating, failed to displace cricket from the top half of the sports pages. On 12 August 2009, the day Saina Nehwal was to open her campaign, the lead sports headline was that the IPL governing council had finalized the schedule for 2009. Most newspapers published the entire schedule in the top half of the page and world badminton was relegated to the bottom half.

Most striking was the coverage of the *Anandabazar Patrika*, one of the better newspapers for sports coverage in the country. *Anandabazar* of 12 August opened its sports section with a lead story of how the IPL schedule can once again affect India's T-20 World Cup preparations. In all of the two pages dedicated to sport, IPL mustered more than a page while world badminton was restricted to one solitary column of not more than 500 words.[20]

HAVE SPORT, WILL CONTROL

Such discrepancies, born out of insurmountable administrative apathy at the highest levels of Indian sport, only add to the despondence of India's sportsmen and women. Blaming the media is the short cut sports administrators often resort to. However, that such a situation has been created in the first place speaks volumes of their efficiency. Unfortunately in India, virtually every sporting body is controlled by a politician or a bureaucrat and, once entrenched, most manage to stay on for years, if not for decades.

The list, as we have detailed elsewhere, is long: Congress MP Suresh Kalmadi, president of the Athletics Federation since 1989; BJP MP V.K. Malhotra, president of the Archery Federation since 1972; Congress MP Priya Ranjan Dasmunsi, president of the Football Federation since 1989 and former Congress MP K.P. Singh Deo, president of the Rowing Federation for twenty-four years. In addition, BJP leader Yashwant Sinha has been running the Tennis Federation since 2000, V.K. Verma has been in charge of badminton since 1998, the Indian National Lok Dal's Ajay Chautala has been running table tennis since 2001 and Samata Party's Digvijay Singh has headed shooting since 2000. This is apart from the complete dominance over cricket bodies by politicians. To name just a few, at the time of writing, the NCP's Sharad Pawar continues to be the de facto head of the BCCI and has now also moved on to becoming the president of the International Cricket Council, the BJP's Arun Jaitly runs the Delhi Association, Home Minister Amit Shah heads the Gujarat Cricket Association and National Conference leader Farooq Abdullah is in charge of Jammu and Kashmir cricket.[21]

What is more alarming is that these men have managed to stay on in power despite a high court ruling which decreed that guidelines on tenure of office bearers of the National Sports Federations are maintainable and enforceable. Suggesting that this is in no way a violation of the principles enshrined in the Olympic charter, Justice Geeta Mittal, sitting judge of the Delhi High Court, observed that even the International Olympic Committee had restrictions on the terms of its office bearers.[22] She went on to state:

> Firstly, I see no interference by the stipulation of the tenure condition as a condition for grant of recognition and assistance by the government. Secondly, the same does not enable the government to have any say of any kind in the affairs of running of the sports body ...
>
> If a tenure clause is not enforced, office-bearers could be repeatedly elected from a particular region and continue to dominate the affairs of the association/federation after having created a monopoly over the sport ... Vesting the control (of sports bodies) in authorities from a particular region may result in diversion of funds, selection of players from and development of a sport from only a particular region. The national federation would not then remain representative of the hopes and aspirations of sportspersons of the entire nation ... A limited office tenure will have the impact of minimizing, if not eliminating, allegations, criticism and elements of nepotism, favoritism and bias of any kind.[23]

The court judgment, the *Hindu* noted, had serious ramifications on the tenure of office bearers and stipulated that an office bearer of a federation can have two terms of four years each at a stretch, the second one on a two-thirds majority. However, the same report went on to suggest that 'the IOA took the lead sometime in the mid-1980s to flout the guidelines by amending its constitution and almost all NSFs followed suit. The Indian Hockey Federation (IHF) told the court that it had amended its constitution in February 2004 to allow more than two terms on a simple majority vote. The government affidavit stated that the guideline regarding tenure was not being insisted upon in the "interest of sportspersons"'.[24]

Commenting on the impact of the ruling, the *Times of India* reported: 'Most of them do not believe in handing over the baton. Perched securely as heads of various sporting federations, sports bosses have been virtually unmovable. But maybe not for long. The Delhi High Court has now ruled that the Centre's guidelines on restricting the tenure of office-bearers in sports bodies to two terms should be strictly enforced. Many sporting chiefs, including several politicians, may have to rework their plans as the HC ruling means that the government funds to these organizations may dry up if they cling to office for more than eight years. The ruling could lead to changes in the Indian Olympic Association as well as other sports bodies.'[25]

ROUND AND ROUND, LIKE A FOOTBALL

Despite the Delhi High Court's argument that 'what is the interest of sportspersons is neither detailed nor spelt out ...',[26] nothing has been done to remedy the situation. Rather, we have witnessed the bizarre state of affairs where, despite being seriously ill for more than a year, Priya Ranjan Dasmunsi continues to be the president of the All India Football Federation. It is as if Indian football's apex body is doing its best to buy time and is waiting for Dasmunsi to recover when it is apparent that his illness, which appeared terminal to start with, has made it impossible for him to return to active social life.[27]

That Indian football is plagued by an ineffective administration at its helm was best evident when Urs Zanitti, head of the development division of FIFA, lamented in January 2004: 'It's a scandal from an outsider's point of view. FIFA's job is to provide the money but, in countries like India, we are forced to deal directly with the people to whom the money is paid eventually.'[28]

Pointing to the FIFA House project, the plan to build a permanent office and much more for the All India Football Federation (AIFF) in New Delhi's Dwarka area, he exclaimed: 'We are dealing directly with the architects and contractors, because nothing seems to get done otherwise. It was supposed to have been built a year or so ago, but it's still not in functioning condition.' His experience with the AIFF top brass has made him more aware of the state of affairs: 'They seem interested enough but where's the administration? Where are the administrators? You have some people in Delhi. Some in Kolkata. Some in Goa. There are no people. The human resource is very poor. The financial resources are poor also, but that's where we come in. But here we need to take part in creating the human resource also.'[29]

It can be argued that if there is any worthwhile boost that the AIFF provided to Indian football over the last decade and a half, it was the introduction of the National Football League (NFL) in 1996. The event certainly infused a new vigour into Indian soccer. But the NFL is still found wanting in several key aspects: organization, marketing, publicity, itinerary and, above all, adequate sponsors. While the league has turned out to be keenly competitive in the last few years – the 2008–09 edition, which went down to the wire, being the best of all – it still leaves a lot to be desired on the organizational front.[30] While the AIFF successfully managed to rope in Zee TV as the broadcaster, they haven't done much to give Zee the backing it needs to convert football into an attractive sporting brand. By contrast, there is a far bigger viewing population for the English Premier League or the UEFA Champions League in India. Many in Zee, while not wanting to speak on record, hold AIFF responsible for the shortcomings of the national league.[31] The NFL's itinerary and logistics have been a topic of ridicule as teams have had to crisscross the vast country with very little or no gap between matches.

Also, while promoting the NFL, the AIFF has systematically undermined important and prestigious tournaments like the Durand Cup, DCM Trophy, Rovers Cup and IFA Shield, which used to act as breeding grounds for soccer talent in the country. It is essential to restore them to their erstwhile status and importance to broaden the base of the game throughout India. At present, regular football leagues take place only in a handful of cities like Kolkata, Mumbai, Goa, Bangalore, Kerala, Delhi, Hyderabad and Punjab. The rest of the associations under the AIFF umbrella have proved ineffective, but haven't been strongly reprimanded because they serve as key vote banks. Even with FIFA support, the AIFF has not been able to implement the most rudimentary soccer development programmes across the country. For this, as Bill Adams points out, 'cronyism, ageism and amateur ineffectiveness' are much to blame.[32]

The AIFF has also shown its culpability in the organization of international tournaments in recent times. Its millennium venture, the Millennium Sahara Cup, which was staged in January 2001, was much publicized as the biggest football show in Asia. It, however, turned out to be a white elephant. In fact, it promised much but delivered nothing for Indian football. The coordination between the All India Football Federation and the organizers, Studio 2100, was so poor that they could not compensate for the last-minute withdrawals of teams from Iraq, Indonesia and Cameroon. Among the participants, only the team from Chile brought a few Olympians in their rank while the remaining teams used the tournament to experiment with young players. It was alleged in some quarters that the AIFF did not provide adequate technical information and trained personnel to the organizers of Studio 2100.[33] Henna Juneja, the frustrated CEO of Studio 2100, was said to have remarked that the tournament was sabotaged due to factionalism within the AIFF.[34] Novy Kapadia, in a scathing critique published the day after the tournament, declared that 'the AIFF president and some officials used the build-up for this tournament as part of their election campaign and once their purpose was achieved, shirked all responsibility in organization'.[35]

THE UNHAPPY GHOST OF DHYAN CHAND

If football has suffered at the hands of incompetent administrators, hockey, India's national sport, is hardly better off. For over a year, it was run by an ad hoc body accountable to the Indian Olympic Association. Bundled unceremoniously out of the IHF,[36] former president K.P.S. Gill has tried his best to make a comeback and even dragged the IOA to court. As a result, the organization controlling Indian hockey continues to be fraught with dissension and factional infighting. Nursing the ignominy of humiliation and insult, Gill, the astute politician that he is, has spared no pains in trying to achieve his aims.

That things could go down to such a level was extraordinary. It just isn't sport. Modern-day electoral campaigns with all their dirty power games have much to learn from the IHF saga. Attempts at buying and selling of votes/loyalty are common, as is the use of political clout. Both factions offer lucrative posts, which include managerial positions of touring Indian teams, to win delegates over. In this tug of war the victim has been Indian hockey.

The politicized nature of Indian hockey has been a cause of alarm for the International Hockey Federation as well. With the Hockey

World Cup already allotted to India, the IHF chief Leonardo Negre visited India in March 2009. As reported by C. Rajsekhar Rao, 'The International Hockey Federation (FIH) chief Leandro Negre seems more concerned about the way the game is being run in India rather than security and infrastructure issues ahead of next year's World Cup.'[37] Negre, during the course of his visit, issued an ultimatum to the Indian officials: 'The World Cup had been allotted with the condition that it will be organized by Hockey India, an association merging both the men's (Indian Hockey Federation) and women's (Indian Women's Hockey Federation) bodies. That is one of the most important issues because we have to run hockey according to our commitment ... The merger is very important for the FIH and I am pushing for it. We need to sort out this issue at the earliest.'[38]

The ultimatum eventually turned into a veiled threat when the FIH chief declared before leaving India that it was absolutely essential that the ad hoc committee held elections within six months. 'We have given them a six-month deadline ... The FIH is not here to dictate terms but to offer advice. We will be watching the situation keenly. If [the] worst comes to [the] worst, our Plan B is ready. The World Cup can be shifted to Malaysia. They have the infrastructure ready to host the tournament.'[39]

Negre also expressed apprehensions over whether the Dhyan Chand Stadium, scheduled to hold matches of the Commonwealth Games, would be ready on time. 'The construction of the stadium is a concern but we have been given a guarantee that it will be completed in time. We have not set any time frame but would ideally want it to be completed by October this year (2009). The reports that I have got so far regarding this as well as security seem satisfactory.'[40]

That India finally got its act in order was evident from a report published in the *Hindu* of 27 July 2009. The report, which announced Hero Honda's bagging the title sponsorship rights for the World Cup, went on to quote FIH president Negre as saying, 'For global development of hockey, it is important that India should come up and play to its potential. The FIH hopes that hosting the 2010 World Cup will give a tremendous boost to Indian hockey.'

A.K. Mattoo, president of Hockey India, a body that finally ended the period of ad hocism in Indian hockey, declared on the occasion that he expected 2010 to be a landmark year in the history of Indian hockey for the sheer magnitude of the event to be held in the national capital. 'Hockey India is proud to be associated with FIH in hosting the 12th Men's Hockey World Cup. We have taken the right step towards the revival of the game.'

However, it wasn't smooth going for Hockey India because the inaugural game of the third IPL was expected to clash with the final of the World Cup. Accordingly, there was some talk of advancing the tournament by a week, as is evident from the following report published by the Press Trust of India:

> Organizers of the 2010 Hockey World Cup are afraid that advancing the event by a week may not be enough and the final of the event may still coincide with the third edition of the Indian Premier League. 'In all likelihood, they are starting IPL 2010 from March 12, a day before our final. Since March 13 is a Saturday, we fear they would slot an IPL double-header and that would mean that the final of the 2010 hockey World Cup would go virtually unnoticed,' one of the organizers told PTI on condition of anonymity.[41]

True to their fears, the World Cup, though finally held on schedule, lost out on coverage because of its clash with the build-up for the third edition of the Indian Premier League. While the IPL is nothing more than a domestic T-20 competition, that it could edge out a World Cup in terms of hype and media coverage, just months before the country plays host to the Commonwealth Games in Delhi, speaks much about the ground reality of Indian sport.

If the picture off the field in 2008–09 was an adequate reflection of the sad plight of Indian hockey, on the field, India has battled hard to overcome the ignominy of failing to qualify for the Beijing Olympic Games, the first such occasion in history. With a slew of new captains at the helm, the results, since the Beijing qualifying debacle, have been mixed. Following a good show at the four-nation Punjab Gold Cup at home in January 2009, where India lost a closely fought final against the Dutch 1-2, India travelled to Australia and New Zealand for a twin Test series in February 2009. While the side performed poorly in Australia, losing to the Australian Development Squad, they won the four-match Test series in New Zealand 2-0.

India followed this up with an excellent showing at the Azlan Shah Tournament in Malaysia, winning the competition after a hiatus of thirteen years. In doing so, India beat arch rivals Pakistan 2-1 in the last group match and followed this with a convincing 3-1 rout of Malaysia in the final. Sandeep Singh, with six goals, was adjudged the player of the tournament.

In the junior Asia Cup, too, India made it to the finals but eventually lost to Pakistan, conceding a last-minute goal. Lamenting this old malady of Indian hockey, former skipper Gurbux Singh maintained:

> It pains to talk time and again about conceding last-minute penalty corners and goals. Falling at the last hurdle is something the junior team have now done in back-to-back finals. They lost in the youth Olympics in Australia before losing the Asia Cup final. In the youth Olympics final, after a series of outstanding results in the group stages, our boys were pipped at the post by the hosts. The senior team, too, suffered the same fate in the Punjab Gold Cup and on their tour of Australia.[42]

However, the string of good performances dried up at the Asia Cup, with India failing to make the semifinals, losing out 2-3 to Pakistan and drawing 2-2 with China. Under new coach Jose Brasa, the European tour had a steep learning curve. If victories against England allowed for celebration, a 2-8 defeat against Spain was a real low.

Unfortunately for Indian hockey, the years 1980–2009, which witnessed cricket's spectacular rise, also witnessed the slide of hockey from its position of pre-eminence. Sadly for hockey, every major cricketing achievement has followed a singular hockey disaster. The 1983 Prudential Cup Triumph followed India's disastrous 1–7 defeat in the hands of Pakistan in the 1982 Asian Games. Again, the failure to make the semifinals at the Los Angeles Games of 1984 was followed by the 1985 Benson and Hedges win in Australia. More recently, a disappointing seventh place showing at the Sydney Games in 2000 ensured that hockey was unable to take advantage of cricket's match-fixing phase.

India's World Cup final showing at South Africa in 2003 and the away series win in Pakistan in 2004 was followed by a seventh place showing at the Athens Olympics in 2004. And the defeat to Great Britain, which resulted in India not qualifying for the summer Olympics for the first time in her hockey history, came immediately after Dhoni's men had made history Down Under, defeating the Australians in a one-day series after two decades. And with the cricket team at an all-time high, following their success in New Zealand in March–April 2009, it was almost impossible that India's showing at the Azlan Shah Tournament or the junior Asia Cup would be taken note of by the country's sporting fraternity. So much so that not a single newspaper reported the Azlan Shah triumph on the first page and some, like the *Anandabazar Patrika*, the leading Bengali daily, attributed only a 500-word news report to the win.[43] In contrast, it covered the spat between Sunil Gavaskar and John Buchanan over the latter's innovative captaincy theories at substantial length.[44] While most English newspapers published Sandeep's photos with the trophy, all of these reports and photographs were restricted to the sports pages in poll season.

What was worse was that the team wasn't even given a warm welcome on their return to India. The *Hindu* headline, 'Victorious team returns home to a lukewarm welcome', best summed up the mood back home. The report went on to state that 'if one thought that a cup win after a thirteen-year gap would lead to a warm, even boisterous, welcome, one was in for disappointment at the Indira Gandhi International Airport as just one sports administrator and an Olympian were on hand to receive the team. Of course, the media was in full strength to make up the numbers, though the team's homecoming seemed to have evoked little interest among the onlookers at the airport'.[45]

What was, however, good to hear was coach Harendra Singh's cautious words. Not getting emotional over the triumph, he exercised restraint while speaking to the press:

> I don't think we need to go ga-ga over what we have done. I had said before departing that we stood a very good chance of winning the tournament. The win is good. It will mean a lot to the players, some of whom are at the best stage of their careers. Winning is always important and it will add to the team's strength and help us plan

better ... The players can do much better. At the end of the day, what matters is the result. We have won, but remember that it is just a small step in the long journey. Changes can't happen overnight and we have made a beginning ... I have been repeatedly saying that we need to aim and join the league of the top six. So please don't read much into this win.[46]

He was, indeed, proved right when he had to give way to Jose Brasa, who, since taking charge, has produced mixed results.

Finally, the muddle in Indian hockey resulting in the sacking of president K.P.S. Gill and suspension of the Indian Hockey Federation had come at a time when the IPL had captured the nation's imagination. While the disorder looked to be temporarily resolved with the suspension of the IHF, further chaos resulted, with nothing coming out of the tussle between the Indian Olympic Association and the Indian Hockey Federation. Ad hocism, as Gurbux Singh argued, 'should be a time-bound affair and the elections to the disaffiliated bodies should be held at the earliest,'[47] something even the FIH was very keen on. Eventually, Indian hockey emerged out of this limbo with the reinstatement of Hockey India with A.K. Mattoo at the helm.

STRAIGHT SHOOTING, IN THE FOOT

The picture hardly improves if we turn our gaze to shooting, India's favourite medal event since Bindra's gold at Beijing. While Gagan Narang, Bindra's compatriot in the 10–metre air rifle, has been in sizzling form since the Olympics and has even broken multiple world marks, his performances are once again the result of individual flair and brilliance. The fact that Narang could win bronze at the world championships in Korea in early April 2009, after a rather ordinary qualifying round, is testament to his skill and mental strength. Experimenting with his technique, Narang lifted his game in the final to make up for a poor 594/600 in the qualifiers and move up from eighth to third in the final rankings.[48]

While Narang's exploits give us ample hope before the Commonwealth Games, in a shocking exposé it was brought to the nation's attention in April 2009 that the fifteen top coaches engaged in training India's shooters for the Commonwealth Games weren't paid between January and March when each of them was entitled to payments of up to Rs 30,000 per month as per the terms of their contract. Also, at the time of appointment, these coaches were promised advanced-level coaching abroad; but till April 2009, none had been sent. In an interview to Ajai Masand and Saurabh Duggal of the *Hindustan Times*, one of these coaches, engaged in training at the national camp in Pune, spilled the beans:

> All of us, barring national coach Sunny Thomas, have not received a paisa from the government for the work we have been putting in to prepare the 150-odd core group shooters … First we were made to sign an undertaking, pledging 305 days in a year to full-time coaching. After that an agreement was prepared on stamp paper, which we duly signed. Strangely, we were also told to disclose our other sources of income. But after that we have been left high and dry.[49]

A shotgun coach asserted, 'We were running from one department to another in the ministry after which we had to leave Delhi for Pune. I think a majority of the coaches associated with other core groups haven't received remunerations as well.'[50]

However, the most disturbing comment came from a pistol coach who challenged the ministry's unfair guidelines:

> One team has already left Indian shores to participate in the World Cup, while another will be leaving shortly for the World Cup in Germany. How do we train them when we ourselves don't know our fate? Tomorrow the ministry might say, 'We'll give you a lump sum rather than the Rs 30,000 we are entitled to under the contract …' The ministry is paying foreign coaches hundreds of dollars by the hour or day and asking us to give away our other source of livelihood. What will we do once the Games are over?[51]

SPORT AND THE MINISTRY

Amidst growing pessimism, almost doing away with the possibilities created at Beijing, a silver lining emerged when the sports ministry, for the first time in years, sent out a circular to all sports federations, whose disciplines are in the 2010 Commonwealth Games, to send details of the past and recent performances of all 'core group' athletes.

The ministry directed the federations to prepare detailed performance charts, including fitness and other test reports, of all the core group athletes undertaking training for the Commonwealth Games. This directive came at the back of growing discord among sportspersons who felt that despite performing at their best they weren't being rewarded in the absence of proper laws and guidelines. Reacting against the groundswell of discontent, a ministry official emphasized that the directive was meant to weed out the non-performers and encourage sportsmen and women to excel with just months remaining for the Games in Delhi.[52]

Carrying on with its objective of identifying talented sportspersons, the government, the *Telegraph* reported, endowed Rs 5 lakh for the Maulana Abul Kalam Azad Trophy, handed out to the best sporting university in India, to encourage talent at the collegiate level. It also identified Ladakh as a fertile ground for archery, ice hockey and figure skating. Interestingly, a twelve-year-old figure skater, Padma Chorol, has already been awarded a Rs 25,000 scholarship under the National Sports Development Fund.[53] As Anirban Das Mahapatra reported:

> The government has upped financial incentives for successful sportspeople. Former medal winners at international events now have their pensions doubled – Vijender Singh can now look forward to a monthly pay of Rs 10,000 after retirement. The monetary carrot for an Olympic gold is now Rs 50 lakh, up by 66 per cent. The annual grant amount for indigent athletes now stands at Rs 2 lakh from Rs 36,000. Financial assistance for medical treatment is now up a whopping 500 per cent to Rs 2 lakh. The government has also released a grant of over Rs 6.5 crore for upgrading all four training centres of the Sports Authority of India, to provide state-of-the-art training facilities.[54]

Finally, for the first time ever in India's sporting history, the government has come forward with a grant of Rs 678 crore to enable our athletes to train abroad with the world's leading professionals and to ensure that they are exposed to the best of facilities before the 2010 Commonwealth Games. In principle, more money for sport is always welcome. The problem lies in the details and in how it is spent.

One statistic is telling. Against an allocation of Rs 678 crore for the Commonwealth Games, the government had spent just over

35 per cent, only Rs 232.19 crores, by November 2009. It takes years of hard commitment to build champions. If the idea of pumping in this money was to create champions for the Commonwealth Games, to use them as a springboard for greater sporting glory, then clearly something was terribly wrong here. According to the sports minister, this money was meant to 'improve the performance of the Indian contingent in the Commonwealth Games'. [55] It doesn't take an expert to know that there is clearly a problem with a system that cannot spend as much as 65 per cent of this allocation with less than a year to go for the Games. Champions, after all, cannot be created overnight.

DELHI'S SPORTING TEST

Talking about the possibility of an Indian sporting renaissance, the IOA Secretary General Randhir Singh has a point: 'It's a Catch-22 situation. You can't produce champions without money, and money doesn't come unless you have champions to flaunt.'[56] India's moribund and deeply politicized sport bureaucracy is usually the first target of opprobrium every time we remember our athletes – which is usually at the once-in-four-years humiliation called the Olympics – but Singh has a point. Individual prodigies aside, the connection between modern sport and commerce is undeniable. This is precisely why nascent private sector initiatives like the Mittal Champions Trust are much needed. By 2009, the Trust had thirty-nine athletes on its rolls and focussed investments were clearly needed. According to Manisha Malhotra, administrator at the Trust, 'During years when there's an Olympic or Commonwealth meet scheduled, the budget can creep up to Rs 8 crore, but that's the kind of investment required if we are to produce results.'[57]

Come October 2010 and the Beijing legacy will be put to its sternest test. If India can overhaul its medal count achieved at the 2006 Melbourne Commonwealth Games, it will give a fillip to Indian Olympic sport two years before the mega spectacle in London. A failed effort in Delhi 2010, on the other hand, organizationally and with regards to medals won, will mean that Beijing's lush promise will be confined to sports history books by the time of the next Olympics.

It is interesting in this context to remember an exchange between a senior television journalist and Abhinav Bindra on his return to India following his gold-medal winning exploit in Beijing. 'Is this Abhinav's gold or India's gold?' an interviewer on Times Now asked him. Abhinav, epitome of political correctness, was quick to suggest that it was India's without question.

If there is a systemic overhaul, thanks to Abhinav and his colleagues, it will certainly be India's gold for all times to come. However, if a fundamental transformation of sporting infrastructure in India is not brought about, as looks likely from the grim realities documented in this chapter, Abhinav's gold will always remain his, a moment of individual brilliance lost amidst countless failures since Independence.

EPILOGUE

This book was initially scheduled to go to press in January 2010. Our publisher was keen to have it out by March and we had just about wrapped up the manuscript when we received a phone call. It was a senior official in the games hierarchy. Their emergency drive to meet the Games deadlines had just started. The target was 31 March and, with the PMO now watching, the pressure was on the administrators. This was where we had ended our narrative of Delhi 2010 – from Delhi's winning bid to its travails up to January 2010. As Delhi's officialdom scrambled to get its act together, the following thought process articulated some of the apprehensions: Was our account of the Games critical? Absolutely. Would we let anyone have a peek before it was published? Of course not. How about waiting to see the results of the last leg of the effort? Well, our working publication schedule was March. No time for that.

But there was something perhaps in that last point that got us thinking a little later that day when we got talking with our publisher, Karthika, at HarperCollins. After all, this book was about the Games, its politics, its organization and its impact. At a purely analytical level, it would be a bit incomplete to leave out the pulls and pressures of the last months of the effort as Delhi struggled to meet its targets. What if there was a twist in the tale? What if we missed something in the last scramble? Would we lose anything by waiting another 4–5 months? We had started this book because we wanted to see what would happen to Delhi. Now, taking a step back, wouldn't it be fair to complete the story as much as we possibly could before the Games commenced?

Overlying all of this, of course, was a serious concern: would it, in any way, mean that we were compromising anything at all if we waited just a bit more?

The answer was crystal clear. The way we saw it: the pre-January 2010 and the post-January 2010 stories were really two distinct parts. We had already researched and documented the first part in detail. It made sense to include as much of the latter as well – whether it was a success or a failure.

So, on our publisher's advice, we decided to write this postscript on the 2010 leg of the work after the March deadline was over, while not changing anything in the rest of the book.

So, what has been the story of the last few months? We write this epilogue with the 100–day countdown knocking at our doors. In the past few months, a number of symposiums have been organized across Commonwealth countries,[1] all trying to figure out if preparations are finally on track or if the political rhetoric of 'Delhi will be the best games ever',[2] is finally beginning to sound hollow to all except those who keep mouthing it.

While the Games Organizing Committee and the politicians continue to be hopeful, the national media discourse on Delhi 2010, the world discourse, and indeed the mood in the city present a rather gloomy picture.

In Canada, for instance, athletes have even been issued warnings that India isn't secure enough amidst recent terror threats from the Lashkar-e-Toiba[3] and instructions that Canadian athletes are not to stay on in Delhi following their event. While some are upset at the prospect of missing out on the cultural experience of India, others concur that it is ultimately the responsibility of the Canadian Olympic Committee to ensure that security concerns are given due importance.[4]

At a recent Commonwealth Games conference in Glasgow, organized, among others, by Louise Martin, vice-chair for the Glasgow Games in 2014, the discourse on Delhi could be symbolized in one word: 'apprehension'. Most, if not all, of the speakers were critical and some were even scathing about Delhi's continued state of under-preparedness.

Similarly, while many may dismiss the Queen's decision to give Delhi a miss — her first non-attendance at the Games in years — as irrelevant to India, it only underscores the negative undercurrent of the discussion in Britain. The BBC World Service's airwaves may be full of Incredible India ads but the only news of the Games on the BBC's domestic networks in May was the damning report alleging a serious scandal about funds assigned for the poor being diverted to the Games.[5] Human rights activists are concerned that the 40,000 families likely to be uprooted between June and September in the lead-up to the Games will not be offered necessary resettlement.[6]

The global discourse is as negative as the domestic discourse in the country's newspapers and TV networks. If anything, the Indian press is even more scathing.

'I AM NERVOUS': BRAVADO, ANXIETY AND DELHI'S POLITICAL DISCOURSE

What about the leaders who are driving the Games? In trying to gauge the thinking in Delhi's political circles in an ambience of growing global apprehension, we conducted a series of interviews with Games stakeholders, members of the Prime Ministerial Committee on the Commonwealth Games and members of the Games Organizing Committee.

Three clear strands emerged in these interviews. First, many of them remain confident but some of the confidence on display is false bravado. Second, they underscored a growing sense of urgency in trying to wrap things up in time. It is this sense of desperation that explains the rapid pace of work in Delhi in the first quarter of 2010, a pace that stands out in sharp contrast with the agonizing apathy witnessed in the years 2003–09. Suresh Kalmadi vehemently insists that there 'is no reason to panic',[7] Sheila Dikshit acknowledges she is 'nervous' but argues that this anxiety is par for the course before an event of this magnitude.[8] Kapil Sibal[9] and Kumari Selja broadly repeat the soft-power argument,[10] akin to the one that is being made in favour of South Africa as it hosts the Soccer World Cup. All assert that India will ultimately pull it off, as the prime minister's report card to the nation after the UPA's first year in office also declares.

In all of the interviews, the one common strand is that the hosting of a sporting event at a scale such as the Commonwealth Games is a matter of international prestige for the country, and is bound to boost 'brand India'. The same sentiment is expressed in the official website for the Delhi Games which also goes on to add that the 'Games will leave behind dramatically improved, world-class sports facilities that generations of Indian sportspersons can use in the future. The establishment of an Olympic-size pool as well as a gym in the Delhi University will boost sports among the youth of Delhi'.

Are such claims tenable at all? As the naysayers say only half in jest, the only thing that playing chess makes you better at is chess, and the only thing that a successful sporting event proves is that country's ability to host it.[11] Greece hosted a great Olympic Games in 2004, see where it is now, says this school of thought. And the argument about the Games turning the host country into a sporting nation is seductive but facile.

The previous chapters examined the rhetoric and the reality in detail but, as Hans Westerbeek rightly argues, the key point to be made here is that 'long-term urban and social planning for a destination needs to coincide with long-term planning and scheduling of capacity building. Key to success remains a long-term vision for the city of Delhi that also fits the plans the government has for it'.[12] Only then can events such as the Commonwealth Games be made into tools that assist in economic development, justify the fast tracking of construction of critical transport and building infrastructure, attract tourists and business investment, provide event spin-off programmes for the local community with socially beneficial outcomes, and so on.

As we write these lines, with less than 100 days to go and because of its heuristic, practical and political value, Delhi 2010 has become a highly sought-after commodity, the long-term impact of which hinges not only on what happens during the Games, but more appropriately on the legacy which it will leave behind. On the plus side of the ledger, to India's credit, Delhi is almost ready to offer the world's athletes a first-rate Games Village alongside good stadiums for most sports competitions. Barring the Jawaharlal Nehru Stadium, construction of which has also picked pace in recent months, and the S.P. Mukherjee Swimming Complex, most venues are likely to be ready on time. But even if they are all ready in time, even if they are gleaming on the day, is that by itself enough? And is that what these Games were about? What after that? And at what cost to the city?

LASTING LEGACIES?

More than the venues or the Games Village, it is our urban infrastructure and more importantly the issue of community integration that is of paramount importance in the time remaining. The key question that we ask in the preceding pages is: do these Games belong to the organizing committee or the Government of India or to the Indian people at large?

If it's the latter, as should be the case, little has been done to give Delhites the feeling that it is their event and that it is being organized to benefit them in the long run. As the auto-rickshaw driver in the opening pages of this book told us, there is a clearly a yawning gap between the city's Games planners and the city itself.

While Delhi's inhabitants haven't yet raised the slogan 'We want bread not circuses', raised by Toronto's citizens in the 1990s and one which had derailed the city's Olympic bid in 1996, the average Delhite, smarting under the impact of the entire city being dug up, is opposed to the biggest event in India's sporting history. Unless the organizing committee is successful in winning over people's confidence, the emotional connect, so very necessary in ensuring a successful legacy, will be extremely difficult to achieve.

Ethnography around Delhi and the NCR region helps demonstrate that the ordinary taxpayer on the street, whose money is being used to fund the Games, is still in the dark about most things pertaining to the event. For the average Delhite, it is an exercise in opulence with little or no benefit in the longer term. Most believe that the sports facilities created for the Games are destined to be white elephants, never to be within the reach of ordinary citizens. The problems facing them on a daily basis far outnumber the gains promised.

Without bridging this gap, the long-term legacy of Delhi 2010 will at best be mixed, nothing more than a marketing slogan gone awry. And as every marketer worth his salt knows, there is nothing worse for a dodgy product than a good slogan.

Finally, can a mega event of this nature really create a sports culture in India? Can CWG 2010 create a rallying cry for 'sport for all'? Or will Indian sport continue to remain a lottery destined only for a few? That is the question that continues to animate experts on the eve of the Games. The notion of sport for all was certainly part of the Delhi 2010 legacy vision, which states: 'More than all, the legacy of the XIX Commonwealth Games 2010 Delhi will be to boost the sports culture as a part of the daily life of every Indian, particularly the youth.' However, the ground reality is very different as Chapter 1 has detailed. With the stakeholders under incessant pressure to ready the infrastructure on time, the vision of sport for all has receded into the background.

It is sobering to see this inability to promote sport nationally in the context of the research done by leading sports historian Bruce Kidd. Studying sport events since the 1960s, Kidd affirms that 'despite the widespread "intuitive" expectation that inspiring performances stimulate new participation, there is no evidence that they automatically lead others in the general population to do so, let alone in ways that address the most difficult challenges of development'.[13]

According to him, research demonstrates that unless those who are meant to be inspired enjoy full access to sustainable programmes with safe, adequate facilities, conducted by competent, ethical leadership, the take-up – and the resulting benefits from mega events – is short-lived and ineffective.

These observations are extremely relevant when studied against the legacy of the 1982 Asian Games in Delhi. While there's little doubt that Delhi was fundamentally transformed as a result of the event, it can definitively be asserted that the legacy of the Asian Games remains negative in terms of nurturing an all-pervasive sports culture in India, a drawback that explains why India has won just a solitary individual Olympic gold after eighty years of competition.

Knowing full well that the tremendous effort and cost of staging major Games militate against the realization of a sustainable legacy for sport and physical activity, Delhi needs to step up and set an example. Only if this is done can Delhi serve as a perfect model of what the Commonwealth Games can do for a host city.

This is especially pertinent in India because, to this day, among most Indian Games organizers, sport is often phrased as somehow being disconnected from its cultural and historical context. While sports officials are keen to espouse the business base of their activities, they are generally reluctant to explore the motivations that made them come into sports administration and how they have evolved in it as a means to help understand and explain present problems and challenges. To illustrate the point, the mainstream sports discourse in

India on the 2010 Commonwealth Games tells us that medals won, records broken and television rights sold are ends in themselves. The point that is lost is that the Games are about the idea of India's emergence as a sporting power, a dream the country has nurtured since independence in 1947. However, as is documented more globally, the Commonwealth Games and their relevant records and statistics are important only if they can affect the societies surrounding them.

In fact, it wouldn't be unfair to suggest that mega events like the Olympics, or the Commonwealth Games on a lesser scale, are still not fully understood in all their dimensions. In recent years, crusading journalists like Andrew Jennings have set out to expose the inner workings of the IOC and what he considers its corruption. The organizational cleanout that followed the Salt Lake City scandal in 2002 confirmed many of Jennings' assertions, even if his recent attacks on the IOC appear motivated rather than searching.

The Commonwealth Games Federation too has been subjected to serious criticism in recent times. Few works on the Olympics like John Macaloon's biography of Pierre de Coubertin and the origins of the Olympic Games are comprehensive and balanced. There is hardly anything on the history and politics of the Commonwealth Games. For the most part, writing on mega events has been sycophantic and idealized.

This is why there's a significant disconnect, as Bruce Kidd argues, between the highly visible mega sports spectacles and the ideal of sport for development:

> Governments, sponsors and the media reward and punish on the basis of the medal count, no matter how courageous, moving or ethical the performance, so the whole culture of high performance sport is increasingly preoccupied with the recruitment and training of champions. As a result, only a fraction of the public and private funds spent on sport goes to grass roots development; even less for sport for development.[14]

GILL VERSUS KALMADI

Amidst such critical commentary globally, the sports pages in India in the past months have been abuzz with the face-off between Sports

Minister M.S. Gill and Suresh Kalmadi. This has been a critical subset of the Commonwealth Games scramble, with the sports ministry training its guns against the IOA on a fairly regular basis. Those running Olympic affairs in India have resorted to the old argument that in case of governmental interference in 'Games' matters, India will be banned by the IOC and will lose its right to participate in international sporting competitions.[15]

This argument, drawing on the principles of the IOC charter, has often been resorted to in the past to diffuse burgeoning crises. In fact, the very same argument has been applied in almost all quarters of the world in trying to stave off statist interference in sporting affairs. What is, however, unique in the most recent controversy is that the IOC appears steadfast in its support for the IOA. In fact, for almost a year now, the IOC has adopted a very radical approach to statist intervention and has even gone on to ban countries like Ghana where sport, historically, has been funded by the government.

It is as if the IOC is determined to stake a claim as a de facto global monitoring agency, which refuses to recognize the legitimacy of individual national governments. Completely ignoring the fact that in many societies across the world sport is government funded, the IOC continues to adhere to its somewhat archaic stand in trying to preserve the autonomy of national Olympic bodies and games organizing committees. For the IOC, state intervention is anathema. While such a policy has long-lasting historical underpinnings and can be traced back to the IOC's determination to ward off dictatorial regimes like the Nazis' in 1936,[16] in the contemporary context where national governments are often in positions to constructively contribute to improving sports governance, such an attitude is arbitrary and dogmatic.

In the case of India, Olympic sports, historically, have been a subject of Central government concern and sports bodies have often been funded by the governments in power. In fact, it is in the IOC's interest to recognize that state interference, on occasions at least, isn't harmful for sport in specific national contexts. Such intervention can act as a corrective against sports administrators who often tend to use the IOC's protection as a shield against public scrutiny.

Having spent the money in bringing the Games to India, and having funded athletes' training and, made tangible contributions in building sporting infrastructure, it is natural that the Central government will want to monitor the actions of sports administrators heading various sports federations. With a system of checks and balances in place, acts of corruption or apathy that have plagued Games organization for years can be done away with.

In the ultimate analysis, there are many in India who look longingly across the border at China's awe-inspiring sporting machine. While we must acknowledge that the organization of Indian sport is far too complicated and far too political to allow the adoption of a unilinear approach like China, the need for synergy between the state and the Games Organizing Committee should not go completely unnoticed.

Like Indian democracy, Indian sport too has evolved its own unique model. When Kapil Dev's unfancied team won the Cricket World Cup in 1983, no one could have predicted that the surprise victory, coinciding with the television revolution, would ignite deeper processes that would ultimately turn India into the throbbing heart of global cricket. If handled right, the prospect of playing host to the world on the occasion of CWG 2010 would have created another opportunity that, if harnessed, could usher in a new era in the history of Indian sport. But with just days to go, Delhi badly needs a miracle to get things back on track.

SELLOTAPE LEGACY

Going by the definition that soft power is the ability to get what you want by attracting others to your values, the Government of India and the Commonwealth Games Organizing Committee have promoted the Games as a tool to attract the West to what they call a truly 'modern India'. At the same time, it is obvious to everyone that there remains a sizeable section of India that chooses to remain beyond the realm of this marketing effort, for whom the Commonwealth Games don't signify much more than lavish spending with little tangible gain in the long run.

Slum dwellers in Kolkata or Kerala, people ravaged by incessant cyclones along the Andhra coast or the thousands who were forcibly resettled owing to the construction of the Games Village, are scathing in their condemnation of the Games. Not to mention a great number of those in Delhi who are ostensibly meant to benefit from the infrastructure being created. As Ashis Nandy has recently argued: 'Anybody who spends a few weeks here will know that there is another India which is rebelling against the version of the official India, the ultra-modern India being hammered home by the government. The slums of Delhi, for example, are in a different kind of dialogue with the mainstream discourse on the Commonwealth Games.'[17]

For Nandy, the contradiction between the official rhetoric on India championed by the government, and the 'dissent' that is so easily noticeable in the slums of Delhi are too obvious not to be taken note of by global commentators and policymakers interested in studying the legacy of the Games. Such comments are gaining in strength as the clock ticks on, once again drawing attention to the issue of a sustainable legacy.

In the final analysis, despite all the contradictions surrounding the legacy rhetoric, the Commonwealth Games, if staged well, will make a statement to a sizeable global audience. A failed Games experience, on the other hand, will add teeth to the murmurs that there remains a serious disconnect between India's new-found modernity and the masses of Indians who still inhabit pitiable conditions of existence – a stereotype championed by commentators intrigued by India's growing economic might and political clout.

At its best, Delhi 2010 was to herald the start of a new journey. At the time of writing, however, such a possibility appears remote. Delhi 2010 was meant to reorder the city, herald a new era, but it in the end it is about a last-chance dash to finish the stadiums. They may well be ready on time and the Games may well turn into a spectacle to remember, but the larger vision that it was to be about seems a distant memory.

As of now, Delhi 2010 is about plastering the cracks and putting on the spit and polish without necessarily focussing on the deeper issues. As of now, when the magnitude of unfinished work is a daily headline, when less than a 100 days are left for the world to descend on India's capital, the long-term legacy of Delhi 2010 is questionable. As of now, it is, at best, a 'sellotape legacy'.

NOTES AND REFERENCES

1 FEAR AND THE CITY

1 Till April 2008, the Delhi Government had given permission to remove 6,949 trees in the capital to facilitate infrastructure development for the Games effort. M.S. Gill, Minister of State (Independent Charge) Youth Affairs and Sport, Government of India, Lok Sabha Unstarred Question No. 4233 (asked by Shri Prabhunath Singh), answered on 23.04.2008, 'Commonwealth Games 2010'.

2 C.A. Bailey, *Empire & Information: Intelligence Gathering and Social Communication in India, 1780-1870*, (Cambridge: Cambridge University Press, 1996), p. ix.

3 Kadambari Murali Wade and Shivani Singh, 'Trailing Badly in Final Lap', *The Hindustan Times*, 18 February 2009.

4 The advertisements were published in the Delhi editions of English-language national dailies on 6 and 7 March 2009.

5 See Express News Service, 'Games Ads in Poll Code Soup, EC Says Get Money From Officers Who Issued', *The Sunday Express, Delhi Newsline* (New Delhi: 8 March 2009).

6 The apology was made by Commonwealth Games Director General V.K. Verma. Rs 26 lakh were spent on the advertisements by the organizing committee. See J. Balaji, 'EC Lets Three Commonwealth Games Officials Off the Hook', *The Hindu*, 6 May 2009.

7 IANS, 'Poll Panel Asks for Report on Commonwealth Games Ads', 31 March 2009, http://www.thaindian.com/newsportal/politics/poll-panel-asks-for-report-on-commonwealth-games-ads_100173745.html (accessed 1 April 2009).

8 For a detailed discussion on the creation of Chandigarh and its deep linkages with the Nehruvian world view, see Sunil Khilnani, *The Idea of India*, (New York: Farrar, Straus & Giroux, first published 1997).

9 Emphasis is ours. Organizing Committee Commonwealth Games 2010 Delhi, *General Organisation Plan* (New Delhi: Organizing Committee 2010, August 2007), p. 14.

10 *Progress Report on Status of Games Planning By Organising Committee Commonwealth Games 2010* (New Delhi: Organizing Committee, CWG 2010, 2006), p. 53.

11 *Games News: Commonwealth Games, Delhi 2010*, Vol. 1, Issue 2 (2006), p. 10.

12 *Updated Bid Document: Delhi 2010 Commonwealth Games*, December 2003, p. 55–56.

13 *Delhi 2010 Logo Story*, handout by CWG 2010 Delhi Organizing Committee. Given to authors in February 2009.

14 *Games News: Commonwealth Games, Delhi 2010*, Vol. 1, Issue 2 (2006), p. 8.

15 The organizing committee itself consists of two governmental nominees, two Indian Olympic Association (IOA) appointees, two state government nominees and four national federation nominees. *Updated Bid Document: Delhi 2010 Commonwealth Games*, December 2003, p. 37.

16 For example, the Commonwealth Games have been the subject of parliamentary scrutiny since 2003 with successive sports ministers laying out consolidated Games budgets in response to probing questions by Members of Parliament. Given that most funding and a great deal of the implementation are being done by government agencies, these parliamentary records should be the most comprehensive. Yet, not till May 2007 was the Rs 264 crore estimated for security arrangements in the Games included in the overall budget figures produced in Parliament by various sports ministers. This, despite the fact that the organizing committee had always factored these costs in and the Delhi Police has been party to discussions since the very beginning. It had provided the Commonwealth Games Federation a preliminary estimate of its plans even before Delhi won the bid! Even this Rs 264 crore security budget, when it was ultimately reported in Parliament, did not include the cost of CCTV cameras, perimeter security and a PA system. The security costs were reported to Parliament by Mani Shankar Aiyar, Minister of Panchayati Raj, Youth Affairs and Sports and Development of North-Eastern Region, Government of India, Rajya Sabha Unstarred Question No. 413 (asked by Ravi Shankar Prasad, Ram Jethmalani), answered on 03.05.2007, 'Amount Sanctioned for Commonwealth Games'. The breakdown of the cost is referred to in Organizing Committee Commonwealth Games 2010 Delhi, *General Organisation Plan* (New Delhi: Organizing Committee 2010, August 2007), p. 88.

17 This included Rs 399.05 crore estimated by the Indian Olympic Association (IOA) as operating expenditure for the Games, Rs 186 crore estimated by the Govt of Delhi for Games Village and Rs 32.05 crore estimated by the DDA for creating new infrastructure and upgrading existing facilities. Annexure 1, Sunil Dutt, Minister of Youth Affairs and Sports, Government of India, Lok Sabha Unstarred Question No. 3180 (asked by Salarapatty Kuppusamy Kharventhan, Ananta Nayak, Ajit Jogi), answered on 20.12.2004, 'Commonwealth Games'. Also see Sunil Dutt, Minister of Youth Affairs and Sports, Government of India, Rajya Sabha Unstarred Question No. 454 (asked by E.M. Sudarsana Natchiappan, Janardhana Poojary, R.P. Goenka), answered on 03.03.2005, 'Preparation for Commonwealth Games'. Prithviraj Chavan, Minister of State in Prime Minister's Office, Government of India, Rajya Sabha Unstarred Question No. 1261 (asked by Eknath K. Thajur), answered on 04.08.2005, 'Funds for Commonwealth Games'.

18 Sunil Dutt, Minister of Youth Affairs and Sports, Government of India, Rajya Sabha Unstarred Question No. 454 (asked by E.M. Sudarsana Natchiappan, Janardhana Poojary, R.P. Goenka), answered on 03.03.2005, 'Preparation for Commonwealth Games'.

19 *Updated Bid Document: Delhi 2010 Commonwealth Games* (December 2003), pp. 174–78

20 Sunil Dutt, Minister of Youth Affairs and Sports, Government of India, Lok Sabha Unstarred Question No. 3180 (asked by Salarapatty Kuppusamy Kharventhan, Ananta Nayak, Ajit Jogi), answered on 20.12.2004, 'Commonwealth Games'.

21 Organizing committee data for 2003 is from *Updated Bid Document: Delhi 2010 Commonwealth Games* (December 2003), pp. 174–78. 2002 and 2003 government data is from Prithviraj Chavan, Minister of State in Prime Minister's Office, Government of India, Rajya Sabha Unstarred Question No. 1261 (asked by Eknath K. Thajur), answered on 04.08.2005, 'Funds for Commonwealth Games'.

Data for 2005 is from Oscar Fernandes, Minister of State (Independent Charge) Statistics and Programme Implementation, Youth Affairs and Sports and Overseas Indian Affairs, Government of India, Rajya Sabha Unstarred Question No. 3347 (asked by E.M. Sudarsana Natchiappan), answered on 22.12.2005, 'Plan for Commonwealth Games'. Rs 896 crore (US$ 199 million) was the Games operating budget worked out in 2005 by the organizing committee. This was based on CGF Manuals/ Regulations, Host City Contract Obligations and key inputs like air fares, hotel/transport costs, catering costs, etc from service providers.

The organizing committee first submitted its budget for recommendations by the sports ministry and finance ministry in September 2005. The finance ministry on 30 May 2006 laid down some parameters to appraise the proposal for the consideration of the

Expenditure Finance Committee (EFC). EFC on 13 September 2006 arrived at a revised expenditure figure of US$177.4 million (Rs 767 crore), with a provision for escalation up to 15 per cent as against US$199 million (Rs 896 crore). *Progress Report on Status of Games Planning By Organising Committee Commonwealth Games 2010* (New Delhi: Organizing Committee, CWG 2010, 2006), pp. 46–47, 200.

Data for 2006 is from Mani Shankar Aiyar, Minister of Panchayati Raj, and Youth Affairs and Sports and Development of North-Eastern Region, Government of India, Rajya Sabha Unstarred Question No. 239 (asked by C. Perumal, Janardhana Poojary), answered on 23.11.2006, 'Creation of Infrastructure for the Commonwealth Games'. Annexure II; Mani Shankar Aiyar, Minister of Panchayati Raj, Youth Affairs and Sports and Development of North-Eastern Region, Government of India, Rajya Sabha Unstarred Question No. 2722 (asked by Rajeev Chandrashekhar), answered on 26.04.2007, 'Status of Preparation for the Commonwealth Games'. For more information also see Oscar Fernandes, Minister of State (Independent Charge) Statistics and Programme Implementation, Youth Affairs and Sports and Overseas Indian Affairs, Government of India, Lok Sabha Unstarred Question No. 70 (asked by Virendra Kumar, Chandrakant Bhaurao Khaire, Sanat Kumar Mandal, Virchandra Paswan), answered on 23.11.2005, 'Commonwealth Games 2010'; Mani Shankar Aiyar, Minister of Panchayati Raj, and Youth Affairs and Sports and Development of North-Eastern Region, Government of India, Lok Sabha Unstarred Question No. 2153 (asked by Salarapatty Kuppusamy Kharventhan), answered on 06.12.2000 'Preparation for Commonwealth Games'; Mani Shankar Aiyar, Minister of Panchayati Raj, and Youth Affairs and Sports and Development of North-Eastern Region, Government of India, Rajya Sabha Unstarred Question No. 1788 (asked by Vijay Jawaharlal Darda), answered on 10.08.2006, 'Programme to Showcase India at Melbourne Commonwealth Games'; Mani Shankar Aiyar, Minister of Panchayati Raj, and Youth Affairs and Sports and Development of North-Eastern Region, Government of India, Rajya Sabha Unstarred Question No. 413 (asked by Ram Jethmalani, Shri Ravi Shankar Prasad), answered on 03.05.2007, 'Amount Sanctioned for Commonwealth Games'.

Data for 2007 is from Mani Shankar Aiyar, Minister of Panchayati Raj, Youth Affairs and Sports and Development of North-Eastern Region, Government of India, Rajya Sabha Unstarred Question No. 413 (asked by Ravi Shankar Prasad, Ram Jethmalani), answered on 03.05.2007, 'Amount Sanctioned for Commonwealth Games'; Mani Shankar Aiyar, Minister of Panchayati Raj, Youth Affairs and Sports and Development of North-Eastern Region, Government of India, Lok Sabha Unstarred Question No. 4766 (asked by Ramji Lal Suman, Chinta Mohan), answered on 09.05.2007, 'Expenditure for Commonwealth Games'; Ajay Maken, Minister of State in the Ministry of Urban Development, Government of India, Rajya Sabha Unstarred Question No. 3953 (asked by Dara Singh), answered on 10.05.2007, 'CPWD'S Blueprint to Facelift Stadium for Commonwealth Games'; Mani Shankar Aiyar, Minister of Panchayati Raj and Youth Affairs and Sports, Government of India, Rajya Sabha Unstarred Question No. 1358 (asked by Nirmala Deshpande), answered on 23.08.2007, 'Training of Youth for Commonwealth Games'; Mani Shankar Aiyar, Minister of Panchayati Raj and Youth Affairs and Sports, Government of India, Rajya Sabha Unstarred Question No. 1361 (asked by Jai Parkash Aggarwal), answered on 23.08.2007, 'State of Preparedness for Commonwealth Games'; Mani Shankar Aiyar, Minister of Panchayati Raj and Youth Affairs and Sports, Government of India, Rajya Sabha Unstarred Question No. 1980 (asked by T.T.V. Dhinakaran), answered on 30.08.2007, 'Sites for Commonwealth Games'.

Data for 2008 is from Dr M.S. Gill, Minister of State (Independent Charge) for Youth Affairs and Sports, Government of India, Rajya Sabha Unstarred Question No. 1234 (asked by Jai Prakash Aggarwal), answered on 11.12.2008, 'Expenditure on Commonwealth Games'; Mani Shankar Aiyar, Minister of Panchayati Raj, Youth Affairs and Sports and Development of North-Eastern Region, Government of India, Rajya Sabha Unstarred Question No. 292 (asked by Rajeev Chandrashekhar), answered on 28.02.2008, 'Preparation for Commonwealth Games'; Mani Shankar Aiyar, Minister of Panchayati Raj, Youth Affairs and Sports and Development of North-Eastern Region, Government of India, Rajya Sabha Starred Question No. 202 (asked by Dr Vijay Mallya), answered on 13.03.2008, 'Status of Commonwealth Games'; Mani Shankar Aiyar, Minister of Panchayati Raj, Youth Affairs and Sports and Development of North-Eastern Region, Government of India, Lok Sabha Starred Question No. 35 (asked by Asaduddin Owaisi, K. Dhanaraju), answered on 27.02.2008, 'Preparation for Commonwealth Games'.

July 2009 data, unless marked otherwise (and except for expenditure on Melbourne Games), is from the Comptroller and Auditor General of

India, *A Report on the Preparedness for the XIX Commonwealth Games 2010* (New Delhi: July 2009), pp. 5, 57–58, henceforth CAG 2009.

†This includes cost of civic infrastructure (Rs 134.32 crore) and security (Rs 7.16 crore) for Commonwealth Youth Games.

★CAG 2009 listed a total of Rs 749 crore in the 'Others' column. We assume that it included the Rs 344 crore that were spent on the Pune Youth Commonwealth Games as the CAG noted this figure in a separate chart on funding sources. Since we have a separate column for the Pune Games here, we have subtracted that amount from said column.

★★CAG 2009 did not have a separate category for expenditure on 'Athletes' in its activity-wise breakdown (though it did note it in its funding sources) and this figure is from Parliamentary records cited above.

Final 2009 cost estimate for infrastructure is from Government of Delhi, internal note on Commonwealth Games, handed to authors by a senior government officer on condition of anonymity, May 2009. The note, we were informed, was prepared by the Office of the Chief Secretary. Subsequently published by Directorate of Information and Publicity, Delhi Government, *Creating Commonwealth for All: Status Report on Infrastructure* (New Delhi: 2009).

22 GoI provided flexibility of up to 15 per cent in organizing committee's budget of Rs 676 crore to Ministry of Youth Affairs and Sports, up to 10 per cent to Sports Authority of India budget of Rs 1,000 crore and 25 per cent variation to DDA in its Rs 325 crore budget for Games Village. In May 2007, a flexibility of Rs 300 crore was envisaged in the overall budget. For sources see ibid.

23 The CAG budget calculation did not include cost of DMRC, Airports Authority of India and several other agencies. Comptroller and Auditor General of India, *A Report on the Preparedness for the XIX Commonwealth Games 2010* (New Delhi: July 2009), p. v.

24 Government of Delhi, internal note on Commonwealth Games, handed to authors by a senior government officer on condition of anonymity, May 2009. Subsequently published by Directorate of Information and Publicity, Delhi Government, *Creating Commonwealth for All: Status Report on Infrastructure* (New Delhi: 2009).

25 Oscar Fernandes, Minister of State (Independent Charge) Statistics and Programme Implementation, Youth Affairs and Sports and Overseas Indian Affairs, Government of India, Rajya Sabha Unstarred Question

No. 3347 (asked by E.M. Sudarsana Natchiappan), answered on 22.12.2005, 'Plan for Commonwealth Games'. By August 2007 the Delhi government's action plan had gone up to Rs 1352 crore for spending on health, transport, roads, horticulture, water, electricity and infrastructure according to records submitted in Parliament. Mani Shankar Aiyar, Minister of Panchayati Raj and Youth Affairs and Sports, Government of India, Rajya Sabha Unstarred Question No. 1361 (asked by Jai Parkash Aggarwal), answered on 23.08.2007, 'State of Preparedness for Commonwealth Games'.

26 See footnote for Table 1.1. 2009 data is from Government of Delhi, internal note on Commonwealth Games, handed to authors by a senior government officer on condition of anonymity, May 2009.The note, we were informed, was prepared by the Office of the Chief Secretary. Subsequently published by Directorate of Information and Publicity, Delhi Government, *Creating Commonwealth for All: Status Report on Infrastructure* (New Delhi: 2009).

27 Interview with V.K. Verma, Director General, Commonwealth Games, President, Badminton Federation of India, January 2009.

28 Government of Delhi, internal note on Commonwealth Games, handed to authors by a senior government officer on condition of anonymity, May 2009. Subsequently published by Directorate of Information and Publicity, Delhi Government, *Creating Commonwealth for All: Status Report on Infrastructure* (New Delhi: 2009).

29 Mani Shankar Aiyar, Minister of Panchayati Raj and Youth Affairs and Sports, Government of India, Rajya Sabha Unstarred Question No.1930 (asked by Prasanta Chatterjee, Tarini Kanta Roy), answered on 09.03.2006, 'Cost of Commonwealth Games'.

30 Mani Shankar Aiyar, Minister of Panchayati Raj and Youth Affairs and Sports, Government of India, Rajya Sabha Unstarred Question No. 3030 (asked by S.G. Indra), answered on 24.08.2006, 'Private Sector Contribution for Organising Commonwealth Games'.

31 *Ministry of Youth Affairs and Sports: Outcome Budget 2008-2009* (New Delhi: Government of India, 2008), p. 41.

32 Ajai Masand, 'We Will Return Every Penny to the Government', *The Hindustan Times* (New Delhi: 21 February 2009).

33 Melbourne had estimated an expenditure of $2,895,021,000 and ended up spending only $18,136,000 more than this. In actual operations in Melbourne, they spent *less* than they had estimated ($938 million), as opposed to an estimate of $1,036 million. It was only in construction

that they went over the estimates: an extra $45 million was spent under this head. KPMG, *Office of Economic Impact Study of the Melbourne 2006 Commonwealth Games: Post-event Analysis*, Office of Commonwealth Games Coordination, October 2006, pp. 47–49.

34 Interview with Sheila Dikshit. Abantika Ghosh, 'Games Security is a Big Concern', *The Times of India* (New Delhi: 3 January 2009).

35 Interview with V.K. Verma, Director General, Commonwealth Games, President, Badminton Federation of India, January 2009.

36 See Sonia Gandhi, Leader of Opposition, Lok Sabha, letter to Michael Fennell, Chairman, Commonwealth Games Federation, 1 May 2003. Reproduced in *Updated Bid Document: Delhi 2010 Commonwealth Games* (December 2003), p. 11.

37 See Vijai Kapoor, Lieutenant Governor of Delhi, Letter to Michael Fennell, Chairman, Commonwealth Games Federation, 14 May 2003. Reproduced in *Updated Bid Document: Delhi 2010 Commonwealth Games* (December 2003), p. 13.

38 See Sheila Dikshit, Chief Minister Delhi, Letter to Suresh Kalmadi, President, Indian Olympic Association, 3 April 2003. Reproduced in *Updated Bid Document: Delhi 2010 Commonwealth Games* (December 2003), p. 15.

39 See Jaishree Panwar, Mayor–Delhi, Letter to Suresh Kalmadi, President, Indian Olympic Association, 4 April 2003. Reproduced in *Updated Bid Document: Delhi 2010 Commonwealth Games* (December 2003), p. 16.

40 For a detailed account of the makeover of Delhi in 1982, see Nalin Mehta, Boria Majumdar, *Olympics: The India Story* (New Delhi: HarperCollins, 2008), Ch. 7.

41 Stephen Evans, 'The Olympics and the Need to Make Money', 6 July 2005, http://news.bbc.co.uk/2/hi/business/4653491.stm (accessed 29 January 2009).

42 Express News Service, 'In Deficit, Govt. Seeks Funds From DDA Now', *The Indian Express: Express Newsline* (New Delhi: 27 May 2009), p. 1.

43 Express News Service, 'Though there Was an Increase of Rs. 1,600 cr in the Budget, Sources Say Commonwealth Games Projects Will Need Much More', *The Indian Express* (New Delhi: 17 February 2009).

44 Express News Service, 'In Deficit, Govt. Seeks Funds From DDA Now', *The Indian Express: Express Newsline*, (New Delhi: 27 May 2009), p. 1.

45 'More Funds for C'wealth Games', *Mail Today* (New Delhi: 17 February 2009).

46 Delhi Government's total revenue receipts in 2009–10 were estimated at Rs 23,353 crore. Times News Network, 'Downturn costs Delhi Rs 1,300 cr', *The Times of India* (New Delhi: 26 February 2009). Interim budget and JNNURM figures are from Express News Service, 'Though there Was an Increase of Rs. 1,600 cr in the Budget, Sources Say Commonwealth Games Projects Will Need Much More', *The Indian Express* (New Delhi: 17 February 2009).

47 The allocation of the National Rural Health Mission, the Union health ministry's flagship programme in the Union Budget of 2009–10 was Rs 14,127 crore. Of these Rs 12,070 crore were provided in the Interim Budget and 2057 crore later by the finance ministry in its budget. PIB Press Release, 'Budget 2009-10', 6 July 2009.

48 The poverty figures are Planning Commission estimates. Times News Service, '50% Indians Living Below Poverty Line: Govt. Panel', *The Times of India* (New Delhi: 1 July 2009).

49 The estimate was by Shankar Acharya, former Chief Economic Advisor. Quoted in Swaminathan S. Anklesaria Aiyar, 'One-Night Stand or a Prolonged Affair?', *Sunday Times of India* (New Delhi: 12 July 2009).

50 *Updated Bid Document: Delhi 2010 Commonwealth Games* (December 2003), p. 165.

51 Anita Soni, 'Urban Conquest of Outer Delhi: Beneficiaries, Intermediaries and Victims The Case of Mehrauli Countryside', in Denis Vidal, Emma Tarlo, Veronique Dupont (eds.), *Delhi: Urban Spaces and Human Destinies* (New Delhi: Manohar, CSH, 2000), p. 79.

52 Pranab Mukherjee, Union Budget Speech, 6 July 2009, reproduced on rediff.com.

53 David Black, 'Dreaming Big: The Pursuit of "Second Order" Games as a Strategic Response to Globalisation', *Sport in Society: Cultures, Commerce, Media, Politics,* Vol. 11, No. 4, Special Issue: *Sport and Foreign Policy in a Globalising World,* July 2008, pp. 472–73. Also see, D. Black and J. van der Westhuizen, 'The Allure of Global Games for "Semi-Peripheral" Polities and Spaces: A Research Agenda', *Third World Quarterly,* Vol. 25, No. 7 (2004), pp. 1195–1214; P. Dimeo and J. Kay, 'Major Sports Events, Image Projection and the Problem of "Semi-Periphery": A Case Study of the 1996 South Asia Cricket World Cup', *Third World Quarterly,* Vol. 25, No. 7 (2004), pp. 1263–76; M. Muda, 'The Significance of Commonwealth Games in Malaysia's Foreign Policy', *The Round Table,* 346 (1998), pp. 211–26.

54 R. Cashman, K. Toohey, S. Darcy, C. Symons and R. Stewart, 'When the Carnival is Over: Evaluating the Outcomes of Mega Sporting Events in Australia', *Sporting Traditions*, 21, No. 1 (2004), p. 26.

55 See David Black, 'Dreaming Big: The Pursuit of "Second Order" Games as a Strategic Response to Globalisation,' *Sport in Society: Cultures, Commerce, Media, Politics,* Vol. 11, No. 4, Special Issue: *Sport and Foreign Policy in a Globalising World*, July 2008, p. 473.

56 Interview with V.K. Verma, Director General, Commonwealth Games, President, Badminton Federation of India, January 2009.

57 For a detailed examination of India's moon mission, see Pallava Baghla, Subhadra Menon, *Destination Moon: India's Quest for Moon, Mars and Beyond* (New Delhi: HarperCollins, 2008).

58 See for instance, R. Suryamurthy, 'Cabinet Clears 2014 Asiad Bid', *The Tribune*, (Chandigarh: 13 April 2007).

59 Organizing Committee Commonwealth Games 2010 Delhi, *General Organisation Plan* (New Delhi: Organizing Committee 2010, August 2007), p. 15.

60 Vikram Verma, Minister, Youth Affairs and Sports, Government of India, Letter to Michael Fennell, Chairman, Commonwealth Games Federation, 24 May 2003. Reproduced in *Updated Bid Document: Delhi 2010 Commonwealth Games* (December 2003), p. 10.

61 *Updated Bid Document: Delhi 2010 Commonwealth Games* (December 2003), p. 22.

62 *IX Asian Games Delhi 1982, Official Report Vol. 1* (New Delhi: IX Asian Games Special Organizing Committee, 1985), p. 27.

63 Ibid., unlisted page number.

64 Ibid., p. 60.

65 *Ministry of Youth Affairs and Sports: Outcome Budget 2008-2009* (New Delhi: Government of India, 2008), p. 24.

66 Organizing Committee Commonwealth Games 2010 Delhi, *General Organisation Plan* (New Delhi: Organizing Committee 2010, August 2007), p. 20.

67 *Ministry of Youth Affairs and Sports: Outcome Budget 2008-2009*, (New Delhi: Government of India, 2008), pp. 24–25.

68 Ibid., p. 26. PYKKA (Panchayat Yuva Krida Aur Khel Abhiyan) was to cover 250,000 villages and 6,373 blocks and of this Rs 1567 crore was to be spent in the 11th Plan from the Planning Commission's funds. *Ministry of Youth Affairs and Sports: Outcome Budget 2008-2009* (New Delhi: Government of India, 2008), p. 29.

69 *Ministry of Youth Affairs and Sports: Outcome Budget 2008-2009* (New Delhi: Government of India, 2008), p. 28.

70 This is the third scheme/programme listed in the ministry's work in its 2008-09 Budget Outcomes report, as per its work in the Tenth Five Year Plan and what it intends to do in the Eleventh Five Year 'Plan. *Ministry of Youth Affairs and Sports: Outcome Budget 2008-2009* (New Delhi: Government of India, 2008), p. 6.

71 In contrast, the ministry's spending target for the CWG in that year was Rs 15000 lakh and it managed to spend Rs 14500 lakh. *Ministry of Youth Affairs and Sports: Outcome Budget 2008-2009* (New Delhi: Government of India, 2008), pp. 45–57.

72 In the ministry outlay Rs 890 crore was Plan and Rs 221.81 crore was Non–Plan expenditure. CWG got Rs 224 crore in Plan and Rs 132.74 crore in Non–Plan expenditure; centres of sports excellence got Rs 51 crore in Plan and 3 crore in Non–Plan Expenditure; SAI got Rs 148 crore in Plan and Rs 33 crore in Non–Plan; while LNIPE (Lakshmibai National Institute of Physical Education) got a total of Rs 30 crore. *Ministry of Youth Affairs and Sports: Outcome Budget 2008-2009* (New Delhi: Government of India, 2008), pp. 45–47.

73 Of this amount, 0 was budgeted for rural sports programme, Rs 54 crore in assistance to sports of excellence (51 Plan and 3 non–plan+10+8), CWG (224 cr+132.74 cr), assistance to rural sports clubs 0, SAI (148+33 cr), LNIPE (22+8 cr). See *Annual Report 2007–08*, pp. 104–6. A detailed look at the Outcome Budget for 2008–09 tells us the real picture. In the ministry's work plan, every activity has a column next to it, specifying the quantifiable deliverables/physical outputs. But in the item for CWG 2010, this column has a telling legend: 'Since the items of work for the CWG 2010 are not quantifiable, no physical targets were fixed as such.' *Ministry of Youth Affairs and Sports: Outcome Budget 2008-2009* (New Delhi: Government of India, 2008), p. 110.

74 Visit to Goutri–Bowli Sports Complex on 22 September 2008.

75 *Updated Bid Document: Delhi 2010 Commonwealth Games* (December 2003), p. 33.

76 Charu Pant, 'One Toilet, 120 Users', *Metro Now* (New Delhi: 24 December 2008), pp.1–2.

77 Letter by Amit Bhandari, 'Is This How We Prepare for CWG?', *Metro Now* (New Delhi: 26 December 2008), pp. 1–2.

78 Interview with V.K. Verma, Director General, Commonwealth Games, President, Badminton Federation of India, January 2009.

79 Mani Shankar Aiyar, Minister of Panchayati Raj, Youth Affairs and Sports and Development of North-Eastern Region, Government of India, Rajya Sabha Unstarred Question No. 292 (asked by Rajeev Chandrashekhar), answered on 28.02.2008, 'Preparation for Commonwealth Games'.

80 Dr M.S. Gill, Minister of State (Independent Charge) Youth Affairs and Sports, Government of India, Rajya Sabha Unstarred Question No. 1234 (asked by Jai Parkash Aggarwal), answered on 11.12.2008, 'Expenditure on Commonwealth Games'. The minister said: 'For enhancing the playing capabilities and medal prospects of Indian sportspersons in the context of the Commonwealth Games, 2010, an amount of Rs 678 crore has been approved by the Government towards training; domestic/international competitions in India; foreign exposure; equipments and scientific back-up for the sportspersons.' The target of providing state-of-the-art training is to about 1280 players belonging to 18 sports, in which competition would take place during CWG 2010. Out of total of Rs 678 crore, Rs 375 crore were to be spent on training, Rs 85 crore on renovation/upgradation of SAI centres and Rs 216 crore on sports science back/medical facilities.

81 Mani Shankar Aiyar, Minister of Panchayati Raj and Youth Affairs and Sports and Development of North-Eastern Region, Government of India, Rajya Sabha Unstarred Question No. 2566 (asked by Dara Singh), answered on 14.12.2006, 'Setting Up of Special Cell for the Commonwealth Games'.

82 *Ministry of Youth Affairs and Sports: Outcome Budget 2008-2009* (New Delhi: Government of India, 2008), p. 30.

83 HT Sports Bureau, 'Chaos Theory', *The Hindustan Times* (New Delhi: 21 February 2009).

84 In conjunction with this, GoM in 2007–08 (until December 2007), had spent Rs 1,42,00,217 on 146 sportspersons and 39 supporting staff through its SAI Talent Scheme. This was in addition to the Rs 51.2968 crore spent in same period (until February 2008) on NSFs (National Sports Federations). *Ministry of Youth Affairs and Sports Annual Report 2007-08* (New Delhi: Government of India), p. 86; *Ministry of Youth Affairs and Sports: Outcome Budget 2008-2009* (New Delhi: Government of India, 2008), p. 36.

85 *Ministry of Youth Affairs and Sports: Outcome Budget 2008-2009* (New Delhi: Government of India, 2008), p. 39.

86 Dr M.S. Gill, Minister of State (Independent Charge) Youth Affairs and Sports, Government of India, Lok Sabha Starred Question No. 344 (asked by K. Jayasurya Prakash Reddy), answered on 16.04.2008, 'Training Schemes for Commonwealth Games'.

87 *Ministry of Youth Affairs and Sports: Outcome Budget 2008–2009*, p. 32. The range for Commonwealth Games is Rs. 3000–3500 per month. *Ministry of Youth Affairs and Sports Annual Report 2007-08* (New Delhi: Government of India), p. 91

88 *Ministry of Youth Affairs and Sports Annual Report 2007-2008* (New Delhi: Government of India), p. 91.

89 Ibid., p. 151–153.

90 Vijai Kapoor, Lieutenant Governor of Delhi, Letter to Michael Fennell, Chairman, Commonwealth Games Federation, 14 May 2003. Reproduced in *Updated Bid Document: Delhi 2010 Commonwealth Games* (December 2003), p. 13.

91 Dean Nelson, 'New Delhi to Hide Slums with "Bamboo Curtains" During 2010 Commonwealth Games', *The Telegraph* (London: 17 August 2009), http://www.telegraph.co.uk/sport/othersports/commonwealthgames/6043719/New-Delhi-to-hide-slums-with-bamboo-curtains-during-2010-Commonwealth-Games.html (accessed 18 August 2009).

92 'Verma Soars Again', 10 June 2007, http://www.badmintonasia.org/newspage.aspx?newsID=223 (accessed 21 August 2009).

93 Interview with V.K. Verma, Director General, Commonwealth Games, President, Badminton Federation of India, January 2009.

94 Ibid.

95 Denis Vidal, Emma Tarlo, Veronique Dupont, 'The Alchemy of an Unloved City', in Denis Vidal, Emma Tarlo, Veronique Dupont (eds), *Delhi: Urban Spaces and Human Destinies* (New Delhi: Manohar, CSH, 2000) p. 15.

96 Steven J. Jackson and Stephen Haigh, 'Between and Beyond Politics: Sport and Foreign Policy in a Globalising World', *Sport in Society: Cultures, Commerce, Media, Politics,* Vol. 11, No. 4, Special Issue: *Sport and Foreign Policy in a Globalising World*, July 2008, p. 351.

97 L. Allison, *The Changing Politics of Sport*, Manchester: Manchester University Press, p. 17, quoted in Steven J. Jackson andStephen Haigh, 'Between and Beyond Politics: Sport and Foreign Policy in a Globalising World', *Sport in Society: Cultures, Commerce, Media, Politics,* Vol. 11, No. 4, Special Issue: *Sport and Foreign Policy in a Globalising World*, July 2008, p. 351.

98 Quoted in David Black, 'Dreaming Big: The Pursuit of "Second Order" Games as a Strategic Response to Globalisation', *Sport in Society: Cultures, Commerce, Media, Politics,* Vol. 11, No. 4, Special Issue: *Sport and Foreign Policy in a Globalising World,* July 2008, p. 467.

99 David Black, 'Dreaming Big: The Pursuit of "Second Order" Games as a Strategic Response to Globalisation', *Sport in Society: Cultures, Commerce, Media, Politics,* Vol. 11, No. 4, Special Issue: *Sport and Foreign Policy in a Globalising World,* July 2008, pp. 468, 472.

100 Ibid., p. 470.

101 Quoted in Abhinav Garg, 'HC's Wake-up Call to MCD for Games', *The Times of India* (New Delhi: 22 December 2008).

2 DELHI'S SELLOTAPE LEGACY

1 Shekhar Gupta, 'Stop Fighting the 1962 War', *The Indian Express* (New Delhi: 19 September 2009).

2 Comptroller and Auditor General of India, *A Report on the Preparedness for the XIX Commonwealth Games 2010,* (New Delhi: July 2009).

3 Rajya Sabha Department-Related Parliamentary Standing Committee on Transport, Tourism, and Culture, *One Hundred and Forty-Ninth Report on Development of Tourism, Infrastructure and Amenities for the Commonwealth Games 2010,* presented to the Rajya Sabha on 24 February 2009; laid on the table of the Lok Sabha in February, 2009 (New Delhi: Rajya Sabha Secretariat, February 2009).

4 TNN, 'Concerned PM Asks Gill to Step In', *The Times of India* (New Delhi: 6 October 2009).

5 V.K. Malhotra, quoted in 'Call it Imperial?' *The Indian Express* (New Delhi: 17 October 2009).

6 Conversation with Charu Sharma, Times Now studio (Mumbai: August, 2008)

7 PTI, 'Gill, CWG is Like the "Great Indian Wedding"', *The Times of India* (New Delhi: 20 February 2009).

8 IANS, 'Court Pulls Up Commonwealth Games Organizing Panel' (New Delhi: 23 December 2008).

9 Rakesh Sood, 'Accountability Issues Put Games' Organizing Panel, Sport Min on Collision Course', *The Financial Express* (New Delhi: 30 December 2008).

10 Times News Network, 'Games Panel Moves HC Against Public Body Tag', *The Times of India* (New Delhi: 11 December 2008).

11 CIC, *RTI Manual: Guide For the Public Authority*, http://rti.india.gov. in/manual1.php

12 http://www.cwgdelhi2010.org/Template3.aspx?pageid=P:1187

13 Commonwealth Games Federation, *The Report of the Commonwealth Games Evaluation Commission for the 2010 Commonwealth Games* (London: CGF, October 2003), p. 13.

14 Ibid., pp. 28, 33.

15 Ibid., p. 6.

16 *Updated Bid Document: Delhi 2010 Commonwealth Games* (December 2003), pp. 174–178.

17 Commonwealth Games Federation, *The Report of the Commonwealth Games Evaluation Commission for the 2010 Commonwealth Games* (London: CGF, October 2003), pp. 83–84.

18 Ibid., p. 84.

19 Ibid., p. 8.

20 Ibid, p. 88.

21 Interview with V.K. Verma, Director General, Commonwealth Games, January 2009.

22 Advertisement for Commonwealth Games Village 2010 by Emaar-MGF in Outlook (New Delhi: 1 December 2008), pp. 18–19.

23 Quote from interview with V.K. Verma, Director General, Commonwealth Games, January 2009. The residential zone of the Commonwealth Games Village was developed as residential apartments through Private Public Participation mode. The Delhi Development Authority (DDA) argues that the development of a residential zone on private public participation mode was envisaged to lessen the requirement of Government funding for the Commonwealth Games. Ajay Maken, Minister of State in the Ministry of Urban Development, Government of India, Lok Sabha Unstarred Question No. 3585 (asked by Shri Shailendra Kumar), answered on 25.08.2006, 'Role of Private Developers for Commonwealth Games'.

24 *Progress Report on Status of Games Planning By Organizing Committee Commonwealth Games 2010* (New Delhi: Organizing Committee, CWG 2010, 2006), p. 77.

25 Vijai Kapoor, Lieutenant Governor of Delhi, Letter to Michael Fennell, Chairman, Commonwealth Games Federation, 14 May 2003. Reproduced in *Updated Bid Document: Delhi 2010 Commonwealth Games* (December 2003), p. 13.

26 *Updated Bid Document: Delhi 2010 Commonwealth Games* (December 2003), p. 135.

27 Ajay Maken, Minister of State in the Ministry of Urban Development, Government of India, Lok Sabha Unstarred Question No. 2304 (asked by Shri Milind Deora), answered on 14.03.2008, 'Commonwealth Games Village'. It has also been suggested by experts that the Safdarjang Airport alternative was rejected because of projected difficulties in getting clearances, but the Urban Development Minister chose only to refer to the CGF's permission in his reply to the Lok Sabha.

28 See for instance, Jhoomur Bose, 'Disaster 2010: Commonwealth Village a Sitting Duck', http://ibnlive.in.com/videos/50590/disaster-2010-commonwealth-village-a-sitting-duck.html (accessed 11 November 2009); Amita Baviskar, 'Commonwealth or Kiss of Death?', http://www.gamesmonitor.org.uk/node/488 (accessed 30 June 2008); Randeep Ramesh, 'Delhi Cleans up for Commonwealth Games but Leaves Locals Without Sporting Chance'; *The Guardian* (London: 8 January 2008), http://www.guardian.co.uk/world/2008/jan/08/sport. india (accessed 10 October 2009).

29 See for instance, Newly Paul, 'A Village of Woes', *India Today*, 2 May 2008, http://indiatoday.intoday.in/site/Story/7753/Sport/A+village+of+woes.html (accessed 28 November 2008).

30 See National Environmental Engineering Research Institute, *Environmental Management Plan for Rejuvenation of River Yamuna in NCT*, sponsor DDA (Nagpur: 2005). Also see *ibid* and Jhoomur Bose, 'Commonwealth Games 2010: Delhi's Death Trap', 18 October 2007, http://ibnlive.in.com/news/commonwealth-games-2010-delhis-death-trap/50715-3.html (accessed 18 November 2009).

31 Newly Paul, 'A Village of Woes', *India Today*, 2 May 2008, http://indiatoday.intoday.in/site/Story/7753/Sport/A+village+of+woes.html (accessed 28 November 2008).

32 Ajay Maken, Minister of State in the Ministry of Urban Development, Government of India, Lok Sabha Unstarred Question No. 2304 (asked by Shri Milind Deora), answered on 14.03.2008, 'Commonwealth Games Village'.

33 Ajay Maken, Minister of State in the Ministry of Urban Development, Government of India, Rajya Sabha Unstarred Question No. 1154 (asked by Shri Motilal Vora, Shri Satyavrat Chaturvedi), answered on 08.03.2007, 'Alterative Site for Commonwealth Games Village'.

34 Ajay Maken, Minister of State in the Ministry of Urban Development, Government of India, Rajya Sabha Unstarred Question No. 1154 (asked by Shri Motilal Vora, Shri Satyavrat Chaturvedi), answered on 08.03.2007, 'Alterative Site for Commonwealth Games Village'. . The Ministry of Environment and Forests conveyed environmental clearance vide letters dated 14 December 2006, 22 January 2007, 29 March 2007 and 23 April 2007. Ajay Maken, Minister of State in the Ministry of Urban Development, Government of India, Lok Sabha Unstarred Question No. 2079 (asked by Shri K.C. Pallani Shamy), answered on 30.11.2007.

35 Ajay Maken, Minister of State in the Ministry of Urban Development, Government of India, Lok Sabha Unstarred Question No. 2079 (asked by Shri K.C. Pallani Shamy), answered on 30.11.2007.

36 Newly Paul, 'A Village of Woes', *India Today*, 2 May 2008, http://indiatoday.intoday.in/site/Story/7753/Sport/A+village+of+woes.html (accessed 28 November 2008).

37 PTI 'SC Green Signal for C'Wealth Games Village Construction', 30 July 2009, http://news.outlookindia.com/printitem.aspx?663613

38 Abhinav Garg, 'HC Panel to Assess Riverbank Projects', *The Times of India* (New Delhi: 4 November 2008). Tribune News Service, 'HC Puts Games Village Under Scanner', *The Tribune* (Chandigarh: 4 November 2008). Express News Service, 'HC: Build on Yamuna Bed at Own Risk', *The Indian Express* (New Delhi: 3 November 2008)

39 Neha Lalchandani, 'Project Never Given Full Clearance: NGO', *The Times of India* (New Delhi: 5 November 2008).

40 Newly Paul, 'A Village of Woes', *India Today*, 2 May 2008, http://indiatoday.intoday.in/site/Story/7753/Sport/A+village+of+woes.html (accessed 28 November 2008). Also see Neha Lalchandani, 'No Relief for Riverbed' *The Times of India* (New Delhi: 7 November 2008). http://timesofindia.indiatimes.com/Delhi/No_relief_for_riverbed/articleshow/3673907.cms (accessed 28 November 2009).

41 Abhinav Garg, 'HC Panel to Assess Riverbank Projects', *The Times of India* (New Delhi: 4 November 2008).

42 Jhoomur Bose, 'Disaster 2010: Commonwealth Village a Sitting Duck', http://ibnlive.in.com/videos/50590/disaster-2010-commonwealth-village-a-sitting-duck.html (accessed 11 November 2009).

43 Abhinav Garg, 'HC Panel to Assess Riverbank Projects', *The Times of India* (New Delhi: 4 November 2008).

44 See letter obtained from CGWA under RTI. Reproduced on: http://
ibnlive.in.com/videos/50590/disaster-2010-commonwealth-village-
a-sitting-duck.html (accessed 11 November 2009); Neha Lalchandani,
'Project Never Given Full Clearance: NGO', *The Times of India* (New
Delhi: 5 November 2008).

45 Times News Network, 'Games Village Site Developer Seeks DDA
Loan', *The Times of India* (New Delhi: 3 January 2009).

46 Moushumi Das Gupta, 'Games Bailout Plan Ready', *The Hindustan
Times* (New Delhi: 18 February 2009).

47 Ayesha Arvind and Mandakini Gahlot, '2010 Village: DDA Fixes Rates
of Flats in Bailout to Emaar', *The Indian Express: Express Newsline* (New
Delhi: 28 April 2009).

48 Comptroller and Auditor General of India, *A Report on the Preparedness
for the XIX Commonwealth Games 2010* (New Delhi: July 2009), p. 31.

49 Quoted in Gyanant Singh, 'Govt Against Panel on Games Construction',
Mail Today (New Delhi: 25 April 2009).

50 Amita Baviskar, 'Commonwealth or Kiss of Death?' http://www.
gamesmonitor.org.uk/node/488 (accessed 30 June 2008).

51 J. Venkatasen, 'Supreme Court Extends Stay on High Court Order',
The Hindu (New Delhi: 12 December 2008).

52 Quoted in Reuters, 'India Could Lose 2010 Commonwealth Games:
Official', *The Times of India* (11 November 2009), posted online at:
http://74.125.153.132/search?q=cache:81zrjzUF4wEJ:sports.timesofindia.
indiatimes.com/Other-Sports/Others/India-could-lose-2010-
Commonwealth-Games-Official/articleshow/3701087.cms+india+could
+lose+2010+commonwealth+games&cd=5&hl=en&ct=clnk&gl=in

53 PTI, 'SC Green Signal for C'Wealth Games Village Construction', 30
July 2009, http://news.outlookindia.com/printitem.aspx?663613

54 Quoted in Gyanant Singh, 'Govt Against Panel on Games Construction',
Mail Today (New Delhi: 25 April 2009).

55 PTI, 'SC Green Signal for C'Wealth Games Village Construction', 30
July 2009, http://news.outlookindia.com/printitem.aspx?663613

56 *Progress Report on Status of Games Planning By Organizing Committee
Commonwealth Games 2010* (New Delhi: Organizing Committee, CWG
2010, 2006), p.7, 60.0

57 Mani Shankar Aiyar, Minister of Panchayati Raj, Youth Affairs and
Sports and Development of North-Eastern Region, Government
of India, Lok Sabha Starred Question No. 2164 (asked by Pamkaj
Chaudhary), answered on 29.08.2007, 'Commonwealth Games-2010'.

58 *Updated Bid Document: Delhi 2010 Commonwealth Games* (December 2003), p. 44, 59, 64.

59 This included two indoor stadiums for weightlifting and wrestling with a capacity for 4,000 and a 2,000 capacity stadium for lawn bowls. The Games operational plan in the bid was based upon data and study conducted by M/S A. Sharma and Company. The first schedule was drawn up in the original Bid document. That laid down a time frame of 1 January 2004–1 May 2006 to complete the planning process (framework of systems and infrastructure and accurate cost estimates) and stipulated 1 May 2006-1 May 2008 to 'create' the Games. The delivery timeline was May 2008–December 2010. *Updated Bid Document: Delhi 2010 Commonwealth Games* (December 2003), p. 172, 18, 38.

60 The Evaluation Committee estimates for delivery of venues were as follows: 2005: Jawaharlal Nehru Sports Complex (lawn bowls), Indoor Stadium at Saket; 2006: Yamuna Sports Complex (rugby 7s); 2007: Yamuna Sports Complex (boxing), Indira Gandhi Stadium Sports Complex (wrestling); 2008: Jawaharlal Nehru Stadium (athletics), Indira Gandhi Indoor Stadium (netball), the Dr Shyama Prasad Mukherjee Swimming Pool (diving and swimming), the training facilities at the Village; 2009: Yamuna Velodrome Indira Gandhi Sports Complex, the Dhyan Chand National Stadium. Commonwealth Games Federation, *The Report of the Commonwealth Games Evaluation Commission for the 2010 Commonwealth Games* (London: CGF, October 2003), pp. 67–72, 75.

61 Ajay Maken, Minister of State in the Ministry of Urban Development, Government of India, Lok Sabha Unstarred Question No. 146 (asked by Shri Milind Deora), answered on 16.11.2007, 'Status of Commonwealth Games Projects'.

62 Comptroller and Auditor General of India, *A Report on the Preparedness for the XIX Commonwealth Games 2010* (New Delhi: July 2009), pp. 29–31.

63 2007 deadlines are from annexure referred to in reply to Lok Sabha Unstarred Question No. 146 for 16 November 2007. Ajay Maken, Minister of State in the Ministry of Urban Development, Government of India, Lok Sabha Unstarred Question No. 146 (asked by Milind Deora), answered on 16.11.2007, 'Status of Commonwealth Games Projects'. Revised deadlines are from http://www.cwgdelhi2010.org/Template3.aspx?pageid=P:1049 status reports are from Comptroller and Auditor General of India, *A Report on the Preparedness for the XIX Commonwealth Games 2010* (New Delhi: July 2009), pp. vi, 16–19, 63.

64 Six of the original thirty-five Games-related flyover and bridge projects had been completed and six were delinked from the Games, which meant that the focus was off them. Comptroller and Auditor General of India, *A Report on the Preparedness for the XIX Commonwealth Games 2010* (New Delhi: July 2009), pp. vi, 36.

65 Kadambari Murali Wade and Shivani Singh, 'Trailing Badly in Final Lap', *The Hindustan Times* (18 February 2009). When the *Hindustan Times* sent its reporters out for a status check on the construction in early 2009, this is what they found: the Talkatora was only 50 per cent finished; the Karni Singh Shooting Range 35 per cent; the Jawaharlal Nehru Sports Complex, 40 per cent; the National Stadium 55 per cent; the R.K. Khanna Complex 50 per cent; the Yamuna Complex 50 per cent; the Velodrome 10 per cent; the Indira Gandhi Complex 40 per cent and the Siri Fort Complex 45 per cent. 'Blocked by Blocks', *The Hindustan Times* (18 February, 2009).

66 IANS, 'India to Invest $10 billion in IMF: Pranab', 4 September 2009, http://timesofindia.indiatimes.com/india/India-to-invest-10-billion-in-IMF-Pranab/articleshow/4973685.cms

67 Figures from Mani Shankar Aiyar, Minister of Panchayati Raj, and Youth Affairs and Sports and Development of North-Eastern Region, Government of India, Rajya Sabha Unstarred Question No. 1788 (asked by Shri Vijay Jawaharlal Darda), answered on 10.08.2006, 'Programme to Showcase India at Melbourne Commonwealth Games'.

68 Comptroller and Auditor General of India, *A Report on the Preparedness for the XIX Commonwealth Games 2010* (New Delhi: July 2009), p. 10.

69 Ibid., p. 9. The organizing committee came into existence only on 10 February 2005. The Group of Ministers on the Commonwealth Games only gave directions to constitute an organizing committee on 29 January 2005.Organizing Committee Commonwealth Games 2010 Delhi, *General Organisation Plan* (Delhi: Organizing Committee 2010, August 2007), p. 48; Sunil Dutt, Minister of Youth Affairs and Sports, Government of India, Rajya Sabha Unstarred Question No. 50 (asked by Shri Pramod Mahajan, Shri Rajkumar Dhoot), answered on 03.03.2005, 'Constitution of Organizing Committee for Commonwealth Games'.

70 Comptroller and Auditor General of India, *A Report on the Preparedness for the XIX Commonwealth Games 2010* (New Delhi: July 2009), p. 10.

71 *Progress Report on Status of Games Planning By Organizing Committee Commonwealth Games 2010* (New Delhi: Organizing Committee, CWG 2010, 2006), p. 60. Also see Organizing Committee Commonwealth

Games 2010 Delhi, *General Organisation Plan* (New Delhi: Organizing Committee 2010, August 2007), pp. 69–70.

72 Comptroller and Auditor General of India, *A Report on the Preparedness for the XIX Commonwealth Games 2010* (New Delhi: July 2009), p. 10.

73 Interview with V.K. Verma, Director General, Commonwealth Games, January 2009.

74 Organizing Committee Commonwealth Games 2010 Delhi, *General Organisation Plan* (New Delhi: Organizing Committee 2010, August 2007), p. 22-23.

75 Comptroller and Auditor General of India, *A Report on the Preparedness for the XIX Commonwealth Games 2010* (New Delhi: July 2009), p. 10.

76 Figure from Suresh Kalmadi, Chairman, Organizing Committee, CWG Delhi 2010, 'A Word From the Chairman', *Annual Report 2008 Organizing Committee Commonwealth Games Delhi 2010*. For details on the governmental structures set up to monitor the Games effort, see Mani Shankar Aiyar, Minister of Panchayati Raj, Youth Affairs and Sports and Development of North-Eastern Region, Government of India, Rajya Sabha Unstarred Question No. 2722 (asked by Rajeev Chandrashekhar), answered on 26.04.2007, 'Status of Preparation for the Commonwealth Games'; Mani Shankar Aiyar, Minister of Panchayati Raj, Youth Affairs and Sports and Development of North-Eastern Region, Government of India, Rajya Sabha Unstarred Question No. 510 (asked by Jai Prakash Aggarwal), answered on 10.05.2007, 'Preparations for Commonwealth Games'; Sunil Dutt, Minister of Youth Affairs and Sports, Government of India, Rajya Sabha Unstarred Question No. 1063 (asked by Shri Raju Parmar, Shri P.K. Maheshwari), answered on 10.03.2005, 'Arrangements for the Commonwealth Games'.

77 Mani Shankar Aiyar, Minister of Panchayati Raj, Youth Affairs and Sports and Development of North-Eastern Region, Government of India, Rajya Sabha Unstarred Question No. 292 (asked by Shri Rajeev Chandrashekhar), answered on 28.02.2008, 'Preparation for Commonwealth Games'; *Progress Report on Status of Games Planning By Organizing Committee Commonwealth Games 2010* (New Delhi: Organizing Committee, CWG 2010, 2006), p. 1.

78 Comptroller and Auditor General of India, *A Report on the Preparedness for the XIX Commonwealth Games 2010* (New Delhi: July 2009), p. 11., Appendix IV.

79 Ibid. The first draft of it was shared with the CGF in November 2006, a presentation made to CGF Executive Board in Kuala Lumpur on 17–18

November 2006. Organizing Committee Commonwealth Games 2010 Delhi, *General Organisation Plan* (New Delhi: Organizing Committee 2010, August 2007), pp. 24–25.

80 Comptroller and Auditor General of India, *A Report on the Preparedness for the XIX Commonwealth Games 2010* (New Delhi: July 2009), p. 11., Appendix IV.

81 See Times News Network, 'Underfire Organisers Present Brave Face', *The Times of India* (New Delhi: 25 February 2009).

82 Comptroller and Auditor General of India, *A Report on the Preparedness for the XIX Commonwealth Games 2010* (New Delhi: July 2009), p. 23.

83 Ibid., p. 24.

84 Ibid., Appendix III, p. 59.

85 Quoted in Richi Verma, 'Games–Bound Govt. Finds DUAC in Slow Lane', *The Times of India* (New Delhi: 1 February 2009).

86 Ibid.

87 Interview with Sheila Dikshit. Abantika Ghosh, 'Games Security is a Big Concern', *The Times of India* (New Delhi: 3 January 2009).

88 Tannu Sharma, '2010 Games: Environment Panel Hauls Up DDA for Siri Fort Projects', *The Indian Express: Express Newsline* (New Delhi: 24 January 2009).

89 Ibid. Also see Dhananjay Mahapatra, 'Rs 5 Cr Fine Likely on DDA for Felling Trees', *The Times of India* (New Delhi: 23 January 2009), http://timesofindia.indiatimes.com/Cities/Rs_5_cr_fine_on_DDA_likely_for_felling_trees/rssarticleshow/4019013.cms

90 Quoted in Express News Service, 'Siri Fort Games Project Gets SC's Okay', *The Indian Express: Express Newsline* (New Delhi: 28 April 2009).

91 Ibid.

92 J. Venkatesan, 'Court orders new look at 2010 Games venue', *The Hindu* (New Delhi: 7 February 2009).

93 Another case in point is the basement in the Siri Fort Complex. 'In June 2007, DDA had applied for a NOC to ASI for construction of a Badminton and Squash Court (including a basement) at Siri Fort Complex, as the site was within the regulated area near a historical monument. ASI initially gave clearance in March 2008. However, in an inspection in December 2008, it noted the construction of a huge basement, for which it claimed that no permission had been given and issued a show cause notice to DDA, threatening to cancel the NOC. On the basis of DDA's response that the basement was part of the originally approved plan, in March 2009,

ASI regularised the basement as a fait accompli.' Comptroller and Auditor General of India, *A Report on the Preparedness for the XIX Commonwealth Games 2010* (New Delhi: July 2009), p. 24.

94 Quoted in Times News Network, 'People's Role Sought in 2010 Games Warm-up', *The Times of India* (New Delhi: 8 March 2009).

95 Transcript of Shekhar Gupta's interview with Suresh Kalmadi on NDTV's *Walk the Talk*, 'Hooper has been a Great Hindrance. He has been Shouting... Throwing Keys at Our Staff... Can't Have Him Here. That is for Sure', *The Indian Express* (New Delhi: 19 October 2009), http://www.indianexpress.com/news/hooper-has-been-a-great-hindrance.-he-has-been-shouting...-throwing-keys-at-our-staff...-cant-have-him-here.-that-is-for-sure/530488/0 (accessed 11 November 2009). This is what he told a reporter in January 2009 for instance, '... I can assure you that all Games projects will be completed on time. The upgradation work is in progress and all stadiums except the Yamuna Velodrome for cycling will be ready by December this year ... The budget for the Games will be increased slightly considering the escalating prices of raw material used in construction. The prices of steel and cement are at present high and we have to take that into consideration ... But let there be no doubt, the Commonwealth Games are happening on time.' Ayesha Arvind, 'Games Venues May Miss Deadline, Says Official; Kalmadi Optimistic', *The Indian Express: Express Newsline* (New Delhi: 5 June 2009), p. 1.

96 'CAG report 6-7 months old: Dikshit on Games 2010', 14 September 2009, http://www.ndtv.com/news/india/cag_report_6-7_months_old_dikshit_on_games_2010.php (accessed 11 November 2009).

97 Ibid.

98 Transcript of Shekhar Gupta's interview with Suresh Kalmadi on NDTV's *Walk the Talk*, 'Hooper has been a Great Hindrance. He has been Shouting... Throwing Keys at Our Staff... Can't Have Him Here. That is for Sure', *The Indian Express* (New Delhi: 19 October 2009), http://www.indianexpress.com/news/hooper-has-been-a-great-hindrance.-he-has-been-shouting...-throwing-keys-at-our-staff...-cant-have-him-here.-that-is-for-sure/530488/0 (accessed 11 November 2009).

99 Brian Stoddart, 'Commonwealth Games: Post-Imperial Conflict', 21 October 2009, http://asiapacific.anu.edu.au/blogs/southasiamasala/2009/10/21/commonwealth-games-post-imperial-conflict/ (accessed 19 November 2009).

100 'Call it Imperial?', *The Indian Express* (New Delhi: 17 October 2009).

101 Brian Stoddart, 'Commonwealth Games: Post-Imperial Conflict', 21 October 2009, http://asiapacific.anu.edu.au/blogs/southasiamasala/2009/10/21/commonwealth-games-post-imperial-conflict/ (accessed 19 November 2009).

102 See, for instance, Shantanu Guha Ray, 'Hoarding the Commonwealth', *Tehelka*, Vol. 6, Issue 43 (New Delhi: 31 October 2009).

103 http://www.cwgdelhi2010.org/newscontent.aspx?newsid=N:190 (accessed 12 November 2009).

104 Conversation in early November 2009 with a senior organizing committee official who prefers to remain unnamed.

105 M. Ramachandran, Urban Development Secretary. Quoted in Express News Service, 'Government to Take Control of Commonwealth Games Finances', *The Indian Express* (New Delhi: 9 November 2009).

106 Transcript of Shekhar Gupta's interview with Suresh Kalmadi on NDTV's *Walk the Talk*, 'Hooper has been a Great Hindrance. He has been Shouting ... Throwing Keys at Our Staff ... Can't Have Him Here. That is for Sure', *The Indian Express* (New Delhi: 19 October 2009), http://www.indianexpress.com/news/hooper-has-been-a-great-hindrance.-he-has-been-shouting...-throwing-keys-at-our-staff...-cant-have-him-here.-that-is-for-sure/530488/0 (accessed 11 November 2009).

107 Conversation in early November 2009 with a senior organizing committee official who prefers to remain unnamed.

108 *Updated Bid Document: Delhi 2010 Commonwealth Games* (December 2003), p. 7. Commonwealth Games Federation, *The Report of the Commonwealth Games Evaluation Commission for the 2010 Commonwealth Games* (London: CGF, October 2003), p. 79.

109 Shantanu Guha Ray, 'Hoarding the Commonwealth', *Tehelka*, Vol. 6, Issue 43 (New Delhi: 31 October 2009).

110 Ibid., p.26.

3 THE NINTH DELHI

1 See for instance, A.G. Krishna Menon, 'The Contemporary Architecture of Delhi: The Role of the State as Middleman', in Denis Vidal, Emma Tarlo, Veronique Dupont (eds.), *Delhi: Urban Spaces and Human Destinies* (New Delhi: Manohar, CSH, 2000), pp. 143–156.

2 Denis Vidal, Emma Tarlo, Veronique Dupont, 'The Alchemy of an Unloved City', in Denis Vidal, Emma Tarlo, Veronique Dupont (eds.), Delhi: Urban Spaces and Human Destinies (New Delhi: Manohar, CSH, 2000), p. 17.

3 See Jagmohan, Rebuilding Shahjahanabad: The Walled City of Delhi (New Delhi: Vikas, 1975).

4 Organizing Committee Commonwealth Games 2010 Delhi, General Organisation Plan (New Delhi: Organizing Committee 2010, August 2007), p. 22.

5 Updated Bid Document: Delhi 2010 Commonwealth Games (December 2003), p. 30.

6 Ibid.

7 Ibid., p. 6.

8 Ibid.

9 Ibid., p. 30.

10 For more on the transformative nature of the 1982 Asian Games, see Nalin Mehta and Boria Majumdar, Olympics: The India Story (New Delhi: HarperCollins, 2008), Chapter 8.

11 Government of Delhi, internal note on Commonwealth Games, handed to authors by a senior government officer on condition of anonymity, May 2009. The note, we were informed, was prepared by the Office of the Chief Secretary. Subsequently published as Directorate of Information and Publicity, Delhi Government, Creating Commonwealth for All: Status Report on Infrastructure (New Delhi: 2009).

12 Speech by Sheila Dikshit, Chief Minister, Delhi, National Development Council Meeting, 9 December 2006.

13 Ibid.

14 Interview with V.K. Verma, Director General, Commonwealth Games, President, Badminton Federation of India, January 2009.

15 Interview with Sheila Dikshit. Abantika Ghosh, 'Games Security is a Big Concern', The Times of India (New Delhi: 03 January 2009).

16 Government of Delhi, internal note on Commonwealth Games, handed to authors by a senior government officer on condition of anonymity, May 2009.

17 '24 New Flyovers by 2010: CM', The Indian Express (26 September 2006).

18 Mani Shankar Aiyar, Minister of Panchayati Raj, Youth Affairs and Sports and Development of North-Eastern Region, Government of

India, Lok Sabha Starred Question No. 230 (asked by Ramdas Athavale, Francis Fanthome), answered on 14.03.2007, 'Pending Projects of Commonwealth Games'.

19 Government of Delhi, internal note on Commonwealth Games, handed to authors by a senior government officer on condition of anonymity, May 2009. For further details on the evolution of these projects, also see Ajay Maken, Minister of State in the Ministry of Urban Development, Government of India, Lok Sabha Unstarred Question No. 3545 (asked by Dr Rajesh Kumar Mishra), answered on 27.04.2007, 'Commonwealth Games 2010'.

20 Government of Delhi, internal note on Commonwealth Games, handed to authors by a senior government officer on condition of anonymity, May 2009. The note, we were informed, was prepared by the Office of the Chief Secretary. Subsequently published as Directorate of Information and Publicity, Delhi Government, *Creating Commonwealth for All: Status Report on Infrastructure* (New Delhi: 2009).

21 *Updated Bid Document: Delhi 2010 Commonwealth Games* (December 2003), p. 55.

22 Government of Delhi, internal note on Commonwealth Games, handed to authors by a senior government officer on condition of anonymity, May 2009. The note, we were informed, was prepared by the Office of the Chief Secretary. Subsequently published as Directorate of Information and Publicity, Delhi Government, *Creating Commonwealth for All: Status Report on Infrastructure* (New Delhi: 2009)

23 Ibid.

24 Quoted in Boria Majumdar, Nalin Mehta, *India and the Olympics* (London: Routledge, 2009), pp. 189–90.

25 Government of Delhi, internal note on Commonwealth Games, handed to authors by a senior government officer on condition of anonymity, May 2009. The note, we were informed, was prepared by the Office of the Chief Secretary. Subsequently published as Directorate of Information and Publicity, Delhi Government, *Creating Commonwealth for All: Status Report on Infrastructure* (New Delhi: 2009).

26 Ibid.

27 Ibid.

28 Ibid.

29 Ambika Soni, Minister for Tourism and Culture, Government of India, Rajya Sabha Unstarred Question No. 230 (asked by Dharam Pal Sabharwal), answered on 07.03.2006, 'Delhi as a Major Tourist Destination for Commonwealth Games'.

30 Ambika Soni, Minister of Tourism and Culture, Government of India, Lok Sabha Unstarred Question No. 1954 (asked by Hemlal Murmu), answered on 29.11.2007, 'Housing Facilities for Commonwealth Games'. Also see Oscar Fernandes, Minister of State (Independent Charge) Statistics and Programme Implementation, Youth Affairs and Sports and Overseas Indian Affairs, Government of India, Rajya Sabha Unstarred Question No. 2573 (asked by Dr M.A.M. Ramaswamy), answered on 15.12.2005, 'Facilities for Commonwealth Games'.

31 The figure of 90,000 hotel rooms was quoted by Ambika Soni in the Rajya Sabha. This differs from the final tourist count for Melbourne, calculated by KPMG for the Melbourne Office of Commonwealth Games Organization (see note 38). Ambika Soni, Minister of Tourism and Culture, Government of India, Rajya Sabha Unstarred Question No. 244 (asked by Jai Parkash Aggarwal), answered on 27.02.2007, 'Action Plan for the Commonwealth Games'.

32 Ambika Soni, Minister of Tourism and Culture, Government of India, Rajya Sabha Unstarred Question No. 244 (asked by Jai Parkash Aggarwal), answered on 27.02.2007, 'Action Plan for the Commonwealth Games'.

33 Ambika Soni, Minister of Tourism and Culture, Government of India, Lok Sabha Unstarred Question No. 1954 (asked by Hemlal Murmu), answered on 29.11.2007, 'Housing Facilities for Commonwealth Games'.

34 Ambika Soni, Minister of Tourism and Culture, Government of India, Rajya Sabha Unstarred Question No. 2385 (asked by Vijay Jawaharlal Darda, Shrimati Syeda Anwara Taimur), answered on 20.03.2007, 'Shortage of Rooms for Commonwealth Games'.

35 Government of Delhi, internal note on Commonwealth Games, handed to authors by a senior government officer on condition of anonymity, May 2009. The note, we were informed, was prepared by the Office of the Chief Secretary. Subsequently published as Directorate of Information and Publicity, Delhi Government, *Creating Commonwealth for All: Status Report on Infrastructure* (New Delhi: 2009).

36 *Updated Bid Document: Delhi 2010 Commonwealth Games* (December 2003), p. 141.

37 TNN and Agencies, 'Six Hoteliers "Withdraw" from Games', *The Times of India* (New Delhi: 28 January 2009).

38 This number differs from the figure of 90,000 tourists officially quoted by the Minister of Tourism and Culture, Government if India (see note 31). KPMG, *Office of Economic Impact Study of the Melbourne 2006 Commonwealth Games: Post-event Analysis* (Office of Commonwealth Games Coordination, October 2006), p. 50.

39 Amita Baviskar, 'Commonwealth or Kiss of Death?' http://www. gamesmonitor.org.uk/node/488 (accessed 30 June 2008).

40 IANS, 'Delhi Monuments to be Illuminated' (4 August 2006).

41 Government of Delhi, internal note on Commonwealth Games, handed to authors by a senior government officer on condition of anonymity, May 2009. The note, we were informed, was prepared by the Office of the Chief Secretary. Subsequently published as Directorate of Information and Publicity, Delhi Government, *Creating Commonwealth for All: Status Report on Infrastructure* (New Delhi: 2009).

42 Times News Network, 'Let There Be Light: Purana Qila Decks Up for Games', *The Times of India* (New Delhi: 23 January 2009).

43 Government of Delhi, internal note on Commonwealth Games, handed to authors by a senior government officer on condition of anonymity, May 2009. The note, we were informed, was prepared by the Office of the Chief Secretary. Subsequently published as Directorate of Information and Publicity, Delhi Government, *Creating Commonwealth for All: Status Report on Infrastructure* (New Delhi: 2009).

44 Ibid.

45 *IX Asian Games Delhi 1982, Official Report*, Vol. II (New Delhi: IX Asian Games Special Organizing Committee, 1985), p. 16.

46 *IX Asian Games Delhi 1982, Official Report*, Vol. 1 (New Delhi: IX Asian Games Special Organizing Committee, 1985), p. 55.

47 *IX Asian Games Delhi 1982, Official Report*, Vol. II (New Delhi: IX Asian Games Special Organizing Committee, 1985), p. 16.

48 'Digital Delhi Gets Ready for 2010 Games', *The Indian Express* (3 October 2006).

49 Government of Delhi, internal note on Commonwealth Games, handed to authors by a senior government officer on condition of anonymity, May 2009.

50 See Dr M.S. Gill, Minister of State (Independent Charge) Youth Affairs and Sports, Government of India, Rajya Sabha Unstarred Question No. 3387 (asked by Jai Parkash Aggarwal), answered on 24.04.2008, 'Preparation for Law and Order During Commonwealth Games'.

51 Government of Delhi, internal note on Commonwealth Games, handed to authors by a senior government officer on condition of anonymity, May 2009.

52 'High Capacity Bus System to be Ready by March 2008', *The Indian Express* (5 October 2006).

53 150 of the 700 new buses were to be air-conditioned, according to then Delhi Transport Minister Haroon Yusuf, 'Modern Low-Floor Buses for Delhi', *The Indian Express* (13 September 2006).

54 Government of Delhi, internal note on Commonwealth Games, handed to authors by a senior government officer on condition of anonymity, May 2009.

55 Ibid. The note, we were informed, was prepared by the Office of the Chief Secretary. Subsequently published as Directorate of Information and Publicity, Delhi Government, *Creating Commonwealth for All: Status Report on Infrastructure* (New Delhi: 2009).

56 Oscar Fernandes, Minister of State (Independent Charge) Statistics and Programme Implementation, Youth Affairs and Sports and Overseas Indian Affairs, Government of India, Rajya Sabha Unstarred Question No. 2573 (asked by Dr M.A.M. Ramaswamy), answered on 15.12.2005, 'Facilities for Commonwealth Games'.

57 Megha Suri, 'Smart Signals on Road to 2010', *The Times of India* (New Delhi: 9 February 2009).

58 This comprises 115 km of Metro (6 corridors), 74 km of LRT (6 corridors), 48 km of monorail (3 corridors) and 307 km of the high capacity bus system (26 corridors). This network is in addition to Phase I and II of Metro and existing BRT corridor from Ambedkar Nagar to Delhi Gate. Government of Delhi, internal note on Commonwealth Games, handed to authors by a senior government officer on condition of anonymity, May 2009.

59 *Updated Bid Document: Delhi 2010 Commonwealth Games* (December 2003), p. 32.

60 Praful Patel, Minister of State (Independent Charge) of Ministry of Civil Aviation, Government of India, Lok Sabha Unstarred Question No. 328 (asked by Pankaj Chaudhary), answered on 06.09.2007, 'Arrangement for Commonwealth Games-2010'.

61 Times News Network, 'New Terminal to be Loaded with Facilities', *The Times of India* (New Delhi: 25 September 2008), p. 4.

62 Neha Lalchandani, 'Delhi's Dream Airport on Fast Track', *The Times of India* (New Delhi: 25 September 2008), p. 4.

63 Praful Patel, Minister of State (Independent Charge) of Ministry of Civil Aviation, Government of India, Lok Sabha Unstarred Question No. 328 (asked by Pankaj Chaudhary), answered on 06.09.2007, 'Arrangement for Commonwealth Games-2010'.

64 Union Civil Aviation Ministry statement quoted in Times News Network, 'Fee to Enable IGI Facelift by 2010: Ministry', *The Times of India* (New Delhi: 10 February 2009).

65 Times News Network, 'CM Gives BSES 4 Days to Fix Electricity Woes', *The Times of India* (New Delhi: 29 June 2009).

66 Sheila Dikshit interview on Times Now, 29 June 2009.

67 'Incentive for Power Companies', *The Hindustan Times* (New Delhi: October 2006).

68 The additional power supply was to be ramped up to 5,960 Mw by December 2011 and in 2006, the projects were estimated to require an investment of Rs 23,840 crore. The details were reported from a high-level monitoring committee headed by Power Secretary R.V. Shahi. 'Delhi Power Supply to Double in Four Years', *Business Standard* (9 October 2006).

69 Government of Delhi, internal note on Commonwealth Games, handed to authors by a senior government officer on condition of anonymity, May 2009. The note, we were informed, was prepared by the Office of the Chief Secretary. Subsequently published as Directorate of Information and Publicity, Delhi Government, *Creating Commonwealth for All: Status Report on Infrastructure* (New Delhi: 2009).

70 Ibid.

71 Indira Gandhi Super Thermal Power Project at Jhajjar, Haryana, was set up as a Joint Venture Company. Aravali Power Company Pvt. Limited has been formed with equity contribution in the ratio of 50:25:25 by NTPC Limited, GNCTD and the Government of Haryana, for development of a 1500 MW coal-based power plant. The power is to be shared equally by Delhi and Haryana. The Prime Minister laid the foundation stone of the plant on 07 October 2007 and it is scheduled for commissioning before Commonwealth Games 2010. The 1500 MW Pragati – III Combined Cycle Gas Turbine Project at Bawana in North-West Delhi is being set up by Pragati Power Corporation Limited. The Prime Minister laid the foundation stone of the plant on 24 March 2008. Turnkey order has been placed on BHEL for setting up and for commissioning of the project before Commonwealth Games 2010. NTPC has been engaged as Consultant. Government of Delhi, internal note on Commonwealth Games, handed to authors by a senior government officer on condition of anonymity, May 2009.

72 These are: National Capital Thermal Power Project, Dadri Stage-II (2x490 MW), Badarpur Thermal Power Station, Stage-III Delhi (2x500

MW), Mejia Ph. II Thermal Power Station, Unit I and II, (2x500 MW), Bokaro 'A' Thermal Power Station (500 MW), Koderma Thermal Power Station, Stage I, Unit I and II (1000 MW). Sushilkumar Shinde, Minister for Power, Government of India, Rajya Sabha Unstarred Question No. 282 (asked by S.M. Laljan Basha), answered on 19.03.2007, 'Action Plan for the Commonwealth Games'.

73　Government of Delhi, internal note on Commonwealth Games, handed to authors by a senior government officer on condition of anonymity, May 2009. The note, we were informed, was prepared by the Office of the Chief Secretary. Subsequently published as Directorate of Information and Publicity, Delhi Government, *Creating Commonwealth for All: Status Report on Infrastructure* (New Delhi: 2009).

74　Ibid.

75　Sheila Dikshit's interview with Rumu Banerjee. 'Outages of 8–10 Hours Can't be Tolerated: CM', *The Times of India* (New Delhi: 28 June 2009), p. 2.

76　Government of Delhi, internal note on Commonwealth Games, handed to authors by a senior government officer on condition of anonymity, May 2009. The note, we were informed, was prepared by the Office of the Chief Secretary. Subsequently published as Directorate of Information and Publicity, Delhi Government, *Creating Commonwealth for All: Status Report on Infrastructure* (New Delhi: 2009).

77　Richi Verma, 'Rain comes to Rescue of BSES, City', *The Times of India* (New Delhi: 30 June 2009).

78　Government of Delhi, internal note on Commonwealth Games, handed to authors by a senior government officer on condition of anonymity, May 2009. The note, we were informed, was prepared by the Office of the Chief Secretary. Subsequently published as Directorate of Information and Publicity, Delhi Government, *Creating Commonwealth for All: Status Report on Infrastructure* (New Delhi: 2009).

79　Government of Delhi, internal note on Commonwealth Games, handed to authors by a senior government officer on condition of anonymity, May 2009.

80　Interview with Sheila Dikshit. Abantika Ghosh, 'Games Security is a Big Concern', *The Times of India* (New Delhi: 03 January 2009).

81　Government of Delhi, internal note on Commonwealth Games, handed to authors by a senior government officer on condition of anonymity, May 2009. The note, we were informed, was prepared by the Office of the Chief Secretary. Subsequently published as Directorate of Information and Publicity, Delhi Government, *Creating Commonwealth for All: Status Report on Infrastructure* (New Delhi: 2009).

82 Ibid.

83 *Updated Bid Document: Delhi 2010 Commonwealth Games* (December 2003), p. 31.

84 Government of Delhi, internal note on Commonwealth Games, handed to authors by a senior government officer on condition of anonymity, May 2009. The note, we were informed, was prepared by the Office of the Chief Secretary. Subsequently published as Directorate of Information and Publicity, Delhi Government, *Creating Commonwealth for All: Status Report on Infrastructure* (New Delhi: 2009).

85 Interview with V.K. Verma, Director General, Commonwealth Games, President, Badminton Federation of India, January 2009.

86 Ibid.

87 Anita Soni, 'Urban Conquest of Outer Delhi: Beneficiaries, Intermediaries and Victims The Case of Mehrauli Countryside', in Denis Vidal, Emma Tarlo, Veronique Dupont (eds.), *Delhi: Urban Spaces and Human Destinies* (New Delhi: Manohar, CSH, 2000), p. 79.

88 Amita Baviskar, 'Commonwealth or Kiss of Death?' http://www.gamesmonitor.org.uk/node/488 (accessed 30 June 2008).

89 Anil Varghee, 'Games Governments Play', *Tehelka*, Vol. 5, Issue 28, 19 July 2008.

90 Vibha Sharma, '150,000 Homeless in Capital', *The Tribune*, 23 February 2008, http://72.14.235.104/search?q=cache:eMLjW5vGrQIJ:www.tribuneindia.com/2008/20080223/delhi.htm+commonwealth+games+delhi+displacement&hl=en&ct=clnk&cd=13&gl=in.

91 Gautam Bhan, 'The Whitewash of Delhi: Where Have all the Poor Gone?', http://infochangeindia.org/Agenda/On-the-move/The-whitewash-of-Delhi-Where-have-all-the-poor-gone.html.

92 Anil Varghese, 'Games Governments Play', *Tehelka*, Vol. 5, Issue 28, 19 July 2008.

93 Cited in Emma Tarlo, 'Welcome to History: A Resettlement Colony in the Making', in Denis Vidal, Emma Tarlo, Veronique Dupont (eds.), *Delhi: Urban Spaces and Human Destinies* (New Delhi: Manohar, CSH, 2000), p. 52.

94 On slum removals and internal colonialism debate see See Claude Alwares, *Science, Development and Violence: The Twilight of Modernity* (New Delhi: OUP, 1992), p. 21.

95 See Jayati Ghosh, 'Delhi, India: On the Margins', People's Democracy, http://www.politicalaffairs.net/article/view/7151/, July 21–July 31, 2008.

96 Kalyani Menon-Sen and Gautam Bhan, *Swept off the Map: Surviving Eviction and Resettlement in Delhi* (New Delhi:Yoda Press, 2008).

97 Gautam Bhan,'TheWhitewash of Delhi:Where Have all the Poor Gone?', http://infochangeindia.org/Agenda/On-the-move/The-whitewash-of-Delhi-Where-have-all-the-poor-gone.html.

98 Anil Varghese, 'Games Governments Play', *Tehelka*, Vol. 5, Issue 28, July 19, 2008.

4 MEGA CITIES, MEGA EVENTS

1 Emma Tarlo, 'Welcome to History: A Resettlement Colony in the Making', in Denis Vidal, Emma Tarlo, Veronique Dupont (eds), *Delhi: Urban Spaces and Human Destinies* (New Delhi: Manohar, CSH, 2000), p. 52.

2 P.R. Emery, 'Bidding to host a major sports event: strategic investment or complete lottery', in Chris Gratton and Ian P. Henry, *Sport in the City* (London, Routledge, 2001), p. 90.

3 Report on the Los Angeles Olympics at www.aafla.org.

4 The Montreal debt took almost three decades to clear and is still referred to in Canadian sporting circles as the prime example of how things can go wrong. Interview with Dean Bruce Kidd at the University of Toronto, 15 May 2008.

5 Van Der Westhuizen, 'Marketing Malaysia as a model Muslim State: The Significance of the 16th Commonwealth Games', in David R Black and Janis Van Der Westhuizen, (eds.), Going Global: *The Promises and Pitfalls of Hosting Global Games,* Special issue of *Third World Quarterly*, Vol. 25, No. 7, (2004), p. 1279.

6 For a close analysis of the politics of the 1982 Asian Games, see Boria Majumdar and Nalin Mehta, *Olympics: The India Story* (New Delhi: HarperCollins, 2008), Chapter 8.

7 Van Der Westhuizen, 'Marketing Malaysia as a model Muslim State: The Significance of the 16th Commonwealth Games', in David R Black and Janis Van Der Westhuizen, (eds.), *Going Global: The Promises and Pitfalls of Hosting Global Games,* Special issue of *Third World Quarterly*, Vol. 25, No. 7, (2004), p. 1277.

8 The cricket experiment, however, was unsuccessful because most leading cricket playing countries sent in second-string sides to the Games. Things may be different in the future with the hugely escalating popularity of T-20 cricket, which was not in vogue then.

9. Van Der Westhuizen, 'Marketing Malaysia as a model Muslim State: The Significance of the 16th Commonwealth Games', in David R Black and Janis Van Der Westhuizen, (eds.), *Going Global: The Promises and Pitfalls of Hosting Global Games,* Special issue of *Third World Quarterly*, Vol. 25, No. 7, (2004), p. 1286.

10 Ibid.

11 For a detailed analysis of the close interplay between Nehruvian diplomacy and international sport, see Boria Majumdar and Nalin Mehta, *Olympics: The India Story* (New Delhi: HarperCollins, 2008), Chapter 7.

12 Van Der Westhuizen, 'Marketing Malaysia as a model Muslim State: The Significance of the 16th Commonwealth Games', *Third World Quarterly,* Vol. 25, No. 7, *Going Global: The Promises and Pitfalls of Hosting Global Games,* (2004), p. 1288.

13 Ibid., p. 1286.

14 *Toronto Star*, 20 August 1930.

15 For details see Katharine Moore, '"The Warmth of Comradeship": The First British Empire Games and Imperial Solidarity', *International Journal of the History of Sport*, Vol. 6, No. 2, September 1989, pp. 244–45.

16 Ibid., p. 246.

17 Ibid., p. 247.

18 Ibid., p. 249.

19 Ibid.

20 *Updated Bid Document: Delhi 2010 Commonwealth Games* (December 2003), p. 6.

21 Vikram Verma, Minister, Youth Affairs and Sports, Government of India, Letter to Michael Fennell, Chairman, Commonwealth Games Federation, 24 May 2003. Reproduced in *Updated Bid Document: Delhi 2010 Commonwealth Games* (December 2003), p. 10.

22 *Updated Bid Document: Delhi 2010 Commonwealth Games* (December 2003), p. 7.

23 *Toronto Star*, 16 August 1930.

24 *The Times of India*, 4 August 1934; also see *Toronto Star*, 4 August 1934.

25 Ibid.

26 *Toronto Star*, 10 August 1934.

27 Ibid.
28 Ibid.
29 Ibid.
30 Vernon Morgan, 'The British Empire and Commonwealth Games', in the *Official Programme* of the Kingston 1966 Games, pp. 8–17.
31 For details see the *Times of India*, 4 February–14 February 1938.
32 Morgan, 'The British Empire and Commonwealth Games', p. 13.
33 *Toronto Star*, 11 February 1938.
34 For details see *Times of India*, 31 January–11 February 1950.
35 *Toronto Star*, 3 February 1950.
36 Morgan, 'The British Empire and Commonwealth Games', p. 13.
37 Ibid.
38 *Toronto Star*, 3 February 1950.
39 *Toronto Star*, 7 August 1954, Also see *Times of India*, 1–13 August 1954.
40 Ibid.
41 Ibid.
42 *The Official History of the British Empire and Commonwealth Games*, published by the Games Organizing Committee, 1958, see section on finance.
43 Ibid.
44 Ibid.
45 Ibid., Appendix.
46 Ibid.
47 Ibid., p. 183.
48 *Toronto Star*, 22 November 1962, also see *Times of India*, 20 November 1962–30 November 1962.
49 *Toronto Star*, 24 November 1962.
50 Interview with Bruce Kidd at the University of Toronto, 15 May 2008.
51 Morgan, 'The British Empire and Commonwealth Games', p. 17.
52 The plan for the closing ceremony was described thus in the *Official Programme* published on the occasion. The elaborate nature of the ritual once again draws attention to the cost-intensive nature of the Games:

CLOSING CEREMONY

The closing ceremony commences with the march into the Arena of the Guard of Honour mounted by the Ist Battalion of the Jamaica Regiment preceded by the Band and Drums of that Regiment.

His Royal Highness Prince Philip, Duke of Edinburgh accompanied by the Officers of the British Empire & Commonwealth Games Federation, the President of the Organizing Committee, the President of the Jamaica Olympic Association, the Commissioners of the City of Kingston and the Equerry to His Royal Highness take up position on the Saluting Dais.

A fanfare of trumpets heralds the arrival into the Arena of Flag Bearers of all participating teams, medal winners, other team members and Technical Officials led by the Jamaica Military Band.

A Jamaican Song is then sung by the choir of massed voices on the conclusion of which the Flag Bearers form a semi-circle behind the Guard of Honour.

Flags are then lowered and the President of the Jamaica Olympic Association symbolizes the return of the flags to participating countries by saying: 'As President of the Jamaica Olympic Association I hand back to you the Flag of your country, both in token of our friendship and goodwill towards you and as a memento of the eighth British Empire Commonwealth Games held in Kingston, Jamaica, in 1966.'

The Flag Bearers then raise their flags and on the request of the Chairman of the British Empire & Commonwealth Games Federation, the Ceremonial Flag is struck, and presented with due ceremony to the Commissioners of the City of Kingston by the Chairman with the following words: 'As Chairman of the British Empire & Commonwealth Games Federation, I entrust this Ceremonial Flag to your care, and I ask that in due time you, or your successor in office, will deliver it to the chief citizen of the City which will be the Host to the ninth British Empire & Commonwealth Games.'

Simultaneous with the striking of the Ceremonial Flag, three flags are raised on the Victory Ceremony Flagpoles, that of the Games in the centre, that of Jamaica on its right and that of the host country for the next Games on its left.

Also at the same time, the choir of massed voices will sing the Games Closing Song.

The Chairman of the British Empire & Commonwealth Games Federation will then invite His Royal Highness to close the Games which he does with the following words: 'In the name of the British Empire & Commonwealth Games Federation I declare the eighth British Empire & Commonwealth Games, Jamaica, 1966 closed and in accordance with tradition I call upon the youths of the Commonwealth and British Empire to assemble in four years time in .... there to celebrate the ninth British Empire & Commonwealth Games. May they display cheerfulness and concord, so that the spirit of our family of nations may be carried on with ever greater eagerness, courage and honour for the good of humanity and the peace of the world.'

The Guard of Honour then gives a general Salute and the Bands play the Anthem of Jamaica the host country, the anthem of the next host country and the anthem of England.

At the conclusion of the Anthems the Flag Bearers will return to their original positions and, with the other groups following, march out of the Arena while the assembly led by the massed choir, sings the Games Farewell Song followed by Auld Lang Syne.

As the last files are entering the Marathon Tunnel, the three Flags on the Victory Ceremony Flagpoles and all the Country Flags on the perimeter wall are lowered.

His Royal Highness the Duke of Edinburgh, His Excellency the Governor-General and the Prime Minister will then depart with due honours, the Guard of Honour will march out, the assembly led by the Bands will sing the Jamaican National Anthem, upon the conclusion of which the Bands will depart. Thus ends the eighth British Empire & Commonwealth Games.

53 *Toronto Star*, 16 July 1970, also see *Times of India*, 10–17 July 1970.
54 *Toronto Star*, 16–17 July, also see 27 July 1970.
55 Ibid., 27 July 1970.
56 Ibid., 2–4 August 1978.
57 Ibid., 11 October 1982.
58 Ibid., 24 July 1986.
59 Ibid., 11 October 1982.
60 Ibid., 18 August 1994.
61 Commonwealth Games 2002: An independent cost and benefit analysis, in http://www.gameslegacy.co.uk/cgi-bin/index.cgi/346 (accessed 10 February 2009).
62 Ibid.
63 Report of the Melbourne Commonwealth Games Organizing Committee, 2006.
64 Media release issued by the Victorian Government, 21 October 2006. Also see Melbourne Commonwealth Games 2006, *Special Purpose*

Financial Report in http://download.audit.vic.gov.au/files/afr2005-06_Com_Games_2006.pdf. (accessed 10 February 2009).

65 Ibid.

66 Hanwen Liao and Adrian Pitts, 'A brief historical review of Olympic urbanization', in Boria Majumdar and Sandra Collins (eds.), *Olympism: The Global Vision: From Nationalism to Internationalism* (London, Routledge, 2008), p. 146.

67 Xu Guoqui, *OIympic Dreams: China and Sports, 1895-2008*, Boston, Harvard University Press, 2008, quoted in 'The Show has Begun' by Boria Majumdar in the *Times of India*, 9 August 2008.

68 Ibid.

69 Beijing was full of thousands of such volunteers during the Games. Most of them had also learnt a smattering of English and were very helpful to tourists.

70 News report published in the *Hindustan Times*, 1 February 2009.

71 Ibid.

72 Liao and Pitts, 'A brief historical review of Olympic urbanization', p. 157.

73 For details see: Richard Cashman, *A Bitter Sweet Awakening: The Legacy of the Sydney 2000 Olympic Games*, Walla Walla Press, Sydney, 2006, Chapter 6, pp. 139–166.

74 Emery, 'Bidding to host a major sports event: strategic investment or complete lottery', p. 91.

75 Interview with John Macaloon at the University of Chicago, 6 April 2008. Prof. Macaloon is currently completing a monograph on the impact of the Olympic Flame Relay.

76 Quoted in Cashman, *A Bitter Sweet Awakening: The Legacy of the Sydney 2000 Olympic Games,* p. 141.

77 Ibid.

78 Liao and Pitts, 'A brief historical review of Olympic urbanization', p. 155.

79 Interview with John Macaloon at the University of Chicago, 6 April 2008.

80 This has been a much quoted statement and among other places was quoted in 'The Show has Begun' by Boria Majumdar in the *Times of India*, 9 August 2008.

81 Gavin Poynter and Iain Mercury, 'Striking Gold: Commodities, gifts and the economics of London 2012', presentation at the Olympic Legacies Conference, St. Antony's College, Oxford, 29–30 March 2008.

82 Ibid.

5 GAMES OF EMPIRE, 1930-1947

1 Vidya Subrahmaniam, 'Indian Disorder and English Precision', *The Hindu* (6 November 2009), http://beta.thehindu.com/opinion/op-ed/article43951.ece (accessed 11 November 2009).

2 This was best evident in the case of football during the Mohun Bagan Club's famous victory against East Yorkshire Regiment in the Indian Football League final of 1911. For a detailed analysis of this historic match and its impact on Indian sport, see Boria Majumdar and Kausik Bandyopadhyay, *Goalless: The Story of a Unique Footballing Nation* (New Delhi: Penguin, 2006), Chapter 3.

3 For a detailed study on the relationship between nationalism and colonial Indian cricket, see Boria Majumdar, *Twenty-Two Yards to Freedom: A Social History of Indian Cricket* (New Delhi: Penguin, 2004), Chapters 1, 3, 5.

4 For a similar argument in the American sporting context, see Boria Majumdar and Sean Brown, 'Why Baseball Why Cricket: Differing Nationalisms Differing Challenges', in *International Journal of the History of Sport*, Vol. 24, No. 2.

5 For a detailed analysis of the close interplay between Nehruvian diplomacy and international sport, see Boria Majumdar and Nalin Mehta, *Olympics: The India Story*, (New Delhi: HarperCollins, 2008), Chapter 7.

6 For details, see Katharine Moore, '"The Warmth of Comradeship": The First British Empire Games and Imperial Solidarity', *International Journal of the History of Sport*, Vol. 6, No. 2, September 1989.

7 Brian Stoddart, 'Sport, Cultural Imperialism and Colonial Response in the British Empire: A Framework for Analysis', *Comparative Studies in Society and History*, Vol. 30, No. 3 (1988), p. 673.

8 For a detailed analysis of the impact of this ideology on Indian sport, see J.A. Mangan, 'The Eton in India', in *The Games Ethic and Imperialism: Aspects of the Diffusion of an Ideal* (London: Frank Cass, 1998).

9 For a detailed analysis of De Coubertin's vision, see John J. Macaloon, revised and updated edition of *This Great Symbol: Pierre de Coubertin and the Origins of the Modern Olympic Games*, Special Issue, *The International Journal of the History of Sport*, Vol. 23, Numbers 3–4, 2006.

10 Moore, '"The Warmth of Comradeship": The First British Empire Games and Imperial Solidarity', p. 243.

11 Ibid., p. 244.

12 *Toronto Star*, 15 August 1928.

13 Ibid.

14 This document has been quoted in several places and is perhaps the most quoted document on the origins of the Commonwealth Games explaining the ideology behind its establishment.

15 Moore, "'The Warmth of Comradeship": The First British Empire Games and Imperial Solidarity', p. 245.

16 A. Berriedale Keith, *The British Commonwealth* (London: Published for the British Council by Longmans Green and Co, 1940), p. 29.

17 Ibid.

18 Moore, "'The Warmth of Comradeship": The First British Empire Games and Imperial Solidarity', p. 246.

19 Ibid.

20 *Toronto Star*, 1 August 1928.

21 Ibid.

22 Ibid.

23 Ibid.

24 Ibid.

25 Ibid.

26 'US Athletes panned for over eating', *Toronto Star*, 2 August 1928.

27 Ibid.

28 Ibid.

29 Ibid.

30 Ibid., 11 August 1928.

31 Ibid., 25 August 1928.

32 Ibid.

33 Ibid.

34 Ibid.

35 Ibid., 28 August 1928.

36 Quoted in, Moore, "'The Warmth of Comradeship": The First British Empire Games and Imperial Solidarity', p. 242.

37 Ibid., p. 249.

38 'Report of the Council for Great Britain and Statement of Account', British Empire Games Canada, 1930, Personal Collection of Prof. Bruce Kidd, Dean, University of Toronto (accessed May 2008).

39 Ibid.

40 Ibid.

41 'Hail Hampson of England as King of Half-Milers', *Toronto Star*, 3 August 1932.

42 For details, see Majumdar and Mehta, *Olympics: The India Story*, Chapter 1.

43 Interview with Raj Singh Dungarpur, Cricket Club of India, 10 October 2007, Quoted in Shantanu Guha Ray and Boria Majumdar, 'A Beautiful Mind', *Tehelka*, 7 March 2009; Dungarpur told Majumdar that that his father was offered Rs 15 lakh sometime in the 1930s by the maharaja of Patiala, the game's richest patron in India, to start a cricket club. The maharaja had felt humiliated on seeing the signboard at the Bombay Gymkhana: Dogs and Indians not allowed. The CCI was once home to the city's washermen but the king of Patiala promised to turn it into a heaven. He told Maharawal of Dungarpur: '*Main yahan chaman banaunga. Iske bad Lord's jhopar patti lagega* (I will create a heaven here. Compared to this, Lord's will look like a shantytown).'

44 When the first British Empire Games were held in 1930, India was only cursorily sent an invite and was offered no subsidy for travel, thus preventing her from competing. However, none of this ignited any angry demonstrations from either the pro–British aristocracy or the nationalist middle classes.

45 We have looked at the *Times of India, The Hindu, Amrita Bazar Patrika* and *The Statesman* of the period for the purposes of this chapter.

46 *Times of India*, 22 August 1930. This report was not only relegated to the sports page but it was a one-column report placed in the lower end of the page.

47 Ibid., 25 August 1930.

48 *The Times of India* and *The Statesman* published a couple of photos each of these athletes training in London.

49 *The Times of India*, 11 August 1934.

50 For details, see *The Times of India*, 1 February 1938.

51 Ibid., 10 February 1938.

52 Anthony S. De Mello, *Portrait of Indian Sport*, (New Delhi: Macmillan 1959). This book is certainly one of the best chronicles of Indian sport in the colonial era and in the immediate aftermath of Independence.

53 Quoted in Priya Jaikumar, 'Introduction', *Cinema at the End of Empire*, Calcutta: Seagull, 2007.

54 Ramachandra Guha, 'Churchill's Indiaspeak', *The Hindu*, 5 June 2005.

55 J.N. Dixit, 'The world has changed, the Commonwealth hasn't: Uneasy sits the crown', in *The Indian Express*, 31 March 2002.

56 Quoted in Jaikumar, 'Introduction', *Cinema at the End of Empire*.

57 Ibid., Jaikumar, in an excellent introduction, has made a similar argument in the context of Indian cinema. She has suggested that the changed

realities of the Empire in the 1920s and 1930s significantly influenced the evolution of Indian cinema as an institution. Britain, trying to stave off threats from Hollywood in the aftermath of the First World War was forced to change its attitude towards cinemas of the Empire, a process that considerably altered the course of the evolution of Indian cinema.

58 Ibid.

6 'MUTUAL BENEFIT ASSOCIATION'

1 H. Duncan Hall, 'The British Commonwealth of Nations', *The American Political Science Review*, Vol. 47, No. 4, December 1953, p. 1003.

2 The Somerset Light Infantry's soldiers were the last British troops to leave India and the public ceremony took place on 28 February 1948. The new Indian Army was represented by a guard of honour from the Bombay Grenadiers, 2 Sikh, and the Indian Navy. Also participating were the 3/5 Gurkhas, and the Maratha Light Infantry.

3 Amitava Ghosh to Sandra Vince, Prizes Manager, Commonwealth Foundation, 18 March 2001. Text reprinted in 'The Conscientious Objector', *Outlook* Online (9 March 2001), http://www.outlookindia. com/full.asp?fodname=20010319&fname=common&sid=1&pn=1 (accessed 10 April 2009).

4 See WD McIntyre, *A Guide to the Contemporary Commonwealth* (London: Palgrave, 2001), p. 201.

5 In 2005, 36 per cent of India's population was below fifteen years of age and estimates suggest that half of all Indians are below the age of thirty. Figures from Carl Haube, O.P. Sharma, 'India's Population Reality: Reconciling Change and Tradition', *Population Bulletin*, Vol. 61, No. 3, September 2006.

6 Michael Brecher, *Nehru: A Political Biography* (London: Oxford University Press, 1959), p.564.

7 *Jawaharlal Nehru's Speeches* (Delhi: Ministry of Information and Broadacsting), Vol. 2, 1954, pp. 313–14.

8 J.D.B. Miller, *Survey of Commonwealth Affairs 1953–1969* (London: OUP, 1974), p. 11.

9 James Brown Scott, 'The British Commonwealth of Nations', *The American Journal of International Law*, Vol. 21, No. 1, January 1927, p. 95.

10 A Brady, 'Dominion Nationalism and the Commonwealth', *The Canadian Journal of Economics and Political Science*, Vol. 10, No. 1, February 1944, p. 9.

11 Ibid., p. 17.

12 James Brown Scott, 'The British Commonwealth of Nations', *The American Journal of International Law*, Vol. 21, No. 1, January 1927, p. 101.

13 Winston Churchill, *Step by Step 1936-1939* (London: 1942) p. 116. Quoted in B.R. Nanda, 'Nehru and the British', *Modern Asian Studies*, Vol. 30, No. 2, 1996. p. 469.

14 Quoted in B.R. Nanda, 'Nehru and the British', *Modern Asian Studies*, Vol. 30, No. 2, 1996, p. 472.

15 Ibid., p. 471.

16 Nehru's letter to Agatha Harrison, quoted in B.R. Nanda, 'Nehru and the British', *Modern Asian Studies*, Vol. 30, No. 2, 1996, p. 474.

17 Quoted in B.R. Nanda, 'Nehru and the British', *Modern Asian Studies*, Vol. 30, No. 2, 1996, p. 472.

18 Ibid., p. 473.

19 Ibid.

20 Jawaharlal Nehru, *Autobiography* (London: 1939), pp. 418–19.

21 John Kenneth Galbraith, *A Life in Our Times: Memoirs*, (New York, London: Ballantine Books, 1981).

22 Nehru to H.K. Kales, 9 November 1933, Quoted in B.R. Nanda, 'Nehru and the British', *Modern Asian Studies*, Vol. 30, No. 2, 1996, p. 476.

23 B.R. Nanda, 'Nehru and the British', *Modern Asian Studies*, Vol. 30, No. 2, 1996, p. 476.

24 Nicholas Mansergh, 'The Commonwealth at the Queen's Accession', *International Affairs (Royal Institute of International Affairs-1944)*, Vol. 29, No. 3, July 1953, p. 288.

25 See A.P. Rana, 'The Intellectual Dimension of Indian Non-Alignment', *The Journal of Asian Studies*, Vol. 28, No. 2, February 1969, pp. 299–312.

26 Report of the Thirty-Ninth Indian National Congress, 1924, p. 26.

27 S.R. Mehrotra, *India and the Commonwealth 1885-1929* (London: Allen and Unwin, 1965), pp. 144–45.

28 Quoted in S.R. Mehrotra, *India and the Commonwealth 1865-1929* (London: Allen and Unwin, 1965), p. 133.

29 Nicholas Mansergh, 'The Commonwealth in Asia', *Pacific Affairs*, Vol. 23, No. 1, March 1950, p. 4.

30 Gwendon M. Carter, 'The Asian Dominions and the Commonwealth', *Pacific Affairs*, Vol. 22, No. 4, December 1949, p. 368–70.

31 Nicholas Mansergh, 'The Commonwealth in Asia', *Pacific Affairs*, Vol.23, No. 1, March 1950, p.10.

32 Gwendon M. Carter, 'The Asian Dominions and the Commonwealth', *Pacific Affairs*, Vol. 22, No. 4, December 1949, p. 372.

33 Anthony H. Richmond, 'The Significance of a Multi-Racial Commonwealth', *Phylon (1940-1956)*, Vol. 16, No. 4 (4th Qtr., 1955), p. 382.

34 C.E. Carrington, 'A New Theory of the Commonwealth', *International Affairs*, Vol. 31, No. 2, April 1955, p. 147.

35 Linda Freeman, Gerald Helleiner, Robert Matthews, 'The Commonwealth at Stake', *The Canadian Journal of African Studies*, Vol. 5, No. 1, 1971, p. 95.

36 Joseph J. Spengler, 'The Commonwealth: Demographic Dimensions; Implications', in Nicholas Mansergh et al, *Commonwealth Perspectives* (Durham: Duke University Press, 1958). The quote is from James G. Allen, untitled book review in *The American Historical Review*, Vol. 64, No. 4, July 1959, p. 941.

37 *Jawaharlal Nehru's Speeches* (Delhi: Ministry of Information and Broadcasting), Vol. 2, 1954, pp. 313–14.

38 Nicholas Mansergh, 'The Commonwealth at the Queen's Accession', *International Affairs (Royal Institute of International Affairs 1944)*, Vol. 29, No. 3, July 1953, p. 278.

39 Nicholas Mansergh, 'The Commonwealth in Asia', *Pacific Affairs*, Vol. 23, No. 1, March 1950, p. 5.

40 Ibid., pp. 4–5.

41 Ibid., pp. 4, 5, 10.

42 K.C. Wheare, 'Is the British Commonwealth Withering Away?', *The American Political Science Review*, Vol. 4, No. 3, September 1950, p. 547.

43 Nicholas Mansergh, 'The Commonwealth in Asia', *Pacific Affairs*, Vol.23, No. 1, March 1950, pp. 4–10.

44 B.R. Nanda, 'Nehru and the British', *Modern Asian Studies*, Vol. 30, No. 2, 1996, p. 477–48

45 16 May 1949, *Indian Constituent Assembly Debates*, Vol. 8, pp. 2–10.

46 Emphasis is ours. Quoted in Zelman Cowen, 'The Contemporary Commonwealth: A General View', *International Organisation*, Vol. 13, No. 2 (Spring 1959), pp. 206–07.

47 H. Duncan Hall, 'The British Commonwealth', *Proceedings of the American Philosophical Society*, Vol. 99, No. 4, August 1955, p. 254.

48 H. Duncan Hall, 'The British Commonwealth of Nations', *The American Political Science Review*, Vol. 47, No. 4, December 1953, p. 1012.

49 Ivor Jennings, 'Crown and Commonwealth in Asia', *International Affairs (Royal Institute of International Affairs 1944)*, Vol. 32, No. 2, April 1956, pp. 145–46.

50 Harry Oppenheimer, *The Fading Commonwealth*, OUP, 1968. Quoted in review, *African Affairs*, Vol. 68, No. 270, January 1969, p. 73.

51 7 May 1949, quoted in Nicholas Mansergh, 'The Commonwealth at the Queen's Accession', *International Affairs (Royal Institute of International Affairs-1944)*, Vol. 29, No. 3, July 1953, p. 282.

52 T.O. Elias, 'The Commonwealth in Africa', *The Modern Law Review*, Vol. 31, No. 3, May 1968, pp. 284–58.

53 James H. Polhemus, 'The Important Commonwealth: A Behavioral Indicator', *International Studies Quarterly*, Vol. 25, No. 3, September 1981, pp. 484–85.

54 N. Mansergh, The *Commonwealth Experience* (London: Weiden Field and Nicholson, 1969), pp. 394–96.

55 Anthony H. Richmond, 'The Significance of a Multi-Racial Commonwealth', *Phylon (1940-1956)*, Vol. 16, No. 4 (4th Qtr., 1955), p. 381.

56 Nicholas Mansergh, 'The Commonwealth in Asia', *Pacific Affairs*, Vol. 23, No. 1, March 1950, p. 18.

57 Meg Gurry, 'Leadership and Bilateral Relations: Menzies and Nehru. Australia and India. 1949–1964', *Pacific Affairs*, Vol. 65, No. 4, Winter 1992–1993, p. 512.

58 Britain argued that there was no time for consultation and that Suez was the lifeline to its economy. During the crisis, for instance, the British representative in India suffered from a 'four-day blackout' of information and the British case was never put to the Indian public during the crisis period. *Third Report from the Select Committee on Estimates*, 1958-9 (HMSO, 1959), p. xiv.

59 In A.W. Martin, 'RG Menzies and the Suez Crisis', *Australian Historical Studies*, Vol. 23, No. 92, April 1989, p. 170.

60 Meg Gurry, 'Leadership and Bilateral Relations: Menzies and Nehru. Australia and India. 1949-1964', *Pacific Affairs*, Vol. 65, No. 4, Winter 1992–1993, p. 511.

61 Ibid., p. 514.

62 J.A .Munro, A.I. Inglis, *Mike: The Memoirs of Lester B. Pearson* (Toronto: University of Toronto Press, 1973), Vol. 2, pp. 106–07.

63 General Smuts, 'The Constitution of the British Commonwealth', referred to in H. Duncan Hall, 'The British Commonwealth of Nations', *The American Political Science Review*, Vol. 47, No. 4, December 1953, p. 1004.

64 H. Duncan Hall, 'The British Commonwealth', *Proceedings of the American Philosophical Society*, Vol. 99, No. 4, August 1955, p. 251.

65 Ibid. Also see H. Duncan Hall, 'The British Commonwealth as a Great Power', *Foreign Affairs*, July 1945.

66 See H. Duncan Hall, 'The British Commonwealth', *Proceedings of the American Philosophical Society*, Vol. 99, No. 4, August 1955, p. 251.

67 *National Herald*, Lucknow, 29 July 1956. Quoted in Meg Gurry, 'Leadership and Bilateral Relations: Menzies and Nehru. Australia and India. 1949-1964', *Pacific Affairs*, Vol.65, No. 4, Winter 1992–1993, p. 515.

68 Nicholas Mansergh, 'The Commonwealth in Asia', *Pacific Affairs*, Vol. 23, No. 1, March 1950, p. 19.

69 F.H. Soward, 'The Commonwealth Countries and World Affairs', *International Affairs (Royal Institute of International Affairs 1944)*, Vol. 27, No. 2, April 1951, p. 198.

70 This was a conference of the Institute of Pacific Affairs. F.H. Soward, 'The Commonwealth Countries and World Affairs', *International Affairs (Royal Institute of International Affairs 1944)*, Vol. 27, No. 2, April 1951, p. 199.

71 See T.A. Keenleyside, 'Nationalist Indian Attitudes Towards Asia: A Troublesome Legacy for Post-Independence Indian Foreign Policy', *Pacific Affairs*, Vol. 55, No. 2, Summer 1982.

72 Minutes of Prime Ministers' Conference 1951, Australian Archives, A5954/1: 1813/9.

73 Meg Gurry, 'Leadership and Bilateral Relations: Menzies and Nehru. Australia and India. 1949-1964', *Pacific Affairs*, Vol. 65, No. 4, Winter 1992–1993, p. 518.

74 Ibid., p. 520.

75 Anthony H. Richmond, 'The Significance of a Multi-Racial Commonwealth', *Phylon (1940-1956)*, Vol. 16, No. 4 (4th Qtr., 1955), pp. 383–84.

76 *Nehru's Speeches*, Vol. 2, 1954, pp. 265–73.

77 Randall Hansen, 'Kenyan Asian, British Politics and the Commonwealth Immigrants Act, 1968', *The Historical Journal*, Vol. 42, No. 3, September 1999, pp. 809–34.

78 Nehru's Speeches, Vol. 4, 1964, p. 338.
79 Hedley Bull, 'What is the Commonwealth?', *World Politics*, Vol. 11, No. 4, July 1959, p. 577.
80 Ibid., pp. 581–82.
81 Quoted in Trevor R. Reese, 'Keeping Calm About the Commonwealth', *International Affairs (Royal Institute of International Affairs-1944)*, Vol. 41, No. 3, July 1965, p. 461.
82 Ibid., p. 462.
83 *The Economist*, 11 July 1964, p. 136.
84 James Mayall, 'Democratising the Commonwealth', *International Affairs (Royal Institute of International Affairs-1944)*, Vol. 74, No. 2, p. 382.
85 'Commonwealth', *The International and Comparative Law Quarterly*, Vol. 15, No. 2, April 1966, p. 578. Also see *Agreed Memorandum on the Commonwealth Secretariat*, Cmnd. 2713 (July 1965).
86 Arnold Smith with Clyde Sanger, *Stitches in Time: The Commonwealth in World Politics* (London: Andre Deutsch, 1981).
87 Timothy M. Shaw, 'The Commonwealth(s): Inter- and Non-State: At the Start of the Twenty-First Century: Contributions to Global Development and Governance', *Third World Quarterly*, Vol. 24, No. 4 (August 2003), p. 733.
88 Private conversation with an Australian diplomat in New Delhi, 21 January 2009.
89 W.D. McIntyre, *A Guide to the Contemporary Commonwealth* (London: Palgrave, 2001), p. 117.
90 Hedley Bull, 'What is the Commonwealth?', *World Politics*, Vol. 11, No. 4, July 1959, p. 583, 586.
91 *Report of the Commonwealth Secretary General*, 1997 (London: Commonwealth Secretariat, 1997), p. 8.
92 James H. Polhemus, 'The Important Commonwealth: A Behavioral Indicator', *International Studies Quarterly*, Vol. 25, No. 3 (September 1981), p.479.
93 Ibid., pp. 477, 481.
94 See Timothy M. Shaw, 'The Commonwealth (s): Inter- and Non-State: At the Start of the Twenty-First Century: Contributions to Global Development and Governance', *Third World Quarterly*, Vol. 24, No. 4 (August 2003), pp. 737–78.
95 http://www.thecgf.com/games/intro.asp (accessed 29 June 2009).
96 Van Der Westhuizen, 'Marketing Malaysia as a model Muslim State: The Significance of the 16th Commonwealth Games', in David R Black

and Janis Van Der Westhuizen, (eds.), Going Global: *The Promises and Pitfalls of Hosting Global Games,* Special issue of *Third World Quarterly,* Vol. 25, No. 7, (2004), p. 1279.

97 Ibid., p. 1278.

98 Ibid., p. 1279.

99 Amitava Ghosh to Sandra Vince, Prizes Manager, Commonwealth Foundation, 18 March 2001. Text reprinted in 'The Conscientious Objector', http://www.outlookindia.com/full.asp?fodname=2001031 9&fname=common&sid=1&pn=1 (March 9, 20

100 All figures in table unless otherwise stated are from the Commonwealth Games Federation website, http://www.thecgf.com/games/ (accessed 29 June 2009) and 'The Story of the Friendly Games', pp. 10–11. Some of the Manchester 2002 figures are from *Manchester 2002-The XVII Commonwealth Games, Post-Games Report , Vol. 1.* Some of the Melbourne 2006 figures are from http://www.melbourne2006.com. au/Media+Centre/Fact+Sheets/20+things+History+of+the+Games. htm (accessed 1 September 2009).

101 Frank H. Underhill, untitled review article in *The Canadian Journal of Economics and Political Science,* Vol. 26, No. 1 (February 1960), pp. 165–66.

102 Paul O'Higgins, 'Extradition within the Commonwealth', *The International and Comparative Law Quarterly,* Vol. 9, No. 3 (July 1960), p. 487.

103 Ivor Jennings, 'Crown and Commonwealth in Asia', *International Affairs (Royal Institute of International Affairs–1944),* Vol. 32, No. 2 (April 1956), p. 141.

104 *The Economist,* 6 June 1964.

105 Robert R. Wilson, 'Commonwealth Prime Ministers' Conference of 1964', *The American Journal of International Law,* Vol. 59, No. 3 (July 1965), p. 571.

106 Timothy M. Shaw, 'The Commonwealth(s): Inter- and Non-State: At the Start of the Twenty-First Century: Contributions to Global Development and Governance', *Third World Quarterly,* Vol. 24, No. 4 (August 2003), pp. 729–44.

107 Ibid., pp. 729–30.

108 D. Armstrong, 'From International Community to International Organisation?', *Commonwealth and Comparative Politics,* Vol. 39, No. 3, pp. 46–47.

7 THE COMMONWEALTH, SPORT DIPLOMACY AND THE SOUTH AFRICAN BOYCOTT, 1961-94

1 Most of the leading Commonwealth nations were engaged in movements of decolonization in the 1930s and 1940s. While India won her independence in 1947, a slew of Caribbean nations won theirs in the 1960s.

2 In N. Mansergh (ed.) *Documents and Speeches on Commonwealth Affairs 1952-1962* (London: OUP, 1963), pp. 389–91.

3 Sunanda K. Dutta-Ray, 'Where Good Anglo-Indians Go to Die', *Sydney Morning Herald*, 28 November 1983, p. 9.

4 Anthony H. Richmond, 'The Significance of a Multi-Racial Commonwealth', *Phylon (1940-1956)*, Vol. 16, No. 4 (4th Qtr., 1955), pp. 380–86.

5 Ibid., pp. 380–386.

6 India correspondence files at the IOC museum in Lausanne, IOC Archives, IDD Chemise 9404 CIO CNO INDE CORR, Correspondence India 1924–1963.

7 K. Durr, 'South Africa and the Commonwealth', *The Round Table* (1994), p. 172.

8 Bruce Kidd, 'Boycotts that worked: the campaign against apartheid in the Commonwealth', in the *CAHPER Journal* (July–August 1983) p. 8.

9 Sam Ramsamy, *Apartheid: The Real Hurdle*, (International Defence Aid Fund for Southern Africa, London, 1982), p. 10; For details on South African sport of the period, also see Richard Lapchick, *The Politics of Race and International sport*, (Greenwood, Westport Connecticut, 1975), A. Boullion and R. Archer, *The South African Game*, (London: Zed Press, 1982).

10 Ramsamy, *Apartheid: The Real Hurdle,* p. 11.

11 Ibid.

12 Ibid., p. 12.

13 Ibid., p. 20.

14 Interview with Anthony Suze, University of Toronto, 22 May 2008. Suze, an ANC member, was imprisoned for fifteen years at Robben Island prison for his role in the anti-apartheid movement.

15 Ibid.

16 E.S. Reddy, 'United Nations, India And Boycott of Apartheid Sport', paper presented at the seminar of the Sports Authority of India and the Arjuna Awardees Association (New Delhi: July 28–29, 1988).

17 Lapchick, *The Politics of Race and International Sport,* p. 196.

18 Bruce K. Murray, *The Sports Boycott and Cricket: The Cancellation of the 1970 South African Tour of England,* www. http://wiserweb.wits.ac.za/PDF%20Files/wirs%20-%20murray.PDF (accessed 15 February 2008); Also see, Bruce Murray and Christopher Merett, *Caught Behind: Race and Politics in Springbok Cricket* (Capetown: University of Kwa Zulu Natal Press, 2004).

19 Donald Macintosh and Donna Greenhorn, 'Canadian Diplomacy and the 1978 Edmonton Commonwealth Games', *Journal of Sport History,* Vol. 19, No. 1 (Spring 1989), p. 27.

20 Linda   Freeman,   Gerald   Helleiner,   Robert   Matthews,   'The Commonwealth at Stake', *The Canadian Journal of African Studies,* Vol. 5, No. 1 (1971), p. 94.

21 For a fascinating account of South African Cricket of the period, see Jon Gemmell, *The Politics of Race in South African Cricket* (Routledge: London, 2005).

22 Murray, *The Sports Boycott and Cricket.*

23 Interview with Mike Brearley at Lord's, 26 February 2009.

24 Murray, *The Sports Boycott and Cricket.*

25 Ibid.

26 Ibid.

27 Ibid.

28 E.S. Reddy, 'United Nations, India And Boycott of Apartheid Sport'.

29 *Toronto Star,* 27 July 1970.

30 Ramsamy, *Apartheid: The Real Hurdle,* p. 20.

31 Ibid.

32 Kidd, 'Boycotts that worked', p. 13.

33 Macintosh and Greenhorn, 'Canadian Diplomacy and the 1978 Edmonton Commonwealth Games', p. 39.

34 For details on New Zealand's role in the anti-apartheid struggle, see Trevor Richards, *Dancing on our Bones: New Zealand, South Africa, Rugby and Racism* (Bridget William Books), pp. 181–204.

35 Macintosh and Greenhorn, 'Canadian Diplomacy and the 1978 Edmonton Commonwealth Games', p. 41.

36 Ibid.

37 We are grateful to Bruce Kidd for giving us a copy of the release.

38 Personal interview with Sam Ramsamy at the University of Toronto at the conference on Olympic Reform, 20–22 May 2009. We met

once again at Lord's in London on 21 June 2009. For Ramsamy's views on the Gleneagles Agreement, also see Sam Ramsamy with Edward Griffiths, *Reflections on a Life in Sport* (Greenhouse, Capetown, 2004), Chapter 7.

39 Macintosh and Greenhorn, 'Canadian Diplomacy and the 1978 Edmonton Commonwealth Games', p. 44.

40 Ibid., p. 45.

41 Ibid.

42 Ibid., p. 48.

43 Ibid., p. 50.

44 Ramsamy, *Apartheid: The Real Hurdle,* p. 21.

45 Richards, *Dancing on our Bones*, p. 190.

46 Ibid., p. 196.

47 Ibid.

48 Ibid., p. 197.

49 Ibid., p. 198.

50 Kidd, 'Boycotts that worked', p. 13.

51 Ibid.

52 Ibid.

53 Ibid., p. 14.

54 Ibid., pp.13–14.

55 Ibid.

56 *Toronto Star*, 11 October 1982.

57 Ibid.

58 This is how Ramsamy describes the events of July 1985 in his book, *Reflections on a Life in Sport*.

59 Interview with Sam Ramsamy at the University of Toronto, 20–22 May 2009.

60 To understand the intensity of the evolving boycott campaign, see *Toronto Star* and *Hamilton Spectator* of July 1986 and the *Times of India* of July 1986.

61 *Toronto Star*, 15 July 1986.

62 Ibid.

63 Ibid., 14 July 1986.

64 Ibid., 15 July 1986.

65 Ibid., 19 July 1986.

66 Ibid.

67 Ibid., 22 July 1986.

68 Ibid.

69 Ibid., 15 July 1986.

70 Ibid., 20 July 1986.

71 Ibid.

72 Ibid.

73 Ibid., 22 July 1986.

74 Ibid.

75 Ibid.

76 *Times* (London), 22 July 1986.

77 Ibid.

78 *Toronto Star*, 22 July 1986.

79 Ibid., 19 July 1986.

80 Quoted in E.S. Reddy, 'United Nations, India And Boycott of Apartheid Sport'.

81 For details, see *Toronto Star* reporting of the Auckland Commonwealth Games for the duration of the competition.

82 Quoted in Boria Majumdar, *Twenty-Two Yards to Freedom: A Social History of Indian Cricket* (New Delhi: Penguin, 2004), p. 410.

83 *Toronto Star*, 19 August 1994.

84 Ibid.

85 Ibid.

86 Ibid.

87 Rohit Mahajan, 'Ah The Human Race', in *Outlook*, 28 April 2008.

88 Boria Majumdar and Nalin Mehta, *Olympics: The India Story* (New Delhi: HarperCollins, 2008), pp. 313–14.

8 BEIJING TO DELHI: INDIAN SPORT 2010

1 Personal interview with Randhir Singh, 10 September 2008. He said the exact same things to the *Telegraph* reporter Anirban Das Mahapatra on 1 February 2009.

2 Nalin Mehta, 'Smile, Sir Dorabji', *The Indian Express*, 12 August 2008.

3 For the astonishing expansion of Indian satellite television, see Nalin Mehta, *India on Television: How Satellite News Channels Have Changed the Way We Think and Act* (New Delhi: HarperCollins, 2008). For the massive expansion of the Indian newspaper industry and its 'mass-ification', see Robin Jeffrey, *India's Newspaper Revolution: Capitalism, Politics and the Indian Language Press* (New Delhi: Oxford University Press, 2003, 2nd ed.).

4 Saina Nehwal made the quarterfinals in women's singles before losing a closely fought match against Maria-Kristine Yulianti of Indonesia. In archery, Mangal Singh Champia raised expectations before failing to deliver and in tennis, Leander Paes and Mahesh Bhupathi lost in the quarterfinals to eventual winners Roger Federer and Stanislas Wawrinka of Switzerland.

5 India won four bronze medals at the Moscow Championships, a first for Indian sport.

6 Boria Majumdar, 'Seize this moment', *The Times of India*, 25 August 2008.

7 Kalmadi expressed caution when speaking at the launch of our book, *Olympics: The India Story* in Delhi on 21 July 2008.

8 Quoted in Nalin Mehta, 'Smile, Sir Dorabji', *The Indian Express*, 12 August 2008.

9 It was plain unfortunate that Ranjan Sodhi, despite equalling a world record in Men's Double Trap in June 2008, could not make it to Beijing in the absence of a quota place. Sodhi, many feel, stands a very good chance in the upcoming Commonwealth Games and also in London 2012.

10 For the Chinese model of sporting success, see, for instance, Fan Hong, Duncan Mackay, Karen Christensen (eds.), *China Gold: China's Quest for Olympic and Global Glory* (Great Barrington, M.A.: Berkshire, 2008).

11 Personal interview with Raj Kumar Sangwan, 8 September 2008.

12 'Inside India's Fight Club', *The Indian Express*, 24 August 2008.

13 Ibid.

14 His rustic yet pleasant statements to the media have endeared him to the nation's sports fraternity. When one of us asked him a question in English after his win against the Russian world number one, his candid confession was startling. 'If I could speak English that well, I'd be doing what you are,' he had retorted in jest.

15 Personal interview with Jagdish Singh, 6 April 2009.

16 There is a telling television commercial which shows village folk sitting huddled together in front of a television set operating on battery watching their local lad in action. This inverter advertisement is a pithy comment on the realities of Bhiwani.

17 *The Telegraph*, 1 April 2009.

18 Ibid.

19 This discrepancy was noticeable across the media. We have consulted ten leading national newspapers and not a single one had the Indian Open as its first headline.

20 *Anandabazar Patrika*, 12 August 2009.

21　For details, see Boria Majumdar and Nalin Mehta, *Olympics: The India Story* (New Delhi: HarperCollins, 2008), 'Epilogue'.

22　For details, see *The Hindu*, 7 March 2009, also see *The Times of India*, 7 March 2009.

23　*The Hindu*, 7 March 2009.

24　Ibid.

25　*The Times of India*, 7 March 2009.

26　Quoted in *The Hindu*, 7 March 2009.

27　Dasmunsi suffered a serious cardiac arrest in October 2008. Yet, the All-India Football Federation has done nothing to replace him.

28　Shamya Dasgupta, 'India is the loser, AIFF scoring the own-goal of corruption. Football: FIFA official slams unprofessional, corrupt system', *Indian Express*, 13 January 2004.

29　Ibid.

30　The 2008–09 competition was decided on the last day of the competition, on 16 April 2009 with both Mohun Bagan and Churchill Brothers in striking distance of the title. It was an unparalleled media opportunity that the AIFF should have cashed in on. Yet, nothing much was done to generate hype around the competition.

31　A series of interviews with senior Zee officials made it evident that Zee is thoroughly dissatisfied with the AIFF and its treatment of Indian football.

32　Bill Adams, 'Saving Soccer in India', www.indianfootball.com.

33　Novy Kapadia, 'The Millennium Cup Flop', indya.com football diary, January 2001.

34　Ibid.

35　Ibid.

36　In a dramatic development after India had failed to qualify for Beijing, the IOA, under pressure from the sports fraternity and the fans, met in Delhi to declare the IHF defunct and assumed the reigns of Indian hockey in March 2008.

37　*DNA*, 9 April 2009.

38　Ibid.

39　*Hindustan Times*, 9 April 2009.

40　*DNA*, 9 April 2009.

41　For details see: http://www.ptinews.com/news/222347_Organisers-fear-IPL-may-mar-hockey-World-Cup-final (accessed 12 August 2009).

42　Gurbix Singh, 'Stickwork' in *The Telegraph*, 2 April 2009.

43 *Anandabazar Patrika*, 13 April 2009.

44 Ibid.

45 *The Hindu*, 14 April 2009.

46 Ibid.

47 Singh, 'Stickwork'.

48 Narang also shot a career best 597 out of 600 in the 50-m prone category and finished fourth – his best performance ever in the category.

49 *The Hindustan Times*, 10 April 2009.

50 Ibid.

51 Ibid.

52 Ibid., 3 April 2009.

53 *The Telegraph*, 1 February 2009.

54 Ibid.

55 Dr M.S. Gill, Minister of State in the Ministry of Youth Affairs and Sports, Government of India, Rajya Sabha Unstarred Question No. 894 (asked by Shrimati T. Ratna Bai), answered on 26.11.2009, 'Training to Participants of Commonwealth Games'. The funding is for the following sport disciplines: Archery, Athletics, Aquatics, Badminton, Boxing (M), Cycling, Gymnastics, Hockey, Lawn Bowls, Netball (W), Rugby 7s (M) Shooting, Squash, Table Tennis, Tennis, Weightlifting, Wrestling, Elite Athletes with Disability, Power lifting, and Swimming.

56 Personal interview with Randhir Singh, 10 September 2008.

57 *The Telegraph*, 1 February 2009.

EPILOGUE

1 The two most prominent are the ones held at the India Habitat Centre, New Delhi on 29–30 March titled, 'Delhi 2010: The Games and the Commonwealth' and the one held at Glasgow on 3–4 June, comparing preparations for Delhi 2010 and Glasgow 2014.

2 This slogan has almost become synonymous with Suresh Kalmadi for the last two years. Even at moments of extreme adversity, Kalmadi has gone on to say that the Delhi Games will be the best ever.

3 *Open* magazine cover story 27 May–3 June 2010.

4 Personal interview with three Canadian athletes – Crispin Duenas, Alana Macdougall and Vanessae Lee – at the University of Toronto, on 1 June 2010.

5 http://news.bbc.co.uk/today/hi/today/newsid_8700000/8700010.stm (accessed 1 June 2010).

6 Ibid.

7 Ibid.

8 For the full text of the interview, see the *Times of India* special supplement on the Commonwealth Games, 29 March 2010.

9 Ibid.

10 Interview with Boria Majumdar, *The Times of India*, 30 March 2010.

11 Michael Skapinker, 'A Thirst for Reality Eclipses the World Cup', *The Financial Times* (London), 8 June 2010, p. 11.

12 Hans Westerbeek, Unpublished presentation at the Commonwealth Games Summit, India Habitat Centre, New Delhi, 29–30 March 2010.

13 Bruce Kidd, Unpublished keynote address at the Commonwealth Games Summit, India Habitat Centre, New Delhi, 29–30 March 2010.

14 Ibid.

15 Boria Majumdar, 'The Games are Serious Business', in the *Times of India*, 26 May 2010.

16 Even Hitler wasn't allowed to speak for long at the opening ceremony in Berlin in 1936. For details, see *Olympia*, directed by Leni Reifenstahl.

17 http://www.bbc.co.uk/iplayer/episode/p007qdkn/The_Monday_Documentary_Soft_Power_India/ (accessed 3 June 2010).

INDEX

ACKNOWLEDGEMENTS

Trying to document the history of the Commonwealth Games appeared daunting to start with. It was our close friend and mentor Bruce Kidd who helped with the first insights and also handed over all of his own material and research to give the project a kick-start.

At the Indian end, we wish to acknowledge the support of Suresh Kalmadi and his office, Raja Randhir Singh, Lalit Bhanot, Manish Kumar and Yaduraj Singh. We are deeply appreciative of the help provided by Sheila Dikshit who has always been receptive to our concerns and has given us many long interviews at her home and office. Kapil Sibal and Jaipal Reddy have always encouraged serious academic research on critical issues and have been sounding boards at difficult times of writing on many an issue of government involvement.

We also wish to thank Mitali Nikore, who worked as our research assistant, conducted field interviews with those displaced, and enthusiastically dug up newspaper articles; Upahar Pramanik, who helped arrange some of the interactions at Bhaleswa Gaon; Priyanka Chakravarty, who helped in research; Uday Sahay, a dear friend with much wisdom; P.K. Srivastava, who was always courteous and helpful; Karin Lundback, who remembered to provide the press dossier on Games security; and our students at the University of Toronto, some of whom will be representing Canada in Delhi.

Research in the UK, key to the writing of this book, wouldn't have been possible without the generous contribution of the University of Central Lancashire. We deeply appreciate the support of DVC Angela Murphy, Dean Dharma Kowuri, Head of school John Minten and Prof. John Hughson.

Thanks are due to our dear friend Karthika for believing in us and to Shantanu and Prema for their careful and critical editing of the manuscript. They were always there to help and adjust timelines and cope with our weird travel commitments.

Finally, it may be silly to thank him, but Brigadier Rakesh Mehta has read more drafts and commented more than anyone else on the overall scope of this project.

Boria Majumdar   Nalin Mehta
Kolkata   Geneva
July 2010   July 2010